Between God and Man
AN INTERPRETATION OF JUDAISM

Between
God and Man

AN INTERPRETATION OF JUDAISM

From the Writings of
ABRAHAM J. HESCHEL

SELECTED, EDITED, AND INTRODUCED BY

Fritz A. Rothschild

THE FREE PRESS, *New York*
COLLIER-MACMILLAN LIMITED, *London*

For information, address:

THE FREE PRESS
A DIVISION OF THE MACMILLAN COMPANY
60 Fifth Avenue, New York, N. Y. 10011

Collier-Macmillan Canada, Ltd., Toronto, Ontario

Library of Congress Catalog Card Number: 59-7161

FIRST FREE PRESS PAPERBACK EDITION 1965
Reprinted by arrangement with Harper and Row, publishers of the first hardcover edition.

PREFACE

The object of this book is to present, within the compass of a single volume, the substance of Heschel's work, hitherto available only in a number of books, articles and addresses.

Heschel's writings deal with the whole range of Israel's religious tradition. He has not only written on the world-view of the Bible, but has expounded its embodiment in Jewish law and custom, prayer and ritual. Thus this book may also serve as a comprehensive exposition of Jewish religion by an authoritative contemporary interpreter. By translating into the idiom of present-day thought the basic insights of Judaism Heschel has correlated the Biblical message with the aspirations and problems of our age. His work can prove helpful to all those who strive to recapture the religious dimension of life.

Even readers who are acquainted with Heschel's writings will, I trust, not find unwelcome the introductory essay which presents an exposition of the basic philosophical categories and arguments that underlie his thought. Those readers whose primary interest is not in the field of philosophy may, however, prefer to begin their reading with the first chapter.

I wish to express my gratitude to Professor Heschel for his friendly cooperation; I am indebted to him for helping me in the compilation of the bibliography and for making available to me the manuscript of his forthcoming work on prophecy. And finally, I wish to thank my wife who assisted me in the task of proof-reading and whose help and encouragement have meant so much to me.

January, 1959   FRITZ A. ROTHSCHILD

CONTENTS

5

Contents

PART III: MAN AND HIS NEEDS

PART IV: RELIGIOUS OBSERVANCE

PART V: THE MEANING OF THIS HOUR

INTRODUCTION

by Fritz A. Rothschild

I

When the first volume of Heschel's philosophy of religion (*Man Is Not Alone*) appeared in 1951, Reinhold Niebuhr predicted that its author would soon become "a commanding and authoritative voice not only in the Jewish community but in the religious life of America."[1] Today, having followed this work with its successor volume, *God in Search of Man*, and studies dealing with prayer and symbolism and the Sabbath, as well as with numerous articles and addresses on a variety of subjects, he has firmly established himself as one of the outstanding religious thinkers of our generation.

Abraham Joshua Heschel is the product of two different worlds. His life and work can perhaps best be understood as an attempt to achieve a creative viable synthesis between the traditional piety and learning of Eastern European Jewry and the philosophy and scholarship of Western civilization. Born in Warsaw, the descendant of a long line of outstanding leaders of Hasidism, he counts among his paternal ancestors the famous rabbi of Apt, Abraham Joshua Heschel, whose name he bears, and Rabbi Dov Ber of Meseritz, the "Great Maggid," the main disciple and successor of the *Baal Shem,* the founder of the Hasidic movement. On his mother's side, he traces lineage to Rabbi Levi Isaac of Berditshev, another famous master of Hasidism.

Growing up in the closed theonomous world of Jewish piety, he gained during the formative years of his childhood and youth two things that are manifest on every page of his published work: a knowledge and an understanding. The *knowledge* of the Jewish religious heritage was acquired through an undeviating attention during most of his waking hours to the study of rabbinical literature. At the age of ten he was at home in the world of the Bible, he had acquired competence in the subtle dialectic of the Talmud, and had also been introduced to the world of Jewish mysticism, the *Kabbalah*. The *understanding* for the realness of the spirit and for the holy dimension of all existence was not primarily the result of book learning but the cumulative effect of life lived among people who "were sure that everything hinted at something transcend-

7

ent";[2] that the presence of God was a daily experience and the sanctification of life a daily task. In his book *The Earth Is the Lord's: The Inner World of the Jew in East Europe,* Heschel has set a lasting memorial to a vanished world—a world exterminated in Hitler's gas chambers and concentration camps during the Second World War.

At the age of twenty Heschel, after having prepared himself in Poland for the requirements of modern academic life, left the closed world of traditional life and lore to enroll as a student at the University of Berlin and the Hochschule für die Wissenschaft des Judentums. Although he developed wide cultural and artistic interests, his studies were concentrated mainly in the fields of Semitics and philosophy. The Hochschule appointed its erstwhile student an instructor in Talmud, and the publication of his *Maimonides* (1935), a biography and interpretation of the great medieval philosopher and codifier, established his reputation as a fine scholar, a gifted and imaginative writer, and a master of German prose. Heschel is one of the rare writers who have a distinguished literary style in whatever language they touch. He writes equally well in English, German, Hebrew, and Yiddish. His study on Hebrew prophetic consciousness, *Die Prophetie,* which had earned him a Ph.D. degree at Berlin University, was published by the Polish Academy of Science in 1936 and hailed as an outstanding contribution by leading Biblical scholars.[3]

In 1937 Martin Buber chose Heschel as his successor at the central organization for Jewish adult education and the Jüdische Lehrhaus. The latter was founded by Franz Rosenzweig in Frankfurt on the Main. There Heschel taught and directed many of the educational activities connected with the last phase of the memorable German-Jewish cultural renaissance that flourished during the Nazi regime only to come to a sudden end with the pogrom of November 10, 1938, and the subsequent extermination policy of the war years.

A mass deportation action in October, 1938, found Heschel himself expelled by the Nazis together with the rest of the Polish Jews resident in Germany. He taught for eight months in Warsaw at the Institute for Jewish Studies, the training school for Jewish teachers and rabbis, before departing for England, where he established the Institute for Jewish Learning in London. In 1940 he received a call from the Hebrew Union College in Cincinnati, where he was Associate Professor of Philosophy and Rabbinics for five years. In 1945 he joined the faculty of the Jewish Theological Seminary of America in New York, where he is Professor of Jewish Ethics and Mysticism.

Heschel's work displays an amazing range of interest and scholarly competence. He has written on the metaphysics of the medieval Neoplatonic philosopher and poet Ibn Gabirol (Avicebron), on *The Quest for Certainty in Saadia's Philosophy,* as well as books on Maimonides, the greatest philosopher and legist of medieval Jewry, and on Isaac Abravanel, the Jewish statesman and Bible commentator of fifteenth-century Spain. He has discovered a hoard of early Hasidic letters and manuscripts, and his subsequent monographs on the history of the Hasidic movement, though not widely known outside the circle of scholars in this subject, have been a major contribution to this little-explored period. He has dealt with the problem of prayer for modern man and the doctrine of the "holy spirit" in medieval Jewish thought. He has completed a Hebrew volume entitled *The Battle of the Book,* a documented history of the manner in which Jewish rabbis and thinkers wrestled with the problems of Mosaic revelation. At present he is working on an English version of his book on Biblical prophecy. He also plans to write a work in English on the intellectual relevance of the Bible. But the central theme of his interest and research has been the clarification of the basic problems of religion as they concern modern man, and it is in his philosophy of religion that we find his most outstanding and original contribution to the world of letters. In his writings on religion he combines the yearning for holiness and spirituality of his Hasidic ancestors with the yearning for free inquiry and objective truth of the modern Western scholar. And he sees no contradiction in this twofold task. True piety must include intellectual honesty. Heschel tells the story of Rabbi Bunam of Przyscha, who pointed out that according to medieval sources a *hasid* (pious man) is he who does more than the law requires. Now the law says: Thou shalt not deceive thy fellow man (Leviticus 25:17). A true *hasid* goes beyond the law; he will not even deceive his own self.[4]

II

Modern man has, by and large, lost contact with the dimension of reality that gives rise to religion. Whether God is dead, as Nietzsche proclaimed, whether he is hiding his face or did not depart of his own volition, but was expelled by man, the fact remains that we no longer live in a world where piety is as "common as knowledge of the multiplication table."[5] The recovery of the once living reality of religion cannot be achieved by the exposition of belief, dogma, ritual, or even *religious experience,* necessary though these are to a complete understanding of the subject. It is well known that the nineteenth century which saw the breakdown of traditional beliefs produced more works dealing with the history of dogma and the description of religious beliefs and practices than any other comparable period in previous history.

Heschel defines religion as *"an answer to man's ultimate questions."*[6]

Introduction

Such ultimate questions arise under the impact of the elemental forces of reality confronting man. Religion originates in a living situation. As an answer religion becomes not only false but meaningless and irrelevant as soon as the question by which it is evoked no longer reflects a challenge. To recover an understanding of religion, one must go beyond the phenomena of religion to that which necessitates religion in one's life: the total situation of man. Only by turning to the reality in which man encounters the significance of ultimate questions and in which he experiences those aspects of life which point to answers can we hope to gain a true understanding of religion. "The inquiry must proceed both by delving into the consciousness of man as well as by delving into the teachings and attitudes of the religious tradition."[7] Both of these sources are equally necessary to accomplish the task. The Bible, which is neither a catechism nor a treatise in dogmatic theology but the classic record of man's encounter with God, is the primary document to which we have to turn for an understanding of Judaeo-Christian faith. But unless the voice which speaks from the pages of Scripture also addresses each person in the experiences of his own life, there is little possibility that the words of the ancient prophets will disclose their meaning. "One must be inspired to understand inspiration," and we could not derive understanding from the Bible if its message did not strike a sympathetic chord in our own soul and allude to aspects and qualities of reality which we have experienced in the events of our own life. By correlating the message of the Biblical and post-Biblical religious literature of Israel with the consciousness of modern individual man, Heschel breathes new life into the ancient documents of the tradition, and by exhibiting their uniqueness discovers their relevance. Theological terms such as "the divine glory," "the word of the Lord," "holiness," and "sin" have become almost meaningless to the majority of our contemporaries. By pointing to the living context in which they originate, Heschel has converted these stumbling blocks to theological understanding into signposts which can help modern man to find his way back to the sources of religious insight.

God and man in their interrelation are the theme of Heschel's philosophy of religion. The concrete reality to which he directs his inquiry can never be exhaustively described by any deductive system of concepts and propositions. Behind almost every sentence of Heschel's works one can sense his awareness that reality is infinitely more rich and complex than any verbal formulation can disclose. It has been said that "the polarity of Heschel's thought, the mosaic of individual insights, and the tendency to stress now one point of view and now another—all make the task of the responsible interpreter and critic a difficult one."[8] But although Heschel has not presented his thought as a systematic treatise *more geometrico,* his various writings exhibit a sustained philosophical analysis[9] which can be understood in terms of a set of basic categories and concepts.

The selections from Heschel's works and their arrangement in this volume are designed to exhibit the central ideas of Heschel's philosophy of religion in as systematic a manner as possible. It is the aim of this essay to present an outline of his philosophy which may be used either as an introduction to or a commentary on the writings of Heschel gathered in this book. Each of the following sections of this Introduction corresponds to a division of the main text: thus, introductory sections III–VI cover in sequence Parts I–IV of the selections from Heschel's works.

III

Religion claims to be a response to a reality beyond our minds. It claims that man is able to surpass himself and that although he is part of the natural world he can enter into relationship with a God who transcends this world. Becoming aware of this higher reality is not, however, the result of a sudden leap of faith; it is engendered by man's perceptive intercourse with the world. What is required, then, is not a turning away from everyday experience but a new openness toward certain aspects of experience to which modern man has generally become oblivious.

Three aspects of nature command our attention: its *power,* its *beauty,* and its *grandeur,* and to each of them there corresponds a way of relating oneself to reality. "We may exploit it, we may enjoy it, we may accept it with awe."[10] In modern technological society the predominant mode of approaching the environment is for purposes of control and use. To recover the sensitivity to that dimension of reality which engenders wonder and worship Heschel turns to the experience of religious men and the classical document of such experience, the Bible. There he finds six terms that describe grandeur and man's reaction to it in three correlative pairs: the sublime and wonder, mystery and awe, the glory and faith.[11] It must be borne in mind that in each of these three pairs of terms the first one refers to an objective aspect of reality and the second one to man's mode of responding to it. All these terms refer to the realm of the ineffable. Heschel opposes the view held by many that only what is definable can be known. We have an awareness that communicates to us aspects of thought and action not accessible to strict definition. This awareness of the ineffable is, of course, no substitute for rational knowledge, but often is the source of insights that can lead to the discovery of new knowledge.

Man has shown two different attitudes toward facts: acceptance and wonder. Acceptance stops with whatever is perceived and sees no good reason for going beyond it. The object is admitted as given (datum) and that is all there is to it. Wonder, on the other hand, is an attitude which, far from being set at ease by a fact, takes it as a stimulus which points beyond what is immediately given. Such wonder can take different forms: it can become the starting point of *science*, which looks beyond individual facts to the laws they exemplify, or it can become the starting point of *religion*, which begins with wonder not only at the fact itself but at there being any facts and acts of awareness of facts. To science a fact points to its antecedents and consequents; to religion a fact points to the ground and power that stands behind all facts and perceptions.[12] We may call the one kind of wonder *curiosity*, the other *radical amazement*.

Wonder is a reaction to an objective aspect of the world we call the sublime. This is not an aesthetic category, opposed to the beautiful (as Burke and Kant thought), but a transcendent allusiveness of all things: "that which we see and are unable to convey."[13] To Biblical man it is never just there as a quality, but appears as a *happening*, a marvel. It is a way in which the presence of God strikes forth.[14] Heschel maintains that within all things an indicativeness of what transcends them is given with the same immediacy as the things themselves.[15]

To the sheer *sublimity* of experience we respond with *radical amazement*, to the *mystery* of reality with *awe*. Awe is not unintelligent fear or abdication of man's rational powers in the face of the unknowable. Human life is the meeting point of mind and mystery, of reason and transcendence. "To surrender to mystery is fatalism, to withdraw into reason is solipsism. Man is driven to commune with that which is beyond the mystery. The ineffable in him seeks a way to that which is beyond the ineffable."[16]

Because Heschel has stressed the ineffable and mysterious aspects of reality, he has been criticized as antirational and has been classified as a "mystic."[17] He is, of course, guilty by association, since it is true that mystic writers always dwell upon the ineffable quality of their experience. But we might equally well label him an "empiricist" for exactly the same reason, since empiricists emphasize against rationalists that thought and its objects, essence and existence, are not identical and that no conceptual system can catch in its net the whole of reality without a remainder. To see the limits of speculative reason, as Kant, for example, did in his critical philosophy is not unreasonable but part of the task of reason. To remember that all knowledge abstracts from reality, that "leagues beyond those leagues there is more sea," does not mean that one has surrendered to irrationalism. It would make the task of the philosopher of religion much easier if he could dispense with the experience of the numinous, which, in the words of Rudolf Otto, is both *tremendum* and *fascinans*, and which so stubbornly refuses to be incorporated into a rational scheme. Yet "the manifestation of something within the context of ordinary experience which transcends the ordinary context of experience"[18] cannot be denied. Sensitive men have always been haunted by the awareness that we apprehend more than we can comprehend, that things point beyond themselves to wider horizons, and behind their façade to the depth of their divine ground. Like the *eros* in Plato's Dialogues, this awareness urges men not to be satisfied with any neat scheme that presumes to catch all of reality by excluding the mystery which is neither the construction nor the object of our controlling reason.

There are three possible attitudes toward the mystery: the fatalist, the positivist, and the Biblical.[19] To the fatalist the mysterious and irrational is the ultimate power controlling the world, a power devoid of purpose and justice and above the gods, such as the Greek Moira (fate). To the positivist mystery does not exist: it is either that which we do not know yet (but which, in principle, may become the object of knowledge) or that which is, in principle, unanswerable and, therefore, meaningless. An awareness of mystery was common to all ancient men, but Biblical thought brought about a revolutionary change by teaching that the mystery is not the ultimate. The ultimate is not a blind power or a law but one who is *concerned* with man.[20]

The experience of the ineffable not only leads to an awareness of the mystery and majesty in and behind all things; it also shatters man's solipsistic pretensions and opens his soul to an attitude in which the question of God can be raised.

The traditional proofs for the existence of God have largely been failures because they confused the claims of science and of religious thought. Religion cannot hope to prove the existence of *un nommé Dieu* the way one proves the existence of the planet Pluto. In fact the greatest obstacle to a genuine understanding of the problem of God is the common notion that he is an object that can be located and analyzed in the way in which other objects are cognized by a human subject. Anticipating Heschel's conclusions, we may say that God can never be understood as the object but only as the subject of which man is the object. To think of God in this way necessitates something analogous to Kant's "Copernican Revolution" in reverse. Paul Tillich, in his article "The Two Types of Philosophy of Religion," dealing with the same difficulty, distinguishes two ways of approaching God: the way of overcoming estrangement and the way of meeting a stranger. "On the first way man discovers *himself* when he discovers God; he discovers something that is identical with himself although it transcends him infinitely, something from which he is estranged, but from which he never has been and never can be separated.

On the second way he meets a stranger when he meets God. The meeting is accidental. . . . He may disappear, and only probable statements can be made about his nature."

Since God is the ultimate subject and not an object, he cannot be "proved" as a conclusion derived from a set of premises. Man's experience of the ineffable can provide the change of inner attitude, the reverse of Kant's "Copernican Revolution," which is a prerequisite for understanding God: the *thaumatic shock* can bring about the awareness in man that reality is not grounded in his individual or generic mind, but that the existence and functioning of his own mind and person are themselves a mystery in need of com-prehension. The reality of God can then be grasped not as the consequent, but rather as the premise of human thought.

In order to ask a question there must be a questioner, a discrete, autonomous self which is the subject, and of which the world, the fellow man, and God can become objects. The question "Who is the subject of all reality?" cannot be significantly raised on the speculative level where man as the subject is presupposed. However, once the question is raised "Who is the self?" and the awareness gained that the conscious self is merely the expression of something never fully expressed, that life and time are not our property but a trust, then it becomes clear that the self "can be distinctly separated only at its branches, namely from other individuals and other things but not at its roots."[21] Realizing that the self did not originate itself, that man is endowed with a will, but that the will is not his, that freedom is something forced upon him, man begins to feel a stranger within the framework of his normal consciousness. Perceiving that he is what is not his, he begins to understand what it means to be an object of transcendent attention rather than a self-contained subject. He even begins to wonder whether the strictly definable "self" which asks the question of God is not itself a high abstraction.

Our conventional ideas about the discrete subject may turn out to be examples of what Whitehead called the fallacy of simple location: human thought is largely based on spatial categories of externality and the notion of an object "outside" the subject may be a case in point. In knowledge the subject "takes" the object and incorporates it into his own self as an "idea"; in practical action man likewise grasps what is external to him and brings it into the domain of his control and power. Thinking about God, however, is different. He is neither a thing nor an idea. "He is within and beyond all things and ideas. Thinking of God is not beyond but within Him."[22] The religious man feels about God as a thought in a man's mind might feel if it had self-consciousness.[23]

Man is aware of allusions to God's concern, intimations of his presence.

But Kant has shown that it is an unwarranted procedure to infer, from an awareness from within our experience, a reality beyond the empirical world. When asserting the reality of God, we do not, however, argue from the idea of God to his existence, possessing first the idea and then postulating its ontal counterpart. Neither do we proceed from the givenness of the world to the God who is needed to explain the world. Such a "God" is derived from the world; and although that does not make him dependent on the world, it makes him merely the sufficient cause of the universe, and as such he cannot transcend the world infinitely. As Tillich points out, the so-called arguments for the existence of God are not arguments at all. Their value lies in that they make possible the question of God, which can be raised only because "an awareness of God is present in the question of God."[24] This awareness, since it precedes the question, is not the result of the argument but its presupposition. Similarly Heschel describes the method of becoming certain of God's reality as an *onto-logical presupposition:* it is not a going forward from premises to God as a conclusion, but a withdrawal from the conceptualizations of everyday life to their underlying premise, a "going behind self-consciousness and questioning the self and all its cognitive pretensions. . . . The ultimate or God comes first and our reasoning about Him second. . . . Just as there is no thinking about the world without the premise of the reality of the world, there can be no thinking about God without the premise of the realness of God."[25] If thinking means the solving of problems, if scientific and practical questions are reactions to challenges posed by the environment, then it stands to reason that the basic question of God can only be framed under the impact of a challenge originating in God's action directed at man. Even the most ludicrous and perverse idols created by primitive tribes are not simply the products of delusion that stand for "nothing," but are genuine reactions to the objective mystery that challenged and addressed them. Their error consisted in relating the transcendent to conventional needs, by making the temporal ultimate and thus distorting both the divine they sought to grasp and the legitimate needs they thus deified.[26]

All human existence and experience can be regarded by the pious man as such divine address and challenge. But as a matter of religious experience this awareness of being the object of a divine challenge is felt only rarely in a clear and unambiguous way. "There are moments in which we feel the challenge of a power that, not born of our will nor installed by it, robs us of independence by its judgment of the rectitude or depravity of our actions. . . ."[27] It is the impact of these intensely stirring moments when the voice reaches us that enables us to ask the question of God. While philosophy begins with man's question, *"religion begins with God's question and man's answer.*"[28] The question of God presupposes the realness of God, just as questions about the world presuppose the experienced realness of the world. But unlike the world the voice of God is not "too much with us"; since it reaches man only at times, it can be forgotten. The awareness that we are open and communicative to someone who transcends us and to whom we are accountable does not remain our permanent possession once we have gained it in a moment of spiritual insight. *Faith* is not assent to a proposition but an attitude of the whole person, of sensitivity, understanding, engagement, and attachment.[29] It includes *faithfulness*—loyalty to the higher moments of insight even during the long periods of ordinary living.

Man knows God because God knows man, and man's purpose is to live in such a way that he may be worthy of being known to God. God knows all of man, but man knows only two things about God: (1) that he is known to God and (2) what God asks of him. Man knows himself, therefore, as the object of God's knowledge and God's demands.[30]

IV

Heschel's analysis of the experiences and thoughts that lead to God awareness has revealed three different approaches to the problem: (1) The awareness of the realm of the ineffable and of God's *glory* ubiquitously sensed in and behind all things leads to a *panentheistic* outlook. (2) The awareness that the discrete conscious self cannot be distinguished at its root and ground but only at its branches tends to lead to a *mystical* world view. (3) The awareness of God's *voice* addressing man and demanding each individual's freely given response leads to a view of God as *transcendent*.

All these three approaches can be found in the Bible and the other classical documents of Jewish tradition, although the emphasis varies in the different sources. Heschel himself has given an English translation of a letter written by a follower of Ḥabad Ḥasidism, the message of which is that *All is God*[31]—a message that differs from pantheism because the phrase is not reversible into "God is the All (the Universe)." Yet it is predominantly the experience of the *transcendent* God whose voice speaks to the living and finds an echo in their hearts that forms the core of prophetic consciousness. The event of *revelation* as described in the Hebrew Bible exhibits in archetypal form what normal religious consciousness has discovered on a lower level. Having traversed the Way of Wonder, we now turn to Heschel's studies on the God of the prophets.

The experience of God as revealing himself in and through the facts of life and nature, and yet infinitely surpassing all reality, is embodied in the

Biblical doctrine of God as essentially transcendent and only accidentally immanent. By denying the pantheistic view of the Deity as essentially immanent and in no way transcendent, it excludes the deification of nature as a whole or of any of her parts which is the outstanding characteristic of paganism and of modern romantic nature worship and cosmic piety.

While Greek philosophy applies the quality of *perfection* to the Divine, Heschel stresses the fact that Biblical thought makes *unity* the most important idea to be associated with God. But the doctrine of God's essential transcendence distinguishes radically the unity of God in Hebrew tradition from the idea of unity in which cosmic piety finds its inspiration.

Religion shares the axiom of unity with science and philosophy.[32] It is not the outcome of empirical investigation but, as Heschel calls it, a "metaphysical insight," whether it expresses itself in the idea of the universe or of God. It is the condition of scientific and religious experience: in knowledge the unity underlying the split of subject and object, in science the unity of the universe in which all interaction takes place, in religion the unity of the source of all beings which implies their common unity of purpose.

The most hallowed statement of Jewish religion is the *Shema* (Deuteronomy 6:4), which may be freely rendered: "Understand, O Israel, the Lord our God, the Lord is One!" Understanding the meaning of *unity* is, however, not a simple matter.[33] According to Heschel this statement, besides denying polytheism, asserts that God is (1) unique, (2) alone (only), (3) the same, and (4) the power of unity with all things.[34]

These four predicates can be reduced to two which I propose to call *uniqueness* and *togetherness,* or, perhaps more precisely, *exclusiveness* and *inclusiveness.* They form a polarity that is of basic importance not only for Heschel's doctrine of God but his whole ontology. Like Plato's sameness and difference (*Sophist,* 254 ff.), they are spread all over reality.

God's uniqueness implies that he is neither an aspect of nature nor an additional reality alongside the universe. God's togetherness means that he is not isolated from reality; that "the natural and the supernatural are not two different spheres, detached from one another as heaven from earth."[35] The exclusive aspect of God is at the bottom of man's experience of the ineffable and leads him to seek an explanation of reality beyond the realm of causality where "explanation" means the discovery of uniformities. The inclusive aspect of God is at the bottom of man's awareness that "no one is ever alone. . . ."[36]

God in his exclusiveness and uniqueness is experienced as *holy,* in his inclusiveness and togetherness as *love.* Since we are dealing with a polar pair of concepts ("scissor words," as Morris R. Cohen called them, since they only cut together like a pair of scissors, and not singly like a knife), each term implies the other: the holy can never be experienced as wholly other and completely isolated from man. In order to become a meaningful human experience it must include the minimum of relatability and togetherness indicated by the pole of inclusiveness. And love which drives toward union presupposes an element of otherness and separation, indicated by the pole of exclusiveness, since that which is the object of love must be different from its subject in order to make the relationship possible.

The notions of uniqueness and togetherness are closely connected with another pair of polar concepts that are fundamental in Heschel's thought: *event* and *process*. Now it is a truism that if two entities were alike in every respect they would not be two different entities (Leibniz' principle of the identity of indiscernibles). And if two entities had nothing whatsoever in common, they could not be compared and perceived as two. It is, therefore, safe but trivial to say that no two things in the universe are alike, and no two things in the universe are without a minimal aspect which they share. But the moment we turn from this innocent commonplace to consider which one of these two aspects predominates in a given domain of reality or in all reality we arrive at sharply divergent types of philosophy.

A mechanistic system, for example, in which all existence is reduced to configurations of identical particles following uniform laws and admitting cyclical repetitions, denies any significant novelty and uniqueness. On the other hand, "contextualist" philosophies such as modern pragmatism emphasize the element of genuine novelty and uniqueness.[37] It is apparently possible to look at reality either as a system of identical entities or repetitive processes which also exhibit accidental traits of difference and novelty, or to see it as a stream of entities and happenings which exhibit substantial differences, novelty and uniqueness, and disclose only accidental traits of uniformity and identity. World views of the latter kind are generally distinguished by the fact that they take the reality of *time* seriously. (Compare, for example, Descartes and Henri Bergson on this point.)

Now Heschel defines a *process* as something which "happens regularly, following a relatively permanent pattern," while an *event* "is extraordinary, irregular." "A process follows a law, events create a precedent."[38] An event is unique and cannot be reduced to a part of a process. It cannot be predicted or fully explained. A process is typical. Nature is largely made up of processes, history of events.[39] The world exhibits both processes and events. But since science is based on the description and prediction of uniform and repetitive series, it tends to look at reality chiefly as a system of processes. The artist and religionist, on the other hand, tend to stress events—the unique and sporadic experiences which, though rare and not reducible to a formula, can become sources of supreme aesthetic and spiritual values.

To the religious mind, which experiences the ground of all being as a person, the idea of *creation* expresses the conviction that neither blind chance nor an impersonal mechanical order is behind the existence of the universe. Behind the orderly processes of nature stands the primordial act of God's concern. There are *processes* because there was an *event* of creation.

To the scientific mind the idea of creation is completely irrelevant. Its task is to look for observable processes. To postulate a unique creative event that, because it is by definition nonrepeatable, could never be verified, would mean the abandonment of the scientific standpoint. But since science and religion deal with different dimensions of reality and since God is not a problem of science, it follows that categories quite irrelevant to science may prove of fundamental importance to a Biblical ontology such as Heschel expounds. Science, proceeding by way of equations and conceiving of cause and effect as changing parts of an unchanging whole,[40] is based on the Greek concept of the cosmos, the totality of things, complete in itself, with an immanent norm that has its foundation in nature. To the Biblical mind the world is neither an ontological necessity nor a brute fact to be taken for granted. In radical amazement the question is raised: Why is there order, being, at all?[41] The answer is that the will of God is responsible, and this voluntaristic outlook conceives of the relation between the Creator and the universe as one "between two essentially different and incompatible entities, and regards creation itself as an *event* rather than as a *process*."[42] Thus, while to Western man reality is *a thing in itself,* it is to Biblical thought *a thing through God.*[43]

Now one may ask why Heschel lays so much emphasis on the unique event character of creation. It is of absolute irrelevance to physical science and seems even to be unnecessary for a religious world outlook. Have not thinkers and religionists developed notions of cosmic piety where the very idea of fixed, eternal, and immutable nature has engendered feelings of awe and reverent submission? The main answer to this question will have to wait until the central relation of God to man, *revelation,* is analyzed in the doctrine of pathos and freedom. The act of revelation—which is not to be construed as an interference with natural processes, but which is the ingression of a new creative moment into the course of history[44]—supplies the key to creation, which is itself an act of primeval revelation. But in addition there are two other considerations that lead Heschel to look upon the *unique* as predominant over the element of repetitiveness.

1. The realm of history shows that the traditional claim for a mechanical self-sufficient universe (which modern science no longer maintains anyhow) is illusory. "What history does with the laws of nature cannot be expressed by a law of nature."[45] Creative and unprecedented novelty is a fact within history. The life of Pericles or Beethoven, considered as a process of birth, maturing, decay, and death, misses the essential significance of the unique, creative events embodied in such a life.[46] Therefore, a time-oriented philosophy finds the sources of truth and reality not only in recurring processes but in "unique events that happened at particular moments in history."[47]

2. Thought, following perception, always deals with posthumous objects and has only memories at its disposal. Hence we develop the tendency to see the present always in the light of the past and to make *comparison,* which abstracts and fixes common features, the basic category of knowledge. (Cf. Aristotle, *Metaphysics,* Book Alpha major, 1.) But although we often forget it, the basis of all knowledge is *presentation*—awareness of the present. The present is always unique, never a mere exemplification of general formulas. It carries an irreducible preciousness, a freight of meaning greater than the general essence which later on knowledge can abstract from it.[48]

Heschel's insistence on the primacy of unique present existence must not be construed as an attempt to posit immediate, unanalyzable emotional experiences against the sober method of scientific analysis. It is rather in line with other modern attempts to distinguish the aims and methods of philosophical analysis from those of physical analysis, where the object of knowledge is uniformities and where diversity can be ignored, except as an aid to the discovery of uniformities, and where the individual is to be understood in terms of its similarity to other members of a class.[49] Modern empiricism has largely neglected the present and individual by focusing its attention on the past (genetic method) and the future (method of consequences). Heschel's statement that "true insight is a moment of perceiving a situation before it freezes into similarity with something else"[50] is not to be taken as an abdication of reason, but as a program to describe the present and unique in a way that neither reduces it to the similarities it shares with uniform processes nor denies it any cognitive relevance by reducing it to an unanalyzable emotional quality. Events, though not reducible to formulas, are not surds but exhibit a structure, point beyond themselves, and connect with past and future processes. The present, though always in some way mysterious, since with awareness there comes an awareness that it is more than can ever be known about it, is never wholly opaque to thought. And to the religious mind it not only points into its past and future but also toward its transcendent source. "For the present is the presence of God."[51]

According to the preponderance of the pole of uniqueness or repetitiveness, a happening is characterized as an event or a process. Each happening partakes of both poles, since even the most unique occurrence must display familiar traits in order to become part of experience, and even the most routine incident is not identical with anything else. The answer to the question whether we are dealing with a process or an event depends in many cases on the context of the inquiry and the interest of the inquirer. To the astronomer each sunrise is part of a regular process; to the poet each experienced sunrise is different and unique.

Viewing the world from a scientific perspective where the "hypothesis" of a transcendent God is not needed, we may look at happenings as *a horizontal line of processes,* in which the powers of nature condition one another in ways that exhibit broad uniformities of cause and effect. Viewing the world as the product of God's *concern,* we may become aware of the *vertical line* that leads beyond every happening and being to its transcendent ground. This *dimension of depth* never enters the domain of knowledge, yet for religious consciousness it is as much a fact of experience as any causal sequence of the horizontal line. It is the source for man's sense of the ineffable, the sensitivity to the mystery of being and the uniqueness of each being.

The world thus conceals and reveals God. The repetitiveness of nature and life tends to stifle the sense of wonder that is the root of God-awareness, and makes one forget that "all actions are not only agencies in the endless series of cause and effect; they also effect and concern God."[52] The dual aspect of the world in which God is concealed and yet present is not a metaphysical construction but a concrete experience. In the moral domain, too, it points to the fact that the world is neither perfect nor depraved; it is still on the way. Heschel uses the terminology of the Lurianic Kabbalah, in which *tzimtzum* (contraction) is the category that accounts for creation.[53] "God is within the world, present and concealed in the essence of things. If not for His presence, there would be no essence; if not for His concealment, there would be no appearance."[54] Only the idea of divine immanence within the rational order of things, an allusiveness that points to the depth of all reality without negating the structures and processes encountered by empirical knowledge, can give us a world view compatible with science and, in accord with the sense of the ineffable, the awareness of divine concern.[55]

It is this idea of *personal concern* that forms the key concept in Heschel's philosophy. God's essence is inaccessible to man, but his dynamic modes of action in relation to the world and man are an empirical datum. "The certainty of being exposed to a presence not of the world is a fact of human existence."[56] It is usually thought that religion, including Israelite religion, is based on the experience of divine power or sovereignty. But Heschel has shown that it is not power—whether of the regular, and therefore predictable, or of the erratic, and therefore irrational and unpredictable, type—but the mode of *concern* or directed attention that is the ultimate datum of prophetic religiosity.[57] He takes this fundamental fact of religious experience, analyzes its structure, and employs it as the *root metaphor* of his ontology. Thus the idea of concern becomes the basic philosophical category, a conceptual tool to render intelligible such different fields of inquiry as theology, ontology, and ethics. *To be* means to be the object of divine concern. Berkeley's statement *"esse est percipi"* (to be means to be perceived) would well summarize Heschel's ontology if the word "percipere" were given a broader meaning, so as to include not only sensation and intellection but any type of directed activity.[58]

Heschel begins with the category of divine concern rather than with being because he is convinced that any adequate philosophy of religion must avoid a bifurcation between God and man, since that would render both terms unintelligible in their isolation. He therefore starts with the total situation in which religion takes its rise: man's awareness of being the object of God's concern. The religious man realizes that to be means to stand for a divine concern, and that *being* only signifies existence in a physical world because it implies participation in a divine world of meaning.[59]

We must distinguish two kinds of concern: *reflexive concern,* referring to one's own self and rooted in anxiety for the self's future, and *transitive concern,* a regard for others.[60] Reflexive concern cannot be attributed to God since there is no threat to his being. His chief attribute is transitive concern.[61] The divine concern expresses itself in three different ways, as creation, revelation, and redemption. Creation conceived as a voluntary expressive activity shows concern with that which is coming into being and is maintained. It is not to be confused with the concept of causality in science, but is rather an explanation for the fact that there is a realm of causality.

According to the type of concern, reality exhibits two levels of being: the subject of pure transitive concern, who is God, and the objects of pure transitive concern, which comprise all created things. Among created things three types of existence can be distinguished: inanimate, animate, and spiritual. Animate is distinguished from inanimate existence by reflexive concern: every living organism abhors its own destruction.[62] In

22

addition to the active, reflexive concern that is the essence of life, man exhibits transitive concern, a regard for others. "Human is he who is concerned with other selves. . . . A stone is self-sufficient, man is self-surpassing. . . . Man cannot even be in accord with his own self unless he serves something beyond himself."[63] Transitive concern is not merely an extension of self-concern; it opens up a new ontological dimension, *the dimension of the holy.* We share reflexive concern with plants and animals and transitive concern with God; it is in this latter that the *imago Dei* (*tzelem elohim*) consists.

The concept of divine concern and perception (*göttliches Gewahren*) plays the same role in the philosophy of religion that the concept of being plays in the philosophy of nature.[64] An adequate Biblical ontology, though taking as its starting point the polarity of God as both infinitely other and incomprehensible and yet the spirit of concern and directed action, must be based on the second element of this polarity, the divine concern. God and the world *in relation,* and not God in isolation, is the subject matter of human experience and thought. Strictly speaking, there is no such thing as *theology* (the logos about God). Heschel calls the Bible "God's anthropology" rather than "man's theology" since it deals with man as standing in relation to God and under his demand and not with the divine nature or essence.[65] And just as Biblical ontology cannot deal with God apart from the world, it is also unable to look at the world in isolation from God. The divine concern is, therefore, a more basic category than being.[66]

The idea of *pathos,* which forms the main theme of Heschel's penetrating study of prophetic consciousness (*Die Prophetie,* Cracow, 1936), expresses the conviction that the Deity cannot be understood through a knowledge of timeless qualities of goodness and perfection, but only by sensing the living acts of God's concern and his dynamic attentiveness in relation to man, who is the passionate object of his interest.[67] The prophets did not inquire into God's essence and they never experienced him in abstract absoluteness, but always in a specific and unique way—in a personal and intimate relationship to the world. He does not simply command and expect obedience but is moved and affected by the actions of men and reacts to them in joy and sorrow, pleasure and wrath. "This notion that God can be intimately affected, that he possesses not merely intelligence and will, but also feeling and pathos, basically defines the prophetic consciousness of God."[68]

The divine pathos is not passion, a mere feeling operating blindly, but an act formed with intention and will. It is also not a self-contained, self-centered state (reflexive concern) but transitive concern. While the emotions of the gods of mythology are determined by their own interests and pleasures, the divine pathos is motivated by its regard for man's dignity, nobility, and the quest for human righteousness. It is, therefore, inextricably involved in human history and human affairs. While in primitive religion divine wrath is often a primary and ultimate phenomenon and the enigma of divine power is experienced as a constant threat, the divine pathos of prophetic religion is conditioned in a twofold manner. In the first place, the pathos does not come "out of the blue," so to speak, but is itself a reaction of God to the behavior of man. In the second place, the prophets communicate God's wrath to the people, not that it may be fulfilled, but so that the people may take warning and return from their evil ways, thereby transforming the divine pathos of anger. This ability to change the divine pathos emphasizes the uniquely important position that man occupies in relation to God. But though human action can condition the divine pathos, it cannot force it. God remains free, yet his pathos is not an attitude arbitrarily taken. Its inner law is the moral law; *ethos* is inherent in pathos. Prophetic experience knows two different kinds of divine pathos: from the human point of view the pathos of redemption and affliction, from the divine point of view the pathos of sympathy and rejection. Experienced in various forms and changing with each unique occasion, the divine pathos points to a connection between God and man, originating with God but not disclosing his essence, directed at man and concerned with his life and well-being.[69]

The pathetic God as distinguished from the God of Aristotle is not the Unmoved Mover but the *Most Moved Mover*. To Aristotle, whose thought began with the notion of the cosmos and whose question was not *why* the universe exists, but *how* it functions, the First Mover was the principle needed to explain the fixed order of reality, its inner *logos*. If the world is eternally necessary and necessarily eternal, then the problem is not to understand how it came into being but what it is, i.e., what goes on within it. The Divine as self-thinking thought is then proclaimed as the theological cause because it provides the scientific solution to the cosmological problem.[70] To Biblical thought, which does not accept being as the unquestioned *a priori* of all reality but is aware of the "unexpectedness of being as such,"[71] the concept of *being through creation* expresses in symbolic form the truth that the world is the outcome of a divine act of freedom, of transcendental concern.

The experience of being the object of divine attention has a twofold effect on man: he becomes aware that he is ineluctably placed within the field of divine perception, from which he cannot escape, and he realizes that he is at all times safe and sheltered within God's care.[72] Man experiences "the joy of being found by God and the terror of being found out by him."[73] But the divine pathos creates in sensitive men not only a passive state of joy and terror; it also effects a powerful active response, based on the feeling of voluntary self-alignment with the divine pathos. Seeing that God has a stake in the human situation and that the human predicament is also a predicament of God, man responds with *sympathy* and makes God's concern his own. Against the *mystical union* where man attains a state of identity with the divine, and against the idea of *incarnation* where the divine becomes man, stands the *sympathetic union.* Here man's personality is not annihilated or identified with the divine essence, but a feeling of complete solidarity with God's purpose and will engenders a new kind of divine-human partnership in which the attainment of God's aims depends on human co-operation and effort.[74]

The sympathetic union must be clearly distinguished from the view of speculative theology which sees the culmination of the quest for the divine in a *knowledge* of God. The Biblical term *"da'at elohim,"* which is usually translated as "knowledge of God," ought to be rendered as "understanding" or "sympathy for God."[75] The experience of the divine pathos, mediated through the Word or the events of history that are interpreted as expressions of the divine attitude, leads to sympathetic understanding (*Verständnis*), which, in turn, results in solidarity (*Einverständnis*).[76] But owing to the nature of the divine pathos as an ever-changing reaction of the Deity to human behavior, understanding for God—unlike "knowledge of God"—cannot, once attained, remain man's permanent and safe possession. The voice speaks to man not in timeless abstraction but in singular moments of life and history.[77] Attentive to the unique demand of the hour, man becomes a partner in the work of creation, not by withdrawing from the temporal, but by sensing and meeting the challenge of the time.

The concept of the divine pathos implies that man's quest for God presupposes God's quest for man. Thus God is always experienced and thought of as subject and never as mere object. To emphasize that he is not to be conceived as an abstract principle or process but as the *living God,* he is called a person. But it must be understood that this is not strictly correct. The terms "person" and "personality" usually denote the essential structure of a human being which determines his modes of behavior. God, whose essence is incomprehensible and who is known only by his acts and expressions, cannot properly be called a person in this sense.[78] Yet, though used with this reservation, we have no more adequate way of referring to him than as a person: the closest analogue to the prophetic encounter with the Deity is the encounter that takes place between human persons. Unlike the knowledge of objects, which depends only on the knower's will, a human person can be known only to the extent that

25

he is willing to reveal himself. In encountering other selves we are met by a will whose spontaneous, self-revealing activity offers resistance to our will and makes us realize that we are confronted by a being whose creative and inaccessible center can never be exhaustively known through its manifestations. Its reactions can never be completely predicted because in its interaction with its environment it produces always novel reactions. Every encounter with another human self discloses some of the traits that are experienced in the revelatory encounter with God. While a consistent tradition in Greek philosophy thought of man as a *microcosm,* it is characteristic of Biblical thought to recognize in man the *imago Dei* and to describe the experience of the divine by the traits that constitute his kinship with the Creator: life, freedom, responsibility, will, passibility.

The notion of a God of pathos whose chief characteristic is concern for and participation in the lives of his creatures is diametrically opposed to the main stream of Jewish, Moslem, and Christian metaphysical theology throughout the last two millennia. The "dogma of the philosophers," as Sextus Empiricus called the idea that the Deity is impassible, was taken over by the speculative theologians, who, since Philo of Alexandria, endeavored to show by means of allegorization and various other exegetical devices that the anthropopathic descriptions of God in the Hebrew Bible have to be reinterpreted so as to make him identical with the self-sufficient, impassible Deity of the philosophers. The difference between the Biblical and Greek concepts of the Deity can largely be traced back to the fact that Greek philosophy takes its rise from the experience of reality as an ordered cosmos,[79] while the Biblical mind begins with the experience of a divine *subject* whose creative act is the ground of all reality. Heschel's ontology recognizes that an adequate understanding of reality presupposes both the category of uniqueness and of repetitiveness, but sees in uniqueness the dominant and decisive element for those aspects of man's experience that concern his relationship with the transcendent and his fellow man. Creation and revelation as *events* underline the divine freedom as against the Greek concepts of cosmos and Moira, and the awareness of this divine freedom by man makes him free too. It is, therefore, necessary to treat briefly Heschel's views on the nature of freedom.

V

But before we can understand the full significance of Heschel's doctrine of human freedom, we must recall some of his teachings on the nature of man and his needs, since freedom implies the ability to be somewhat independent of needs. As we have seen, man is distinguished from other animals by his *transitive concern*—his regard for others. Human nature,

though functioning within the framework of certain biological requirements, is not circumscribed by a fixed set of "needs" which must be fulfilled. Man is "concerned with ends, not only with needs."[80] Thus morality
and religion are not just feelings within man but responses to goals and
situations beyond him. Human happiness does not consist in satisfying
one's personal wishes but in the certainty of *being needed,* in having the
vision of goals still unattained.[81] Living is not a private affair; it is "what
man does with God's time . . . with God's world."[82] Thus at the bottom
of ethical action stands the element of uniqueness that enables man to
react to stimuli beyond the established set of biological needs. Yet unless
this element of uniqueness and exclusiveness were supplemented by the
element of togetherness and inclusiveness, man's reaction would remain
idiosyncrasy and would not attain the level of ethical and responsible
action. The unique sensitivity liberates the individual from the tyranny
of egocentric patterns, but in order to become ethical it must be integrated
into patterns of wider context and more pervasive togetherness.

Human freedom cannot be treated as a quality that can be predicated
of man in isolation. Just as the problem of God can neither be raised nor
solved except in the concrete situation in which Creator and world are
mutually implicated, so man and his freedom cannot be abstracted from
the total context of man-world-God.

If freedom means man's ability to act according to his nature, then it
is tautologously true to assert it. But as soon as the self or the will is seen
to be an abstraction or "solipsistic pretension," and the freedom which the
self experiences is forced upon it, it becomes clear that the question of
human freedom can be satisfactorily treated only in the context of man's
existence as both the object of transcendent concern and as immersed in
the processes of nature.

According to Heschel, freedom is not (1) to be dominated by one's own
will, since the will is not an ultimate and isolated entity, but determined
by motives beyond its control. To be what one wants to be is also not true
freedom, since the wishes of the ego are largely determined by external
factors.[83] (2) Freedom is not a principle of uncertainty, the ability to act
without a motive. Such action would be chaotic and subrational rather
than free. (3) Although freedom includes an act of choice, it is by no
means identical with choice between alternate motives.[84]

To understand Heschel's positive doctrine of freedom, one must bear in
mind that man not only stands in the horizontal line of natural processes
but also participates in the "dimension of depth," the vertical line of
divine concern. Freedom then means not the denial of physiological and
psychological determining factors but the ability to react to the unique

and novel beyond the routine of repetitive factors. It means that man is capable of "expressing himself in events beyond his being involved in the natural processes of living."[85] Man's ability to surpass himself, which is the premise of religion,[86] is the essence of freedom.[87] It is the liberation from the tyranny of the self-centered ego. It comes about in moments of transcending the self as an act of *spiritual ecstasy*, of stepping out of the confining framework of routine reflexive concern.[88] Although all men are potentially free, the actuality of freedom is not a permanent state, but rather an act, an event, which happens in rare creative moments.[89]

The distinction between the horizontal line of processes and the vertical line of divine attention which we made, though valid for purposes of exposition, must not be understood as indicating a "realminess" in Heschel's thought that would make the "natural" and the "supernatural" two different domains. Much of his work is concerned with combating just this type of bifurcation and showing that there is not nature and super-nature but only God's creation which exhibits repetitive traits that lead to attempts to explain it as a system of immanent regularities, and unique and novel traits that point to its transcendent ground. "To assume that the entire complex of natural laws is transcended by the freedom of God, would presuppose the metaphysical understanding that the laws of nature are derived not from a blind necessity but from freedom, that the ultimate is not fate but God. Revelation is not an act of interfering with the normal course of natural processes but the act of instilling a new creative moment into the course of history."[90]

Freedom then, just as revelation, can be understood only within the context of the polarity of uniqueness and repetitiveness, of event and process, in which all human life participates. The *thaumatic shock* that liberates man from looking only at the routine and regular features of experience opens his soul to the unique and transcendent. This sensitivity to the novel and unprecedented is the foundation of God-awareness and of the awareness of the preciousness of all beings. It leads from reflexive concern and the moral and spiritual isolation that is the result of ego-centricity to a mode of responding to each new and unique experience in terms of broader considerations, wider interests, deeper appreciation, and new, as yet unrealized, values.

As the object of divine transitive concern, man *is;* as knowing himself to be the object of divine concern and responding through acts of his own transitive concern, he *is free*. The meaning of freedom is not exhausted by deliberation, decision, and responsibility,[91] although it must include all these; it presupposes an openness to transcendence, and man has to be *responsive* before he can become *responsible*. Heschel finds that each challenge from beyond the person is unique, and that each response must be new and creative. And yet each act of freedom is more than an individual idiosyncrasy: *"Freedom is an act of self-engagement of the spirit, a spiritual event."*[92]

The characterization of freedom as an event once more draws attention to the importance of time in Heschel's philosophy. Existence is more intimately tied to time than to space and the objects of space. Man is free to exchange the place he occupies for another one and he can even return to his previous place, but time is uniquely assigned to each existent and is irreversible. The relation of existence to time is characterized by two polar elements: *temporality* and *uninterruptedness*. Existence is evanescent and always faces the prospect of annihilation, of being thrown out of the stream of time, yet it also exhibits some degree of permanence as a continuous duration in time. Without an element of constancy there could be no permanence within temporality and no knowledge of reality, since our categories of reason are "mirrors, in which the things are reflected in the light of their constancy."[93] Values are likewise measured by their endurance. Even the consciousness of time and the ability to measure it presuppose a standard and a measure that is itself not temporal.[94]

The secret of human existence lies in this relation of temporality to abidingness.[95] Man's reflexive concern is not the reason but the consequence of this abiding element of reality. A postulated "vital force" or "subconscious will to live" does not explain it either. Man has a will to live, but he did not will to have it; he must live. "Existence is a compliance, not a desire. . . . *In being we obey.*"[96] Man's yearning for the abiding is not a wish to conserve his own life forever. He does not aspire that the self and all it contains should last, but rather that what the self stands for should last.[97] In treating the polarity of temporality and abidingness, which are instances of the basic polarity of *exclusiveness* and *inclusiveness,* Heschel draws attention to a paradox of our experience of time and space: we usually associate time with change, and things of space with permanence. Time flies, things last. But it would be more relevant to speak of the passage of space through time than the other way round, since it is things which perish within time, while time itself is everlasting. "To the spiritual eye space is frozen time, and all things are petrified events."[98] The pole of exclusiveness manifests itself as detachment and isolation: "Two instants can never be together, never contemporary."[99] But from the pole of inclusiveness, seen as *eternity,* the essence of time is attachment and communion. Such communion does not begin beyond but within time. To be lasting does not mean to endure through a long stretch of time in isolation, but rather to commune with God. If reality is experienced as the act of God's concern, then every instant is seen not as an abstraction but as the presence of God. And the present moment is not a terminal but a signal of beginning, an act of creation. "Time is perpetual innovation, a synonym for continuous creation."[100] The vivid intuition of the realness of time changes man's everyday outlook, in which things of space are seen as real and substantial, while time is thought of as devouring them and bringing them to nought. The experience of reality as the continuous action of God and the reaction of man opens the way for the insight that reality is not a dead and closed system but a continuous process of creation. Both God's new ingressions into reality and man's creative responses to the voice and demand that address him through the happenings in time open up "new roads for ultimate realizations."[101] As a partner of God man is privileged to participate in the creation of new values and ideal consummations.

Heschel says that religion is characterized by a consciousness of *ultimate commitment* and *ultimate reciprocity;* that something is asked of man and that God needs man. This statement requires that in addition to his doctrine of the divine *pathos* his views on the nature of time must be taken into consideration. The awareness of God's interest in man, expressed in Judaism through the idea of the *covenant,* presupposes that God needs man for the attainment of his ends in the world, that religion is a way by which man identifies himself with these ends and serves them, and that this mutual relation imposes a responsibility on God as well as on his human partners. Human insight and creativity are correlative with human obedience and obligation: "We have rights, not only obligations; our ultimate commitment is our ultimate privilege."[102]

VI

The conceptual framework of Heschel's philosophy as set forth briefly in the preceding pages serves as the foundation for his views on the meaning of Jewish law (*halakhah*). His exposition is a masterly synthesis in which elements from the whole of Jewish religious tradition from the Bible, Talmud, Midrash, medieval philosophy, Kabbalah, and Ḥasidism are welded into an organic whole that is held together by the central framework of his philosophy of religion. Thus, for example, his views both on ethics and on religious observance are based on the experience of *divine concern,* and they are both dominated by the polarity of uniqueness and togetherness, of exclusiveness and inclusiveness. Man in his relation to his fellows or to God, as expressed in the practice of the *mitzvot* (religious commandments), cannot be understood if either of these polar elements is neglected.

Heschel deals with the problem of religious observance in terms of the tension between law and inwardness, pattern and spontaneity. Where the pole of regularity predominates, there is the continual danger of religion degenerating into mere habit and mechanical performance. Yet where fixed pattern is abandoned and religious life is confined to moments when the spirit moves the individual, the result is frequently a spiritual vacuum. "What may seem to be spontaneous is in truth a response to an occasion. The soul would remain silent if it were not for the summons and reminder of the law."[108] Perhaps the most instructive example of this fusion of law and love, and of holiness and happiness, is the institution of the *Sabbath*. A reminder of the unique event of creation, it is yet a regular day, repeated every week. Devoted to the service of God, it is yet a day of human "delight." A truce in the struggle for existence, it is the climax of living. Subject to numerous rules and regulations that circumscribe his actions, the Jew yet feels free on this as on no other day. Called "queen" and "bride," it calls for both obedience and love. Set within the pattern of ordinary temporal life, it is yet a piece of eternity.

Our examples from the field of religious observance have illustrated how Heschel finds, in the concepts of uniqueness and repetitiveness, the categories that inform the polar character of all human experience. God's essence is forever inaccessible to man, but wherever we meet the Divine in life our experience reveals this polarity. Stability and order in finite beings presuppose a high degree of repetitive regularity. Within a temporal career the unique can be preserved only if it can become incorporated in an enduring pattern. Although from the divine point of view every being is unique and every happening an *event,* human life requires the abstraction of common and recurrent traits (*processes*) for cognition and action.

God's concern, seen from the pole of the envisaged end of the *togetherness* of all beings with him and one another, appears dominated by the element of repetitiveness and hence of compulsion, as law, justice (*middat ha-din*), and the order of nature.

God's concern, seen from the pole of the envisaged end of the *uniqueness* and the irreplaceable preciousness of every creature, appears dominated by the element of freedom as spontaneity, pathos, compassion (*middat ha-rahamim*), and creative novelty.

Human life at its best is involved in a perpetual dialectic between these two poles. Living within an order and a pattern that opens his soul to the call of the transcendent and unique, he reconverts unique and novel in-

31

sights into a wider and more enduring pattern of living. And having risen to a higher plane of spiritual living, he opens his soul to new and richer experiences of transcendence. For the unique will perish unless it can point to a way, and a way will not serve us unless it remains open.

Part I

Ways to His Presence

1. THREE STARTING POINTS

It is customary to blame secular science and anti-religious philosophy for the eclipse of religion in modern society. It would be more honest to blame religion for its own defeats. Religion declined not because it was refuted, but because it became irrelevant, dull, oppressive, insipid. When faith is completely replaced by creed, worship by discipline, love by habit; when the crisis of today is ignored because of the splendor of the past; when faith becomes an heirloom rather than a living fountain; when religion speaks only in the name of authority rather than with the voice of compassion, its message becomes meaningless.

Religion is an answer to ultimate questions. The moment we become oblivious to ultimate questions, religion becomes irrelevant, and its crisis sets in. The primary task of religious thinking is to rediscover the questions to which religion is an answer, to develop a degree of sensitivity to the ultimate questions which its ideas and acts are trying to answer.

Religious thinking is an intellectual endeavor out of the depths of reason. It is a source of cognitive insight into the ultimate issues of human existence. Religion is more than a mood or a feeling. Judaism, for example, is a way of thinking, not only a way of living. Unless we understand its categories, its mode of apprehension and evaluation, its teachings remain unintelligible.

It is not enough to call for good will. We are in desperate need of good thinking.

There are three starting points of contemplation about God; three trails that lead to Him. The first is the way of sensing the presence of God in the world, in things;[1] the second is the way of sensing His presence in the Bible; the third is the way of sensing His presence in sacred deeds. These three ways are intimated in three Biblical passages:

> Lift up your eyes on high and see, Who created these?
> (Isaiah 40:26)

> I am the Lord thy God.
> (Exodus 20:2)

> We shall do and we shall hear.
> (Exodus 24:7)

35

These three ways correspond in our tradition to the main aspects of religious existence: worship, learning, and action. The three are one, and we must go all three ways to reach the one destination. For this is what Israel discovered: the God of nature is the God of history, and the way to know Him is to do His will.

To recapture the insights found in those three ways is to go to the roots of Biblical experience of life and reality; it means to delve into the religious drama of Israel, to grasp what it was that enabled Job to say:

> As for me, I know that my Redeemer lives,
> That He will witness at the last upon the dust.
> After my skin has been destroyed,
> Out of my flesh I shall see God.
> My own eyes shall behold, not another's.
> My heart faints within me.
>
> (Job 19:25-27)

How does man reach a stage of thinking where he is able to say, "Out of my flesh I shall see God"?

2. THE SUBLIME

How does one find the way to an awareness of God through beholding the world here and now? To understand the Biblical answer, we must try to ascertain what the world means and to comprehend the categories in which the Bible sees the world: the sublime, wonder, mystery, awe, and glory.

Lift up your eyes and see. How does a man lift up his eyes to see a little higher than himself? *The grand premise* of religion is that *man is able to surpass himself;* that man who is part of this world may enter into a relationship with Him who is greater than the world; that man may lift up his mind and be attached to the absolute; that man who is conditioned by a multiplicity of factors is capable of living with demands that are unconditioned. How does one rise above the horizon of the mind? How does one free oneself from the perspectives of ego, group, earth, and age? How does one find a way in this world that would lead to an awareness of Him who is beyond this world?

Small is the world that most of us pay attention to, and limited is our

2. The Sublime

concern. What do we see when we see the world? There are three aspects of nature that command our attention: its *power*, its *beauty*, and its *grandeur*. Accordingly, there are three ways in which we may relate ourselves to the world—we may exploit it, we may enjoy it, we may accept it in awe. In the history of civilization, different aspects of nature have drawn forth the talent of man; sometimes its power, sometimes its beauty and occasionally its grandeur have attracted his mind. Our age is one in which usefulness is thought to be the chief merit of nature; in which the attainment of power, the utilization of its resources is taken to be the chief purpose of man in God's creation. Man has indeed become primarily a tool-making animal, and the world is now a gigantic tool box for the satisfaction of his needs.

The Greeks learned in order to comprehend. The Hebrews learned in order to revere. The modern man learns in order to use. To Bacon we owe the formulation, *"Knowledge is power."* This is how people are urged to study: knowledge means success. We do not know any more how to justify any value except in terms of expediency. Man is willing to define himself as "a seeker after the maximum degree of comfort for the minimum expenditure of energy." He equates value with that which avails. He feels, acts, and thinks as if the sole purpose of the universe were to satisfy his needs. To the modern man everything seems calculable; everything reducible to a figure. He has supreme faith in statistics and abhors the idea of a mystery. Obstinately he ignores the fact that we are all surrounded by things which we apprehend but cannot comprehend; that even reason is a mystery to itself. He is sure of his ability to explain all mystery away. Only a generation ago he was convinced that science was on the way to solve all the enigmas of the world. In the words of a poet:

Whatever there is to know
That we shall know some day.

The awareness of grandeur and the sublime is all but gone from the modern mind. Our systems of education stress the importance of enabling the student to exploit the power aspect of reality. To some degree, they try to develop his ability to appreciate beauty. But there is no education for the sublime. We teach the children how to measure, how to weigh. We fail to teach them how to revere, how to sense wonder and awe. The sense for the sublime, the sign of the inward greatness of the human soul and something which is potentially given to all men, is now a rare gift. Yet without it, the world becomes flat and the soul a vacuum. Here is where the Biblical view of reality may serve us as a guide. Significantly, the theme of Biblical poetry is not the charm or beauty of nature; it is the

37

grandeur, it is the *sublime* aspect of nature which Biblical poetry is trying to celebrate.

What do we mean by the sublime? The sublime is not opposed to the beautiful, and must not, furthermore, be considered an esthetic category. The sublime may be sensed in things of beauty as well as in acts of goodness and in the search for truth. The perception of beauty may be the beginning of the experience of the sublime. The sublime is that which we see and are unable to convey. It is the silent allusion of things to a meaning greater than themselves. It is that which all things ultimately stand for; "the inveterate silence of the world that remains immune to curiosity and inquisitiveness like distant foliage in the dusk." It is that which our words, our forms, our categories can never reach. This is why the sense of the sublime must be regarded as the root of man's creative activities in art, thought, and noble living. Just as no flora has ever fully displayed the hidden vitality of the earth, so has no work of art, no system of philosophy, no theory of science, ever brought to expression the depth of meaning, the sublimity of reality in the sight of which the souls of saints, artists, and philosophers live.

The sublime, furthermore, is not necessarily related to the vast and the overwhelming in size. It may be sensed in every grain of sand, in every drop of water. Every flower in the summer, every snowflake in the winter, may arouse in us the sense of wonder that is our response to the sublime.

> A sense sublime
> Of something far more deeply interfused,
> Whose dwelling is the light of setting suns,
> And the round ocean and the living air,
> And the blue sky, and in the mind of man;
> A motion and a spirit, that impels
> All thinking things, all objects of all thought,
> And rolls through all things.
> (William Wordsworth, "The Old Cumberland Beggar")

It is not the sublime as such of which the Biblical man is aware. To him, the sublime is but a way in which things react to the presence of God. It is never an ultimate aspect of reality, a quality meaningful in itself. It stands for something greater; it stands in relation to something beyond itself that the eye can never see.

The sublime is not simply there. It is not a thing, a quality, but rather a happening, an act of God, a marvel. Thus even a mountain is not regarded as a thing. What seems to be stone is a drama; what seems to be natural is wondrous. There are no sublime facts; there are only divine *acts.*

2. The Sublime

Moreover, the sublime in the Biblical sense is found not only in the immense and the mighty, in the "bold, overhanging, and, as it were, threatening rocks," but also in the pebbles on the road. "For the stone shall cry out of the wall" (Habakkuk 2:11). "The stone which the builders rejected is become the chief cornerstone" (Psalms 118:27). A simple stone that Jacob had put under his head for the night was set up as a pillar to be "God's house" (Genesis 28:18, 22). The sublime is revealed not only in the "clouds piled up in the sky, moving with lightning flashes and thunder peals," but also in God's causing the rain "to satisfy the desolate and waste ground, and to cause the bud of the tender herb to spring forth" (Job 38:27); not only in the "volcanoes in all their violence and destruction," but also in God's "setting up on high those that are low" and in frustrating "the device of the crafty" (Job 5:11–12); not only in "the hurricanes with their track of devastation" but also in "the still small voice" (I Kings 19:12); not only in "the boundless ocean in a state of tumult" but in His setting a bar to the sea, saying, "Thus far shalt thou come, but no further; here shall thy proud waves be stayed" (Job 38:11).

The feeling caused by the sublime is astonishment which Burke defines as "that state of the soul in which all its motions are suspended with some degree of horror," in which "the mind is so entirely filled with its object, that it cannot entertain any other, nor by consequence reason on that subject which employs it." In contrast, the Biblical man in sensing the sublime is carried away by his eagerness to exalt and to praise the Maker of the world.

> Cry out unto God, all the earth,
> Sing of the glory of His name,
> Make His praise glorious:
> Say unto God: How sublime are Thy works!
> (Psalms 66:2-3)

In the face of threatening sights, the Biblical man could say: "Though I walk through the valley of the shadow of death, I will fear no evil, for Thou art with me" (Psalms 23:4).

One more feature sets Biblical man's experience apart from the esthetic experience of the sublime. The most exalted objects such as heaven or the stars and he himself have a mystery in common: they all continually depend on the living God. This is why the reaction to sublime objects is not simply "terrifying astonishment" or "the stupefaction of mind and senses," as Burke described, but wonder and amazement.

39

3. WONDER

Among the many things that religious tradition holds in store for us is *a legacy of wonder*. The surest way to suppress our ability to understand the meaning of God and the importance of worship is *to take things for granted*. Indifference to the sublime wonder of living is the root of sin.

Modern man fell into the trap of believing that everything can be explained, that reality is a simple affair which has only to be organized in order to be mastered. All enigmas can be solved, and all wonder is nothing but "the effect of novelty upon ignorance." The world, he was convinced, is its own explanation, and there is no necessity to go beyond the world in order to account for the existence of the world. This lack of wonder, this exaggeration of the claim of scientific inquiry, is more characteristic of writers of popular science books and of interpreters of science to the laymen than of the creative scientists themselves. Spencer and others "seem to be possessed with the idea that science has got the universe pretty well ciphered down to a fine point; while the Faradays and Newtons seem to themselves like children who have picked up a few pretty pebbles upon the ocean beach. But most of us find it difficult to recognize the greatness and wonder of things familiar to us."[1] "The facts of the case, we venture to say, are so wonderful that from first to last no general impression of Nature reached along scientific or any other lines can be even in the direction of being true that does not sound the note of joyous appreciation and of reverent wonder."[2]

"The history of European thought, even to the present day, has been tainted by a fatal misunderstanding. It may be termed The Dogmatic Fallacy. The error consists in the persuasion that we are capable of producing notions which are adequately defined in respect to the complexity of relationship required for their illustration in the real world. Canst thou by searching describe the universe? Except perhaps for the simpler notions of arithmetic, even our most familiar ideas, seemingly obvious, are infected with this incurable vagueness. Our right understanding of the methods of intellectual progress depends on keeping in mind this characteristic of our thoughts. . . . During the medieval epoch in Europe, the theologians were the chief sinners in respect to dogmatic finality. During the last three centuries, their bad pre-eminence in this habit passed to the men of science."[3]

3. Wonder

Wonder or radical amazement is the chief characteristic of the religious man's attitude toward history and nature. One attitude is alien to his spirit: taking things for granted, regarding events as a natural course of things. To find an approximate cause of a phenomenon is no answer to his ultimate wonder. He knows that there are laws that regulate the course of natural processes; he is aware of the regularity and pattern of things. However, such knowledge fails to mitigate his sense of perpetual surprise at the fact that there are facts at all. Looking at the world he would say, "This is the Lord's doing, it is marvelous in our eyes" (Psalms 118:23).

That "wonder is the feeling of a philosopher, and philosophy begins in wonder" was stated by Plato[4] and maintained by Aristotle: "For it is owing to their wonder that men both now begin and at first began to philosophize."[5] To this day, rational wonder is appreciated as *"semen scientiae,"* as the seed of knowledge, as something conducive, not indigenous to cognition.[6] Wonder is the prelude to knowledge; it ceases, once the cause of a phenomenon is explained.[7]

But does the worth of wonder merely consist in its being a stimulant to the acquisition of knowledge? Is wonder the same as curiosity? To the prophets wonder is *a form of thinking*. It is not the beginning of knowledge but an act that goes beyond knowledge; it does not come to an end when knowledge is acquired; it is an attitude that never ceases. There is no answer in the world to man's radical amazement.

As civilization advances, the sense of wonder declines. Such decline is an alarming symptom of our state of mind. Mankind will not perish for want of information; but only for want of appreciation. The beginning of our happiness lies in the understanding that life without wonder is not worth living. What we lack is not a will to believe but a will to wonder.

Awareness of the divine begins with wonder. It is the result of what man does with his higher incomprehension. The greatest hindrance to such awareness is our adjustment to conventional notions, to mental clichés. Wonder or radical amazement, the state of maladjustment to words and notions, is therefore a prerequisite for an authentic awareness of that which is.

Radical amazement has a wider scope than any other act of man. While any act of perception or cognition has as its object a selected segment of reality, radical amazement refers to all of reality; not only to what we see, but also to the very act of seeing as well as to our own selves, to the selves that see and are amazed at their ability to see.

The grandeur or mystery of being is not a particular puzzle to the mind, as, for example, the cause of volcanic eruptions. We do not have to go to the end of reasoning to encounter it. Grandeur or mystery is something

41

with which we are confronted everywhere and at all times. Even the very act of thinking baffles our thinking, just as every intelligible fact is, by virtue of its being a fact, drunk with baffling aloofness. Does not mystery reign within reasoning, within perception, within explanation? What formula could explain and solve the enigma of the very fact of thinking?

What fills us with radical amazement is not the relations in which everything is embedded but the fact that even the minimum of perception is a maximum of enigma. The most incomprehensible fact is the fact that we comprehend at all.

The way to faith leads through acts of wonder and radical amazement. The words addressed to Job apply to every man:

> Hearken unto this, O Job,
> Stand still and consider the wondrous works of the Lord.
> Do you know how God lays His command upon them,
> And causes the lightning of His cloud to shine?
> Do you know the balancings of the clouds,
> The wondrous works of Him who is perfect in knowledge,
> You whose garments are hot when the earth is still
>   because of the south wind?
> Can you, like Him, spread out the skies,
> Hard as a molten mirror?
> Teach us what we shall say to Him;
> We cannot draw up our case because of darkness.
> Shall it be told Him that I would speak?
> Did a man ever wish that he would be swallowed up?
> And now men cannot look on the light
> When it is bright in the skies
> When the wind has passed and cleared them.
> Out of the north comes golden splendor;
> God is clothed with terrible majesty.
>   (Job 37:14–22)

In radical amazement, the Biblical man faces *"the great things and unsearchable, the wondrous things without number"* (Job 5:9). He encounters them in space and in time, in nature[8] and in history;[9] not only in the uncommon but also in the common occurrences of nature.[10] Not only do the things outside of him evoke the amazement of the Biblical man; his own being fills him with awe.

> I will give thanks unto Thee
> For I am fearfully and marvelously made;
> Wondrous are Thy works;
> And that my soul knoweth exceedingly.
>   (Psalms 139:14)

3. Wonder

The profound and perpetual awareness of the wonder of being has become a part of the religious consciousness of the Jew. Three times a day we pray:

> We thank Thee . . .
> For Thy miracles which are daily with us,
> For Thy continual marvels. . . .

In the evening liturgy we recite the words of Job (9:10):

> Who does great things past finding out,
> Marvelous things without number.

Every evening we recite: "He creates light and makes the dark." Twice a day we say: "He is One." What is the meaning of such repetition? A scientific theory, once it is announced and accepted, does not have to be repeated twice a day. The insights of wonder must be constantly kept alive. Since there is a need for daily wonder, there is a need for daily worship.

The sense for the "miracles which are daily with us," the sense for the "continual marvels," is the source of prayer. There is no worship, no music, no love, if we take for granted the blessings or defeats of living. No routine of the social, physical, or physiological order must dull our sense of surprise at the fact that there *is* a social, a physical, or a physiological order. We are trained in maintaining our sense of wonder by uttering a prayer before the enjoyment of food. Each time we are about to drink a glass of water, we remind ourselves of the eternal mystery of creation, "Blessed be Thou . . . by Whose word all things come into being." A trivial act and a reference to the supreme miracle. Wishing to eat bread or fruit, to enjoy a pleasant fragrance or a cup of wine; on tasting fruit in season for the first time; on seeing a rainbow, or the ocean; on noticing trees when they blossom; on meeting a sage in Torah or in secular learning; on hearing good or bad tidings—we are taught to invoke His great name and our awareness of Him. Even on performing a physiological function we say "Blessed be Thou . . . who healest all flesh and *doest wonders.*"

This is one of the goals of the Jewish way of living: to experience commonplace deeds as spiritual adventures, to feel the hidden love and wisdom in all things.

Said David the king: "I shall testify to the love of the Holy One, blessed be He, and to the benefits He confers upon Israel, hour by hour, and day by day. Day by day man is sold [into slavery], and every day he is redeemed; every day the soul of man is taken from him, and delivered to the Keeper; on the morrow it is returned to him; as it is written: *Into Thy hand I commit my spirit: Thou hast redeemed me, O Lord, Thou God of truth* (Psalms 31:6). Every day miracles such as those that occurred at the

43

Exodus come upon man; every day he experiences redemption, like those who went forth from Egypt; every day he is fed at the breasts of his mother; every day he is punished for his deeds, like a child by his master."[11]

The sense of wonder and transcendence must not become "a cushion for the lazy intellect." It must not be a substitute for analysis where analysis is possible; it must not stifle doubt where doubt is legitimate. It must, however, remain a constant awareness if man is to remain true to the dignity of God's creation, because such awareness is the spring of all creative thinking.

Such awareness was the wellspring of Kant's basic insight. "Two things fill the mind with ever new and increasing admiration and awe, the more often and the more steadily we reflect on them: *the starry heavens above and the moral law within.* . . . The former view of a countless multitude of worlds annihilates, as it were, my importance as an *animal creature,* which after it has been for a short time provided with vital power, one knows not how, must again give back the matter of which it was formed to the planet it inhabits (a mere speck in the universe). The second, on the contrary, infinitely elevates my worth as an intelligence by my personality, in which the moral law reveals to me a life independent of animality and even of the whole sensible world—at least so far as may be inferred from the destination assigned to my existence by this law, a destination not restricted to conditions and limits of this life, but reaching into the infinite."[12]

4. THE MYSTERY

We live on the fringe of reality and hardly know how to reach the core. What is our wisdom? What we take account of cannot be accounted for. We explore the ways of being but do not know what, why or wherefore being is. Neither the world nor our thinking or anxiety about the world are accounted for. Sensations, ideas are forced upon us, coming we know not whence. Every sensation is anchored in mystery; every new thought is a signal we do not quite identify. We may succeed in solving many riddles; yet the mind itself remains a sphinx. The secret is at the core of the apparent; the known is but the obvious aspect of the unknown. No fact in

4. The Mystery

the world is detached from universal context. Nothing here is final. The mystery is not only beyond and away from us. We are involved in it. It is our destiny, and "the fate of the world depends upon the mystery."[1]

There are two kinds of ignorance. The one is "dull, unfeeling, barren," the result of indolence; the other is keen, penetrating, resplendent; the one leads to conceit and complacency, the other leads to humility. From the one we seek to escape, in the other the mind finds repose.

The deeper we search the nearer we arrive at knowing that we do not know. What do we truly know about life and death, about the soul or society, about history or nature? "We have become increasingly and painfully aware of our abysmal ignorance. No scientist, fifty years ago, could have realized that he was as ignorant as all first-rate scientists now know themselves to be."[2] "Can we not see that exact laws, like all the other ultimates and absolutes, are as fabulous as the crock of gold at the rainbow's end?"[3] "Beware lest we say, we have found wisdom" (Job 32:13).[4] "They who travel in pursuit of wisdom, walk only in a circle; and after all their labor, at last return to their pristine ignorance."[5] "No illumination," remarks Joseph Conrad in *The Arrow of Gold*, "can sweep all mystery out of the world. After the departed darkness the shadows remain."

The mystery is an ontological category. What it stands for is to most people most obviously given in the experience of exceptional events. However, it is a dimension of all existence and may be experienced everywhere and at all times. In using the term mystery we do not mean any particular esoteric quality that may be revealed to the initiated, but the essential mystery of being as being, the nature of being as God's creation out of nothing, and, therefore, something which stands beyond the scope of human comprehension. We do not come upon it only at the climax of thinking or in observing strange, extraordinary facts but in the startling fact that there are facts at all: being, the universe, the unfolding of time. We may face it at every turn, in a grain of sand, in an atom, as well as in the stellar space. Everything holds the great secret. For it is the inescapable situation of all being to be involved in the infinite mystery. We may continue to disregard the mystery, but we can neither deny nor escape it. The world is something *we apprehend but cannot comprehend.*

Science does not try to fathom the mystery. It merely describes and explains the way in which things behave in terms of causal necessity. It does not try to give us an explanation in terms of logical necessity—why things *must* be at all, and why the laws of nature *must* be the way they are. We do not know, for example, *why* certain combinations of a definite kind form a constellation which goes with the phenomena of electricity, while others with the phenomena of magnetism. The knowledge of how

45

the world functions gives us neither an acquaintance with its essence nor an insight into its meaning, just as the knowledge of general physiology and psychology does not give us an acquaintance with the Dalai Lama whom we have never met.

Science extends rather than limits the scope of the ineffable, and our radical amazement is enhanced rather than reduced by the advancement of knowledge. The theory of evolution and adaptation of the species does not disenchant the organism of its wonder. Men like Kepler and Newton who have stood face to face with the reality of the infinite would have been unable to coin a phrase about the heavens declaring the glory not of God, but of Kepler and Newton; or the verse: "Glory to man in the highest! for man is the master of things."

Scientific research is an entry into the endless, not a blind alley; solving one problem, a greater one enters our sight. One answers breeds a multitude of new questions; explanations are merely indications of greater puzzles. Everything hints at something that transcends it; the detail indicates the whole, the whole, its idea, the idea, its mysterious root. What appears to be a center is but a point on the periphery of another center. The totality of a thing is actual infinity.

There is no true thinker who does not possess an awareness that his thought is a part of an endless context, that his ideas are not taken from the air. All philosophy is but a word in a sentence, just as to a composer the most complete symphony is but a note in an inexhaustible melody.

Yet, how would we know of the mystery of being if not through our sense of the ineffable, and it is this sense that communicates to us the supremacy and grandeur of the ineffable together with the knowledge of its reality. Thus, we cannot deny the superiority of the ineffable to our minds, although, for the same reason, we canot prove it.

On the other hand, the fact of our being able to sense it and to be aware of its existence at all is a sure indication that the ineffable stands in some relationship to the mind of man. We should, therefore, not label it as *irrational,* to be disregarded as the residue of knowledge, as dreary remains of speculation unworthy of our attention. The ineffable is conceivable in spite of its being unknowable.

The ineffable inhabits the magnificent and the common, the grandiose and the tiny facts of reality alike. Some people sense this quality at distant intervals in extraordinary events; others sense it in the ordinary events, in every fold, in every nook; day after day, hour after hour. The sense of the ineffable is not an esoteric faculty but an ability with which all men are endowed; it is potentially as common as sight or as the ability to form syllogisms. For just as man is endowed with the ability to know certain aspects of reality, he is endowed with the ability to know that there is more than what he knows. His mind is concerned with the ineffable as well as with the expressible, and the awareness of his radical amazement is as universally valid as the principle of contradiction or the principle of sufficient reason.

Just as material things offer resistance to our spontaneous impulses, and it is that feeling of resistance that makes us believe that these things are real, not illusory, so does the ineffable offer resistance to our categories.

What the sense of the ineffable perceives is something *objective* which cannot be conceived by the mind nor captured by imagination or feeling, something real which, by its very essence, is beyond the reach of thought and feeling. What we are primarily aware of is not our self, our inner mood, but a transubjective situation, in regard to which our ability fails. Subjective is the *manner,* not the *matter* of our perception. What we perceive is objective in the sense of being independent of and corresponding to our perception. Our radical amazement responds to the mystery, but does not produce it. You and I have not invented the grandeur of the sky nor endowed man with the mystery of birth and death. We do not create the ineffable, we encounter it.

Our awareness of it is potentially present in every perception, every act of thinking and every enjoyment or valuation of reality. Since it is an incontestable fact, no theory of man would be complete if it were left out. It is attested to by undaunted triumphant explorers who, when they have reached the peak, are more humble than ever before.

Subjective is the absence not the presence of radical amazement. Such lack or absence is a sign of a half-hearted, listless mind, of an undeveloped sense for the depth of things.

The ineffable, therefore, may be verified by every nonsophisticated man who must come upon it in his own unmitigated experience. This is why all words that hint at the ineffable are understandable to everybody.

Without the concept of the *ineffable* it would be impossible to account for the diversity of man's attempts to express or depict reality, for the diversity of philosophies, poetic visions or artistic representations, for the consciousness that we are still at the beginning of our effort to say what we see about us.

The awareness of the ineffable is that with which our search must begin. Philosophy, enticed by the promise of the known, has often surrendered the treasures of higher incomprehension to poets and mystics, although without the sense of the ineffable there are no metaphysical problems, no awareness of being as being, of value as value.

Just as the simple-minded equates appearance with reality, so does the overwise equate the expressible with the ineffable, the logical with the metalogical, concepts with things. And just as critical thought is conscious of its not being identical with things, so does our self-reflecting soul bear in its heart an awareness of itself, distinct from the logical content of its thoughts.

We have characterized the perception of the ineffable as a universal perception. But if its content is not communicable, how do we know that it is the same in all men?

To this we may say that while we are unable either to define or to describe the ineffable, it is given to us to point to it. By means of *indicative* rather than descriptive terms, we are able to convey to others those features of our perception which are known to all men.

Perceptions of beauty are not expressed by definitions either, and because that which we sense is not identical in all regards, the descriptions offered are highly divergent. Yet we assume that they all mean essentially the same. This is because the reader recognizes in the descriptions the essence of a perception in which he shares, although the descriptions themselves differ widely.

The sense of the ineffable, the awareness of the grandeur and mystery of living, is shared by all men, and it is in the depth of such awareness that acts and thoughts of religion are full of meaning. The ideas of religion are *an answer*, when the mystery is *a problem*. When brought to the level of utilitarian thinking, when their meaning is taken literally as solutions to scientific problems, they are bound to be meaningless. Thus the basic *ideas* in Judaism have more than one dimension; what they refer to is a mystery, and they become distorted when taken as matter-of-fact descriptions. The idea of man as a being created in the likeness of God, the idea of creation, of divine knowledge, the election of Israel, the problem of evil, messianism, the belief in the resurrection or faith in revelation become caricatures when transposed into categories of pedestrian thinking.[6]

We have said that the root of worship lies in the sense of the "miracles that are daily with us." There is neither worship nor ritual without a sense of mystery. For worship and ritual imply the ability to address ourselves to God—an implication that cannot be integrated into any system of pure naturalism—and are only meaningful as a mystery we are convinced of, without being able to analyze it or to submit it to experiment. What is more, all worship and ritual are essentially attempts to remove our callousness to the mystery of our own existence and pursuits.

Let us take a loaf of bread. It is the product of climate, soil and the work of the farmer, merchant and baker. If it were our intention to extol the forces that concurred in producing a loaf of bread, we would have to give praise to the sun and the rain, to the soil and to the intelligence of man. However, it is not these we praise before breaking bread. We say,

4. The Mystery

"Blessed be Thou, O Lord our God, King of the Universe, who brings forth bread from the earth." Empirically speaking, would it not be more correct to give credit to the farmer, the merchant and the baker? To our eyes, it is they who bring forth the bread.

Just as we pass over the mystery of vegetation, we go beyond the miracle of cultivation. We bless Him who makes possible both nature and civilization. It is not important to dwell each time on what bread is empirically, namely "an article of food made of the flour of grain, mixed with water, to which yeast is commonly added to produce fermentation, the mixture being kneaded and baked in loaves." It is important to dwell each time on what bread is ultimately.

Firm and abiding are the laws of nature. And yet, we are told that a farmer scattering the seeds in the earth for the purpose of growth must do so by faith in God, not by faith in nature. For this is the essence of faith: even what appears to us as a natural necessity is an act of God.[7]

The mystery of God remains for ever sealed to man. *Thou canst not see My face, for man shall not see Me and live.* Even the seraphim cover their faces with their wings in the presence of God (Isaiah 6:2). Solomon, who built the great Temple in Jerusalem, knew that the Lord who fixed the sun in the heavens decided *"to dwell in deep darkness"* ('arafel) (I Kings 8:12).[8]

All we have is an awareness of the presence of the mystery, but it is a presence that the mind can never penetrate. Such an attitude may be contrasted with Hegel's characterization of the transition of the Egyptian to the Greek religion. "The enigma is solved; the Egyptian sphinx, according to a deeply significant and admirable myth, was slain by a Greek, and thus the enigma has been solved."[9] The extreme hiddenness of God is a fact of constant awareness. Yet His concern, His guidance, His will, His commandment, are revealed to man and capable of being experienced by him.

God is a mystery, but the mystery is not God.[10] He is a *revealer of mysteries* (Daniel 2:47). "He reveals deep and mysterious things; He knows what is in the darkness and the light dwells with Him" (Daniel 2:22). In the words of the liturgy of the Days of Awe: "Thou knowest eternal mysteries and the ultimate secrets of all living." The certainty that there is meaning beyond the mystery is the reason for ultimate rejoicing.

> The Lord reigns; let the earth rejoice;
> Let the many coastlands be glad!
> *Clouds and thick darkness are round about him;*
> *Righteousness and justice are the foundation of his throne.*
> (Psalms 97:1–2)

49

We do not deify the mystery; we worship Him who in His wisdom surpasses all mysteries.

When the great moment arrived and the voice of God became audible at Sinai, what mysteries did it disclose? In apocalyptic visions one is shown "the treasuries of the stars," mountains of gold, seas of glass, cities of jasper. Did Israel learn anything at Sinai about the enigmas of the universe? About the condition of the departed souls? About demons, angels, heaven? The voice they perceive said: Remember the seventh day to keep it holy. . . . Honor thy father and thy mother. . . .

When in response to Moses' request, the Lord appeared to tell him what He is, did He say: I am the all-wise, the perfect, and of infinite beauty? He did say: I am full of love and compassion. Where in the history of religion prior to the age of Moses, was the Supreme Being celebrated for His being sensitive to the suffering of men? Have not philosophers agreed, as Nietzsche remarked, in the deprecation of pity?

There are three attitudes toward the mystery: the fatalist, the positivist, and the Biblical.

To the fatalist, mystery is the supreme power controlling all reality. He believes that the world is controlled by an irrational, absolutely inscrutable and blind power that is devoid of either justice or purpose. The Maat of the Egyptian, Pta and Asha among the Indians and Persians, and the Moira among the Greeks signify a power set over the gods. The stern decrees of Moira are feared even by Zeus. To the notion of fate history is an impenetrable mystery, and man is in dark uncertainty with regard to the future. A tragic doom is hanging over the world, to which gods and men alike are subject, and the only attitude one may take is that of resignation. It is a view that is found in various forms and degrees in nearly all pagan religions, in many modern philosophies of history (history as a cycle of becoming and decay), as well as in popular thinking.

The positivist has a matter-of-fact orientation. To him the mystery does not exist; what is regarded as such is simply that which we do not know yet, but shall be able to explain some day. The logical positivist maintains that all assertions about the nature of reality or about a realm of values transcending the familiar world are meaningless and that, on the other hand, all meaningful questions are in principle answerable.

The awareness of mystery was common to all men of antiquity. It was the beginning of a new era when man was told that the mystery is *not* the ultimate; that not a demonic, blind force but a God of righteousness rules the world. In Greek tragedy man is invariably the victim of some unseen power which foredooms him to disaster. "Awful is the mysterious power of fate." "Pray not at all, since there is no release for mortals from predestined calamity."[11] In contrast, Abraham stands before God, arguing for the salvation of Sodom: "Far be it from Thee to do such a thing, to slay the righteous with the wicked, so that the righteous fare as the wicked! Far be it from Thee! Shall not the judge of all the earth do right?"[12]

The theology of fate knows only a one-sided dependence upon the ultimate power. That power has neither concern for man nor need of him. History runs its course as a monologue. To Jewish religion, on the other hand, history is determined by the covenant: God is in need of man. The ultimate is not a law but a judge, not a power but a father.

The Jewish attitude toward the mystery may be compared with the following statement by Plotinus.

"If a man were to inquire of Nature, 'Wherefore dost thou bring forth creatures?' and she were willing to give ear and to answer, she would say, 'Ask me not, but understand in silence, even as I am silent.' "[13]

The Jew will not accept that answer. He will continue to pray, "O God, do not keep silence, do not hold Thy peace or be still, O God" (Psalms 83:2). "Why dost Thou hide Thy face? Why dost Thou forget our affliction and oppression?" (Psalms 44:25). God is not always silent, and Israel is waiting for the word. "He is our God; He is our Father; He is our King; He is our Deliverer. He will again in His mercy proclaim to us in the presence of all living . . . to be your God—I am the Lord your God."[14]

The most vexing issue in Jewish thinking, furthermore, is not, "wherefore dost Thou bring forth creatures?" but rather, "where is Thy mercy?" "Where is thy zeal and Thy might? The yearning of Thy heart and Thy compassion are withheld from me." "Look down from heaven and see, even from Thy holy and glorious habitation."[15]

5. AWE AND REVERENCE

The message that the Bible conveys is not that of despair or agnosticism. Job does not simply say, "We do not know," but rather that God knows, that "God understands the way to it," He knows where wisdom is. What is unknown and concealed from us is known and open to God. This, then, is the specific meaning of mystery in our sense. It is not a *synonym for the unknown* but rather a name for a *meaning which stands in relation to God.*

Ultimate meaning and ultimate wisdom are not found within the world but in God, and the only way to wisdom is through our relationship to God. That relationship is *awe.* Awe, in this sense, is more than an emotion; it is a way of understanding. Awe is itself an act of insight into a meaning greater than ourselves.

The question, therefore, *where shall wisdom be found?* is answered by the Psalmist: *the awe of God is the beginning of wisdom.* The Bible does not preach awe as a form of intellectual resignation; it does not say, awe is the end of wisdom. Its intention seems to be that awe is a way to wisdom.

The beginning of awe is wonder, and the beginning of wisdom is awe.

Awe is a way of being in rapport with the mystery of all reality. The awe that we sense or ought to sense when standing in the presence of a human being is a moment of intuition for the likeness of God which is concealed in his essence. Not only man; even inanimate things stand in a relation to the Creator. The secret of every being is the divine care and concern that are invested in it. Something sacred is at stake in every event.

Awe is an intuition for the creaturely dignity of all things and their preciousness to God; a realization that things not only are what they are but also stand, however remotely, for something absolute. Awe is a sense for the transcendence, for the reference everywhere to Him who is beyond all things. It is an insight better conveyed in attitudes than in words. The more eager we are to express it, the less remains of it.

The meaning of awe is to realize that life takes place under wide horizons, horizons that range beyond the span of an individual life or even the life of a nation, a generation, or an era. Awe enables us to perceive in the world intimations of the divine, to sense in small things the beginning of infinite significance, to sense the ultimate in the common and the simple; to feel in the rush of the passing the stillness of the eternal.

In analyzing or evaluating an object, we think and judge from a particular point of view. The psychologist, economist, and chemist pay attention to different aspects of the same object. Such is the limitation of the mind that it can never see three sides of a building at the same time. The danger begins when, completely caught in one perspective, we attempt to consider a part as the whole. In the twilight of such perspectivism, even the sight of the part is distorted. What we cannot comprehend by analysis, we become aware of in awe. When we "stand still and consider," we face and witness what is immune to analysis.

Knowledge is fostered by curiosity; wisdom is fostered by awe. True wisdom is participation in the wisdom of God. Some people may regard as wisdom "an uncommon degree of common sense." To us, wisdom is the ability to look at all things from the point of view of God, sympathy with the divine pathos, the identification of the will with the will of God. "Thus says the Lord: Let not the wise man glory in his wisdom, let not the mighty man glory in his might, let not the rich man glory in his riches; but let him who glories glory in this, that he understands and knows Me, that I am the Lord who practises kindness, justice, and righteousness on the earth; for in these things I delight, says the Lord" (Jeremiah 9:22–23).

There are, of course, moments of higher or lower intensity of awe. When a person becomes alive to the fact that God "is the great ruler, the rock and foundation of all worlds, before Whom all existing things are as nought, as it has been said, all the inhabitants of the earth are as nought" (Daniel 4:32),[1] he will be overwhelmed by a sense of the holiness of God. Such awe is reflected in the exhortation of the prophets: "Enter into the rock, hide thee in the dust, from before the terror of the Lord, from the splendor of His majesty" (Isaiah 2:10).

Fear is the anticipation and expectation of evil or pain, as contrasted with hope which is the anticipation of good. Awe, on the other hand, is the sense of wonder and humility inspired by the sublime or felt in the presence of mystery. Fear is "a surrender of the succors which reason offers;"[2] awe is the acquisition of insights which the world holds in store for us. Awe, unlike fear, does not make us shrink from the awe-inspiring object, but, on the contrary, draws us near to it. This is why awe is compatible with both love[3] and joy.[4]

In a sense, awe is the antithesis of fear. To feel "The Lord is my light and my salvation" is to feel "Whom shall I fear?" (Psalms 27:1).[5] "God is my refuge and my strength. A very present help in trouble. Therefore will we not fear, though the earth do change, and though the mountains be moved into the heart of the seas" (Psalms 46:2–3).

Awe precedes faith; it is *at the root of faith.* We must grow in awe in order to reach faith. We must be guided by awe to be worthy of faith. Awe rather than faith is the cardinal attitude of the religious Jew. It is "the beginning and gateway of faith, the first precept of all, and upon it the whole world is established."[6] In Judaism, *yirat hashem,* the awe of God, or *yirat shamayim,* the "awe of heaven," is almost equivalent to the word "religion." In Biblical language the religious man is not called "believer," as he is for example in Islam (*mu'min*), but *yere hashem.*

There is thus only one way to wisdom: awe. Forfeit your sense of awe, let your conceit diminish your ability to revere, and the universe becomes a market place for you. The loss of awe is the great block to insight. A return to reverence is the first prerequisite for a revival of wisdom, for the discovery of the world as an allusion to God. Wisdom comes from awe rather than from shrewdness. It is evoked not in moments of calculation but in moments of being in rapport with the mystery of reality. The greatest insights happen to us in moments of awe.

A moment of awe is a moment of self-consecration. They who sense the wonder share in the wonder. They who keep holy the things that are holy shall themselves become holy.[7]

Ignorance is not the cause of reverence. The unknown as such does not fill us with awe. We have no feelings of awe for the other side of the moon or for that which will happen tomorrow. Nor is it might or mass that arouses such an attitude. It is not the prize-fighter or the millionaire but the fragile old man or our mother whom we find venerable. Nor do we revere an object for its beauty, a statement for its logical consistency or an institution for its purposefulness.

Nor do we ever revere the known; because the known is in our grasp, and we revere only that which surpasses us. We do not revere the regularity of the year's seasons, but that which makes it possible; not the calculating machine, but the mind that invented it; not the sun, but the power that created it. It is the *extremely precious,* morally, intellectually or spiritually, that we revere.

Reverence is one of man's answers to the presence of the mystery.

We do not sense the mystery because we feel a need for it, just as we do not notice the ocean or the sky because we have a desire to see them. The sense of mystery is not a product of our will. It may be suppressed by the will but it is not generated by it. The mystery is not the product of a need, it is a fact.

That sweep of mystery is not a thought in our mind but a most powerful presence beyond the mind. In asserting that the ineffable is spiritually real, independent of our perception, we do not endow a mere idea with existence, just as I do not do so in asserting: "This is an ocean," when I am carried away by its waves. The ineffable is there before we form an idea of it. The objection may be voiced that a psychological reaction is no evidence for an ontological fact, and we can never infer an object itself from a feeling a person has about it. The feeling of awe may often be the result of a misunderstanding of an ordinary fact; one may be over-awed by an artificial spectacle or a display of evil power. That objection is, of course, valid. Yet what we infer from is not the actual feeling of awe but the intellectual certainty that in the face of nature's grandeur and mystery we must respond with awe; what we infer from is not a psychological state but a fundamental norm of human consciousness, a *categorical imperative.*

6. THE GLORY

In his great vision Isaiah perceives the voice of the seraphim even *before* he hears the voice of the Lord. What is it that the seraphim reveal to Isaiah: "Holy, holy, holy is the Lord of hosts; *the whole earth is full of His glory*" (6:3). It is proclaimed not as a messianic promise but as a fact. *Man* may not sense it, but *the seraphim* announce it. It is the first utterance which Isaiah perceived as a prophet. Ezekiel, too, when the heavens were opened by the river Chebar, hears the voice of a great rushing, "Blessed be the glory of the Lord from His place" (3:12). And when again "the hand of the Lord was upon Ezekiel," he saw: "The glory of the God of Israel came from the way of the east; and His voice was like the sound of many waters; and the earth did shine with His glory" (43:2). In the Pentateuch the fact that the glory of God pervades the world is expressed in the name of God. "And the Lord said . . . in very deed, as I live—and as *the earth is filled with the glory of the Lord* . . ." (Numbers 14:21).

Is the presence of the glory in the world a divine secret, something known to God and the seraphim alone? According to the Psalmist, *"The heavens declare the glory of God"* (19:2). How do they declare it? How do they reveal it? *"Day unto day utters speech, and night unto night reveals knowledge."* Speech? Knowledge? What is the language, what are the words in which the heavens express the glory? *"There is no speech, there are no words, neither is their voice heard."* And yet, "Their radiation goes out through all the earth, and their words to the end of the world" (Psalms 19:4–5). The song of the heavens is *ineffable*.

The glory is concealed, yet there are moments in which it is revealed, particularly to the prophets. During the sojourn in the wilderness it happened more than once that "the glory of the Lord appeared unto all the people" (Leviticus 9:23; Numbers 16:19, 17:7, 20:6), so that the Book of Deuteronomy could acknowledge that "the Lord our God hath shown us His glory" (Deuteronomy 5:21).[1]

What is the nature and meaning of the glory or, as it was frequently called in later times, the *Shekhinah?* Since the glory was often revealed in a cloud and its appearance compared with a devouring fire (Exodus 24:17), it was sometimes characterized as a purely external manifestation, entirely divested of inner content; an exhibition of power, never of

55

the spirit.[2] Yet such a conception is erroneous. Is it possible to substitute fire or cloud for glory in the prophecy of Haggai (2:7): "I will fill this house with glory"? Or in the words of the Psalmist (85:10): "Surely His salvation is nigh them that fear Him, that [His] glory may dwell in our land"? Is it, moreover, conceivable that this is what the seraphim proclaim: the whole earth is full of fire or cloud?

What, then, is the nature of the glory? Perhaps this was what Moses was anxious to know when he prayed, "Show me, I pray Thee, Thy glory." His prayer was granted, and the Lord said, "I will make all My goodness pass before thee" (Exodus 33:18-19). The glory, then, is not a physical phenomenon. It is equated with the goodness of God.

And this is how the glory was revealed. Moses stood alone on the top of the mount, the glory passed by, "the Lord descended in the cloud," and the great answer was revealed:

> The Lord, the Lord, God, merciful and gracious,
> long-suffering, and abundant in goodness and
> truth; keeping mercy unto the thousandth
> generation, forgiving iniquity and transgression
> and sin; and that will by no means clear the
> guilty; visiting the iniquity of the fathers
> upon the children and upon the children's children
> unto the third and unto the fourth generation.
>
> (Exodus 34:6-7)

The glory is the presence, not the essence of God; an act rather than a quality; a process not a substance. Mainly the glory manifests itself as a power overwhelming the world. Demanding homage, it is a power that descends to guide, to remind. The glory reflects abundance of good and truth, the power that acts in nature and history.

The whole earth is full of His glory. It does not mean that the glory fills the earth in the way in which the ether fills space or water fills the ocean. It means that the whole earth is full of His presence.

In English the phrase that a person "has presence" is hard to define. There are people whose being here and now is felt, even though they do not display themselves in action or speech. They have "presence." There are other people who may be here all the time, and no one will be aware of their presence. Of a person whose outwardness communicates something of his indwelling power or greatness, whose soul is radiant and conveys itself without words, we say he has presence.

The whole earth is full of His glory. The outwardness of the world communicates something of the indwelling greatness of God, which is radiant and conveys itself without words. *"There is no speech, there are no words, neither is their voice heard."* And yet, *"their radiation goes out through all the earth and their words to the end of the world"* (Psalms 19:4–5).

The glory is neither an esthetic nor a physical category. It is sensed in grandeur, but it is more than grandeur. It is, as we said, a living presence or *the effulgence of a living presence.*

Is the glory something that is seen, heard, or clearly apprehended?

The whole earth is full of His glory, but we do not perceive it; it is within our reach but beyond our grasp.

> Lo, He passes by me, and I see Him not;
> He moves on, but I do not perceive Him.
>
> (Job 9:11)

The earth is filled with the glory; it is not filled with knowledge of the glory. In the time to come, "the earth shall *be filled with the knowledge of the glory of the Lord,* as the waters cover the sea" (Habakkuk 2:14). Now the glory is *concealed;* in the time to come *"The glory of the Lord shall be revealed,* and all flesh shall see it together" (Isaiah 40:5). It is in this messianic sense that the Psalmist prays, "Let the whole world be filled with His glory. Amen and Amen" (72:19).[3] And still, the glory is not entirely unknown to us. That not only the heavens are able to declare it, may be seen from the fact that we are all called upon: "Declare His glory among the nations. His marvels among all the peoples" (I Chronicles 16:24; see also Psalms 145:5). We have no words to describe the glory; we have no adequate way of knowing it. Yet what is decisive is not our knowing it but our awareness of *being known* by it.

> Thou compasseth my path and my lying down,
> Thou art acquainted with all my ways.
> For there is not a word in my tongue,
> But lo, O Lord, Thou knowest it altogether.
>
> Whither shall I go from Thy spirit?
> Or whither shall I flee from Thy presence?
> If I ascend up into heaven, Thou art there;
> If I make my bed in the netherworld, behold Thou art there.
> If I take the wings of the morning,
> And dwell in the uttermost parts of the sea;
> Even there would Thy hand lead me,
> And Thy right hand would hold me.
> And if I say: "Surely the darkness shall envelop me,
> And the light about me shall be night";
> Even the night shineth as the day;
> The darkness is even as the light.
>
> (Psalms 139:3–4, 7–12)

Standing face to face with the world, we often sense a spirit which surpasses our ability to comprehend. The world is too much for us. It is crammed with marvel. The glory is not an exception but an aura that lies about all being, a spiritual setting of reality.

To the religious man it is as if things stood with their backs to him, their faces turned to God, as if the glory of things consisted in their being an object of divine thought.

The perception of the glory is a rare occurrence in our lives. We fail to wonder, we fail to respond to the presence. This is the tragedy of every man: "to dim all wonder by indifference." Life is routine, and routine is resistance to the wonder. "Replete is the world with a spiritual radiance, replete with sublime and marvelous secrets. But a small hand held against the eye hides it all," said the Baal Shem. "Just as a small coin held over the face can block out the sight of a mountain, so can the vanities of living block out the sight of the infinite light."[4]

The wonders are daily with us, and yet "the miracle is not recognized by him who experiences it."[5] Its apprehension is not a matter of physical perception. "Of what avail is an open eye, if the heart is blind?"[6] One may see many things without observing them—"his ears are open, but he does not hear."[7]

"The word of the Lord came to me: 'Son of man, you dwell in the midst of a rebellious house, who have eyes to see, but see not, who have ears to hear but hear not.' "[8]

"Alas for people that they see but do not know what they see, they stand and do not know on what they stand."[9]

7. A QUESTION ADDRESSED TO US

The heavens declare the glory of God. Man is confronted with a world that alludes to something beyond itself, to a truth beyond experience. It is the allusiveness to a meaning which is not of this world, and it is that allusiveness which conveys to us the awareness of a spiritual dimension of reality, the relatedness of being to transcendent meaning.

True, the mystery of meaning is silent. There is no speech, there are no words, the voice is not heard. Yet beyond our reasoning and beyond our believing, there is a *preconceptual* faculty that senses the glory, the presence of the Divine. We do not perceive it. We have no knowledge; we only have an awareness. We witness it. And to witness is more than to give an account. We have no concept, nor can we develop a theory. All we have is an awareness of something that can be neither conceptualized nor symbolized.

The answer to the ultimate question is not found in the notion that the foundations of the world lie amid impenetrable fog. Fog is no substitute for light, and the totally unknown God is not a god but a name for the cosmic darkness. The God whose presence in the world we sense is anonymous, mysterious. We may sense that He is, not what He is. What is His name, His will, His hope for me? How should I serve Him, how should I worship Him? The sense of wonder, awe, and mystery is necessary, but not sufficient to find the way from wonder to worship, from willingness to realization, from awe to action.

There is no answer in the world for man's ultimate wonder at the world. There is no answer in the self to man's ultimate wonder at the self. The question, Who created these? cannot be answered by referring to a cause or a power, since the question would remain, who created the power or the cause? There is nothing in the world to deserve the name God. The world is a mystery, a question, not an answer. Only an idea that is greater than the world, an idea not borrowed from either experience or speculation, is adequate and worthy to be related to the religious problem. The mystery of creation rather than the concept of design; a God that stands above the mystery rather than a designer or a master mind; a God in relation to Whom the world here and now may gain meaning—these are answers that are adequate to the religious problem. The admission that we do not comprehend the origin of the universe is more honest than the acceptance of a designer.

There is another essential difference between the issue of God in speculation and the issue of God in religion. The first is a question *about* God; the second is a question *from* God. The first is concerned with a solution to the problem, whether there is a God and, if there is a God, what is His nature? The second is concerned with our personal answer to the problem that is addressed to us in the facts and events of the world and our own experience. Unlike questions of science which we may if we wish leave to others, the ultimate question gives us no rest. Every one of us is called upon to answer.

To the speculative mind, the world is an enigma; to the religious mind, the world is a challenge. The speculative problem is impersonal; the religious problem is a problem addressed to the person. The first is concerned with finding an answer to the question: what is the cause of being? The second, with giving an answer to the question: what is asked of us?

Thinking is not an isolated phenomenon: it affects all of one's life and is in turn affected by all one knows, feels, values, utters, and does. The act of thinking about God is affected by one's awe and arrogance, humility and egotism, sensitivity and callousness.

We do not think in a vacuum. To think means first of all to reflect upon what is present to the mind. What is present to us in religious thinking is not a hypothesis, but the sublime, the marvel, the mystery, the challenge. To think about God does not mean simply to theorize or to conjecture about something that is inane and unknown. We do not conjure up the meaning of God out of nothing. It is not a vacuum we face, but the sublime, the marvel, the mystery, the challenge.

There is no concern for God in the absence of awe, and it is only in moments of awe that God is sensed as an issue. In moments of indifference and self-assertion, He may be a concept, but not a concern, and it is only *a concern* that initiates religious thinking.

Lift up your eyes on high. Religion is the result of what man does with his ultimate wonder, with the moments of awe, with the sense of mystery.

How did Abraham arrive at his certainty that there is a God who is concerned with the world? According to the Rabbis, Abraham may be "compared to a man who was traveling from place to place when he saw *a palace full of light.*[1] 'Is it possible that there is no one who cares for the palace?' he wondered. Until the owner of the palace looked at him and said, 'I am the owner of the palace.' Similarly, Abraham our father wondered, 'Is it conceivable that the world is without a guide?' The Holy One, blessed be He, looked out and said, 'I am the Guide, the Sovereign of the world.' " It was in wonder that Abraham's quest for God began.

Thus it is not a feeling for the mystery of living, or a sense of awe, wonder, or fear, which is the root of religion; but rather the question *what to do* with the feeling for the mystery of living, what to do with awe, wonder, or fear. Thinking about God begins when we do not know any more how to wonder, how to fear, how to be in awe. For wonder is not a state of esthetic enjoyment. Endless wonder is endless tension, a situation in which we are shocked at the inadequacy of our awe, at the weakness of our shock, as well as the state of being asked the ultimate question.

The soul is endowed with a sense of indebtedness, and wonder, awe, and fear unlock that sense of indebtedness. Wonder is the state of our being asked.

In spite of our pride, in spite of our acquisitiveness, we are driven by an awareness that something is asked of us; that we are asked to wonder, to revere, to think and to live in a way that is compatible with the grandeur and mystery of living.

What gives birth to religion is not intellectual curiosity but the fact and experience of our being asked.

All that is left to us is a choice—to answer or to refuse to answer.

If awe is rare, if wonder is dead, and the sense of mystery defunct, then the problem what to do with awe, wonder and mystery does not exist, and one does not sense being asked. The awareness of being asked is easily repressed, for it is an echo of the intimation that is small and still. It will not, however, remain forever subdued. The day comes when the still small intimation becomes "like the wind and storm, fulfilling His word" (Psalms 148:8).

Indeed, the dead emptiness in the heart is unbearable to the living man. We cannot survive unless we know what is asked of us. But to whom does man in his priceless and unbridled freedom owe anything? Where does the asking come from? To whom is he accountable?

8. I AM WHAT IS NOT MINE

Is it possible to evade the ultimate issue by withdrawing within the confines of the self? The awareness of wonder is often overtaken by the mind's tendency to dichotomize, which makes us look at the ineffable as if it were a thing or an aspect of things apart from our own selves; as if only the stars were surrounded with a halo of enigma and not our own existence. The truth is that the self, our "lord," is an unknown thing, inconceivable in itself. In penetrating the self, we discover the paradox of not knowing what we presume to know so well.

Man sees the things that surround him long before he becomes aware of his own self. Many of us are conscious of the hiddenness of things, but few of us sense the mystery of our own presence. The self cannot be described in the terms of the mind, for all our symbols are too poor to render it.

Beyond my reach is the bottom of my own inner life. I am not even sure whether it is the voice of a definite personal unit that comes out of me. What in my voice has originated in me and what is the resonance of transsubjective reality? In saying "I," my intention is to differentiate myself from other people and other things. But what is the direct, positive content of the "I": the blooming of consciousness upon the impenetrable soil of the subconscious? The self comprises no less unknown, subconscious, than known, conscious reality. This means that the self can be distinctly separated only at its branches; namely, from other individuals and other things but not at its roots.

All we know of the self is its expression, but the self is never fully expressed. What we are, we cannot say; what we become, we cannot grasp. It is all a cryptic, suggestive abbreviation which the mind tries in vain to decipher.

As we shall see, to exist implies to own time. But does a man own time? The fact is that time, the moments through which I live, I cannot own, while the timeless in my temporality is certainly not my private property. However, if life does not belong exclusively to me, what is my legal title to it? Does my essence possess the right to say "I"? Who is that "I" to whom my life is supposed to belong? Nobody knows either its content or its limits. Is it something that withers or is it something that time cannot take away?

As an individual, as an "I," I am separated from external reality, from other men and other things. But in the only relation in which the "I" becomes aware of itself, in the relation to existence, I find that what I call "self" is a self-deception; that existence is not a property but a trust; that the self is not an isolated entity, confined in itself, a kingdom ruled by our will.

What we face in penetrating the self is the paradox of not knowing what we presume to know so well. Once we discover that the self in itself is a monstrous deceit, that the self is something transcendent in disguise, we begin to feel the pressure that keeps us down to a mere self. We begin to realize that our normal consciousness is in a state of trance, that what is higher in us is usually suspended. We begin to feel like strangers within our normal consciousness, as if our own will were imposed on us.

> And God said unto Moses:
> I Am that I Am, and He said:
> Thus shalt thou say to the children of Israel,
> I Am hath sent me unto you.
> (Exodus 3:14)

I am endowed with a will, but the will is not mine; I am endowed with freedom, but it is a freedom imposed on the will. Life is something that visits my body, a transcendent loan; I have neither initiated nor conceived its worth and meaning. The essence of what I am is not mine. *I am what is not mine.* I am that I am not.

Upon the level of normal consciousness I find myself wrapt in self-consciousness and claim that my acts and states originate in and belong to myself. But in penetrating and exposing the self, I realize that the self did not originate in itself, that the essence of the self is in its being a non-self, that ultimately man is not a subject but an *object*.

It is easy to raise verbally the question: Who is the subject, of which my self is the object? But to be keenly sensitive to its meaning is something which surpasses our power of comprehension. It is, in fact, impossible to comprehend logically its implications. For in asking the question, I am always aware of the fact that it is I who asks the question. But as soon as I know myself as an "I," as a subject, I am not capable any more of grasping the content of the question, in which I am posited as an object. Thus, on the level of self-consciousness there is no way to face the issue, to ask the absolute question. On the other hand, when we are overtaken with the spirit of the ineffable, there is no logical self left to ask the question or the mental power to stand as the judge with God as an object, about the existence of whom I am to decide. I am unable to raise my voice or to sit in judgment. There is no self to say: I think that . . .

There is, indeed, no speculative level where the question could be raised. We either do not sense the meaning of the issue or, when realizing what we ought to ask about, there is no logical subject left to ask, to examine, to inquire.

9. AN ONTOLOGICAL PRESUPPOSITION

But how can we ever reach an understanding of Him who is beyond the mystery? How do we go from the intimations of the divine to a sense for the realness of God? Certainty of the realness of God comes about

As a response of the whole person to the mystery and transcendence of living.

As a response, it is an act of raising from the depths of the mind an *ontological presupposition* which makes that response intellectually understandable.

The meaning and verification of the ontological presupposition are attained in rare *moments of insight*.

It is the mystery that evokes our religious concern, and it is the mystery where religious thinking must begin. The way of thinking about God in traditional speculation has been *via eminentiae,* a way of proceeding from the known to the unknown. Our starting point is not the known, the finite, the order, but *the unknown within the known,* the infinite within the finite, *the mystery within the order.*

All creative thinking comes out of *an encounter with the unknown.* We do not embark upon an investigation of what is definitely known, unless we suddenly discover that what we have long regarded as known is actually an enigma. Thus the mind must stand beyond its shell of knowledge in order to sense that which drives us toward knowledge. It is when we begin to comprehend or to assimilate and to adjust reality to our thought that the mind returns to its shell.

Indeed, knowledge does not come into being only as the fruit of thinking. Only an extreme rationalist or solipsist would claim that knowledge is produced exclusively through the combination of concepts. Any genuine encounter with reality is an encounter with the unknown, is an intuition in which an awareness of the object is won, a rudimentary, *preconceptual* knowledge. Indeed, no object is truly known, unless it was first experienced in its unknown-ness.

It is a fact of profound significance that we sense more than we can say. When we stand face to face with the grandeur of the world, any formulation of thought appears as an anticlimax. It is in the awareness that the mystery which we face is incomparably deeper than what we know that all creative thinking begins.

The encounter with reality does not take place on the level of concepts through the channels of logical categories; concepts are second thoughts. All conceptualization is symbolization, an act of accommodation of reality to the human mind. The living encounter with reality takes place on a level that precedes conceptualization, on a level that is responsive, *immediate, preconceptual,* and *presymbolic.*[1] Theory, speculation, generalization, and hypothesis are efforts to clarify and to validate the insights which preconceptual experience provides. "To suppose that knowledge comes upon the scene only as the fruit of reflection, that is generated in and through the symbols and sign manipulations, is, in principle, to revert to that very idol of sheer rationalism against which the whole vigorous movement of modern empiricism has lodged such effective and necessary protest."[2]

All insight stands between two realms, the realm of objective reality and the realm of conceptual and verbal cognition. Conceptual cognition must stand the test of a double reference, of the reference to our system of concepts and the reference to the insights from which it is derived.

Particularly in religious and artistic thinking, the disparity between that which we encounter and that which is expressed in words and symbols, no words and symbols can adequately convey. In our religious situation we do not comprehend the transcendent; we are present at it, we witness it. Whatever we know is inadequate; whatever we say is an understatement. We have an awareness that is deeper than our concepts; we possess insights that are not accessible to the power of expression.

Knowledge is not the same as awareness, and expression is not the same as experience. By proceeding from awareness to knowledge we gain in clarity and lose in immediacy. What we gain in distinctness by going from experience to expression we lose in genuineness. The difference becomes a divergence when our preconceptual insights are lost in our conceptualizations, when the encounter with the ineffable is forfeited in our symbolizations, when the dogmatic formulation becomes more important than the religious situation.

The entire range of religious thought and expression is a sublimation of a presymbolic knowledge which the awareness of the ineffable provides. That awareness can only partly be sublimated into rational symbols.

Philosophy of religion must be an effort to recall and to keep alive *the meta-symbolic relevance of religious terms.* Religious thinking is in perpetual danger of giving primacy to concepts and dogmas and to forfeit the immediacy of insights, to forget that the known is but a reminder of God, that the dogma is a token of His will, the expression the inexpressible at its minimum. Concepts, words must not become screens; they must be regarded as windows.

The roots of ultimate insights are found, as said above, not on the level of discursive thinking, but on the level of wonder and radical amazement, in the depth of awe, in our sensitivity to the mystery, in our awareness of the ineffable. It is the level on which the great things happen to the soul, where the unique insights of art, religion, and philosophy come into being.

It is not from experience but *from our inability to experience* what is given to our mind that certainty of the realness of God is derived. It is not the order of being but the transcendent in the contingency of all order, the allusions to transcendence in all acts and all things that challenge our deepest understanding.

Our certainty is the result of wonder and radical amazement, of awe before the mystery and meaning of the totality of life beyond our rational discerning. Faith is *the response* to the mystery, shot through with meaning; the response to a challenge which no one can for ever ignore. "The heaven" is a challenge. When you "lift up your eyes on high," you are faced with the question. Faith is an act of man who *transcending himself* responds to Him who *transcends the world.*

Such response is a sign of man's essential dignity. For the essence and greatness of man do not lie in his ability to please his ego, to satisfy his needs, but rather in his ability to stand above his ego, to ignore his own needs; to sacrifice his own interests for the sake of the holy. The soul's urge to judge its own judgments, to look for meaning beyond the scope of the tangible and finite—in short, the soul's urge *to rise above its own wisdom*—is the root of religious faith.

The urge of faith is the reverse of the artistic act in which we try to capture the intangible in the tangible. In faith, we do not seek to decipher, to articulate in our own terms, but to rise above our own wisdom, to think of the world in the terms of God, to live in accord with what is relevant to God.

To have faith is not to capitulate but to rise to a higher plane of thinking. To have faith is not to defy human reason but rather to share divine wisdom.

Lift up your eyes on high and see: Who created these. One must rise to a higher plane of thinking in order to see, in order to sense the allusions, the glory, the presence. One must rise to a higher plane of living and learn to sense the urgency of the ultimate question, the supreme relevance of eternity. He who has not arrived at the highest realm, the realm of the mystery; he who does not realize he is living at the edge of the mystery; he who has only a sense for the obvious and apparent, will not be able to lift up his eyes, for whatever is apparent is not attached to the highest realm; what is highest is hidden. Faith, believing in God, is attachment to the highest realm, the realm of the mystery. This is its essence. Our faith is capable of reaching the realm of the mystery.[3]

The sense of wonder, awe, and mystery does not give us a knowledge of God. It only leads to a plane where the question about God becomes an inescapable concern, to a situation in which we discover that we can neither place our anxiety in the safe deposit of opinions nor delegate to others the urgent task of answering the ultimate question.

Such ultimate concern is *an act of worship,* an act of acknowledging in the most intense manner the supremacy of the issue. It is not an act of choice, something that we can for ever ignore. It is the manifestation of a fundamental fact of human existence, the fact of worship.

Every one of us is bound to have an ultimate object of worship, yet he is free to choose the object of his worship. He cannot live without it; it may be either a fictitious or a real object, God or an idol.

There can be no honest denial of the existence of God. There can only be faith or the honest confession of inability to believe—or arrogance. Man could maintain inability to believe or suspend his judgment, if he were not driven by the pressure of existence into a situation in which he must decide between yes and no; in which he must decide what or whom to worship. He is driven toward some sort of affirmation. In whatever decision he makes he implicitly accepts either the realness of God or the absurdity of denying Him.

Understanding God is not attained by calling into session all arguments for and against Him, in order to debate whether He is a reality or a figment of the mind. God cannot be sensed as a second thought, as an explanation of the origin of the universe. He is either the first and the last, or just another concept.

Speculation does not precede faith. The antecedents of faith are the premise of wonder and the premise of praise. Worship of God precedes affirmation of His realness. We *praise* before we *prove*. We respond before we question.

Proofs for the existence of God may add strength to our belief; they do not generate it. Human existence implies the realness of God. There is a certainty without knowledge in the depth of our being that accounts for our asking the ultimate question, a preconceptual certainty that lies beyond all formulation or verbalization. It is *the assertion* that God is real, independent of our preconceptual awareness, that presents the major difficulty. Subjective awareness is not always an index of truth. What is subjectively true is not necessarily trans-subjectively real. All we have is the awareness of allusions to His concern, intimations of His presence. To speak of His reality is to transcend awareness, to surpass the limits of thinking. It is like springing clear of the ground. Are we intellectually justified in inferring from our awareness a reality that lies beyond it? Are we entitled to rise from the realm of this world to a realm that is beyond this world?

We are often guilty of misunderstanding the nature of an assertion such as "God is." Such an assertion would constitute a leap if the assertion constituted an addition to our ineffable awareness of God. The truth, however, is that to say "God is" means less than what our immediate awareness contains. *The statement "God is" is an understatement.*

Thus, the certainty of the realness of God does not come about as a corollary of logical premises, as a leap from the realm of logic to the realm of ontology, from an assumption to a fact. It is, on the contrary, a transition from an immediate apprehension to a thought, from a preconceptual awareness to a definite assurance, from being overwhelmed by the presence of God to an awareness of His existence. What we attempt to do in the act of reflection is to raise that preconceptual awareness to the level of understanding.

In sensing the spiritual dimension of all being, we become aware of the absolute reality of the divine. In formulating a creed, in asserting:

God is, we merely bring down overpowering reality to the level of thought. Our thought is but an after-belief.

In other words, our belief in the reality of God is not a case of first possessing an idea and then postulating the ontal counterpart of it; or, to use a Kantian phrase, of first having the idea of a hundred dollars and then claiming to possess them on the basis of the idea. What obtains here is first the actual possession of the dollars and then the attempt to count the sum. There are possibilities of error in counting the notes, but the notes themselves are here.

In other words, our belief in His reality is not a leap over a missing link in a syllogism but rather *a regaining,* giving up a view rather than adding one, going behind self-consciousness and questioning the self and all its cognitive pretensions. *It is an ontological presupposition.*

In the depth of human thinking we all presuppose some ultimate reality which on the level of discursive thinking is crystallized into the concept of a power, a principle or a structure. This, then, is the order in our thinking and existence: The ultimate or God comes first and our reasoning about Him second. Metaphysical speculation has reversed the order: reasoning comes first and the question about His reality second; either He is proved or He is not real.

However, just as there is no thinking about the world without the premise of the reality of the world, there can be no thinking about God without the premise of the realness of God.

10. FAITH

Most theories of religion start out with defining the religious situation as man's search for God and maintain the axiom that God is silent, hidden and unconcerned with man's search for Him. Now, in adopting that axiom, the answer is given before the question is asked. To Biblical thinking, the definition is incomplete and the axiom false. The Bible speaks not only of man's search for God but also of *God's search for man.* "Thou dost hunt me like a lion," exclaimed Job (10:16).

"From the very first Thou didst single out man and consider him worthy to stand in Thy presence."[1] This is the mysterious paradox of Biblical faith: *God is pursuing man.*[2] It is as if God were unwilling to be alone, and He had chosen man to serve Him. Our seeking Him is not only man's but also His concern, and must not be considered an exclusively human affair. His will is involved in our yearnings. All of human history as described in the Bible may be summarized in one phrase: *God is in search of man*. Faith in God is a response to God's question.

> Lord, where shall I find Thee?
> High and hidden in Thy place;
> And where shall I not find Thee?
> The word is full of Thy glory.
>
> I have sought Thy nearness;
> With all my heart have I called Thee,
> *And going out to meet Thee*
> *I found Thee coming toward me.*
>
> Even as, in the wonder of Thy might,
> In holiness I have beheld Thee,
> Who shall say he hath not seen Thee?
> Lo, the heavens and their hosts
> Declare the awe of Thee,
> Though their voice be not heard.[3]

When Adam and Eve hid from His presence, the Lord called: *Where art thou* (Genesis 3:9). It is a call that goes out again and again. It is a still small echo of a still small voice, not uttered in words, not conveyed in categories of the mind, but ineffable and mysterious, as ineffable and mysterious as the glory that fills the whole world. It is wrapped in silence; concealed and subdued, yet it is as if all things were the frozen echo of the question: *Where art thou?*

Faith comes out of awe, out of an awareness that we are exposed to His presence, out of anxiety to answer the challenge of God, out of an awareness of our being called upon. Religion consists of *God's question and man's answer*. The way *to* faith is the way *of* faith. The way to God is a way of God. Unless God asks the question, all our inquiries are in vain.

The answer lasts a moment, the commitment continues. Unless the awareness of the ineffable mystery of existence becomes a permanent state of mind, all that remains is a commitment without faith. To strengthen our alertness, to refine our appreciation of the mystery is the meaning of worship and observance. For faith does not remain stationary. We must continue to pray, continue to obey to be able to believe and to remain attached to His presence.

Recondite is the dimension where God and man meet, and yet not entirely impenetrable. He placed within man something of His spirit (see

Isaiah 63:10), and "it is the spirit in a man, the breath of the Almighty, that makes him understand" (Job 32:8).

For God is not always silent, and man is not always blind. His glory fills the world; His spirit hovers above the waters. There are moments in which, to use a Talmudic phrase, heaven and earth kiss each other; in which there is a lifting of the veil at the horizon of the known, opening a vision of what is eternal in time. Some of us have at least once experienced the momentous realness of God. Some of us have at least caught a glimpse of the beauty, peace, and power that flow through the souls of those who are devoted to Him. There may come a moment like a thunder in the soul, when man is not only aided, not only guided by God's mysterious hand, but also taught how to aid, how to guide other beings. The voice of Sinai goes on for ever: "These words the Lord spoke unto all your assembly in the mount out of the midst of the fire, of the cloud, and of the thick darkness, with a *great voice that goes on for ever*."[4]

We must first peer into the darkness, feel strangled and entombed in the hopelessness of living without God, before we are ready to feel the presence of His living light.

"And it shall come to pass, when I bring a cloud over the earth, that the bow shall be seen in the cloud" (Genesis 9:14). When ignorance and confusion blot out all thoughts, the light of God may suddenly burst forth in the mind like a rainbow in the sky. Our understanding of the greatness of God comes about as an act of illumination. As the Baal Shem said, "like a lightning that all of a sudden illumines the whole world, God illumines the mind of man, enabling him to understand the greatness of our Creator." This is what is meant by the words of the Psalmist: "He sent out His arrows and scattered [the clouds]; He shot forth lightnings and discomfited them." The darkness retreats, "The channels of water appeared, the foundations of the world were laid bare" (Psalms 18:15–16).[5]

The essence of Jewish religious thinking does not lie in entertaining a concept of God but in the ability to articulate a memory of moments of illumination by His presence. Israel is not a people of definers but a people of witnesses: "Ye are My witnesses" (Isaiah 43:10). Reminders of what has been disclosed to us are hanging over our souls like stars, remote and of mind-surpassing grandeur. They shine through dark and dangerous ages, and their reflection can be seen in the lives of those who guard the path of conscience and memory in the wilderness of careless living.

Since those perennial reminders have moved into our minds, wonder has never left us. Heedfully we stare through the telescope of ancient rites lest we lose the perpetual brightness beckoning to our souls. Our mind has not kindled the flame, has not produced these principles. Still our thoughts glow with their light. What is the nature of this glow, of our faith, and how is it perceived?

In the spirit of Judaism, our quest for God is a return to God; our thinking of Him is a recall, an attempt to draw out the depth of our suppressed attachment. The Hebrew word for repentance, *teshuvah,* means *return.* Yet it also means *answer.* Return to God is an answer to Him. For God is not silent. "Return O faithless children, says the Lord" (Jeremiah 3:14).[6] According to the understanding of the Rabbis, daily, at all times, "A Voice cries: in the wilderness prepare the way of the Lord, make straight in the desert a highway for our God" (Isaiah 40:3). "The voice of the Lord cries to the city" (Micah 6:9).[7]

"Morning by morning He wakens my ear to hear as those who are taught" (Isaiah 50:4). The stirring in man to turn to God is actually a "reminder by God to man."[8] It is a call that man's physical sense does not capture, yet the "spiritual soul" in him perceives the call.[9] The most precious gifts come to us unawares and remain unnoted. God's grace resounds in our lives like a staccato. Only by retaining the seemingly disconnected notes do we acquire the ability to grasp the theme.

Is it possible to define the content of such experiences? It is not a perception of a thing, of anything physical; nor is it always a disclosure of ideas hitherto unknown. It is primarily, it seems, an enhancement of the soul, a sharpening of one's spiritual sense, an endowment with a new sensibility. It is a discovery of what is in time, rather than anything in space.

Just as clairvoyants may see the future, the religious man comes to sense the present moment. And this is an extreme achievement. For the present is the presence of God. Things have a past and a future, but only God is pure presence.

But if insights are not physical events, in what sense are they real?

The underlying assumption of modern man's outlook is that objective reality is physical: all non-material phenomena can be reduced to material phenomena and explained in physical terms. Thus, only those types of human experiences which acquaint us with the quantitative aspects of material phenomena refer to the real world. None of the other types of our experience, such as prayer or the awareness of the presence of God, has any objective counterpart. They are illusory in the sense that they do not acquaint us with the nature of the objective world.

In modern society, he who refuses to accept the equation of the real and the physical is considered a mystic. However, since God is not an object of a physical experience, the equation implies the impossibility of

His existence. Either God is but a word not designating anything real or He is at least as real as the man I see in front of me.

This is the premise of faith: Spiritual events are real. Ultimately all creative events are caused by spiritual acts. The God who creates heaven and earth is the God who communicates His will to the mind of man.

"In Thy light we shall see light" (Psalms 36:10). There is a divine light in every soul, it is dormant and eclipsed by the follies of this world. We must first awaken this light, then the upper light will come upon us. In Thy light which is within us will we see light (Rabbi Aaron of Karlin).

We must not wait passively for insights. In the darkest moments we must try to let our inner light go forth. "And she rises while it is yet night" (Proverbs 31:15).

It is within man's power to seek Him; it is not within his power to find Him. All Abraham had was wonder, and all he could achieve on his own was readiness to perceive. The answer was disclosed to him; it was not found by him.

But the initiative, we believe, is with man. The great insight is not given unless we are ready to receive. God concludes but we commence. "Whoever sets out to purify himself is assisted from above."[10]

11. REVELATION

In our own lives many of us have found that there are channels of knowledge other than those of speculation and observation. When living true to the wonder of the steadily unfolding wisdom, we feel at times as if the echo of an echo of a voice were piercing the silence, trying in vain to reach our attention. We feel at times called upon, not knowing by whom, against our will, terrified at the power invested in our words, in our deeds, in our thoughts.

In our own lives the voice of God speaks slowly, a syllable at a time. Reaching the peak of years, dispelling some of our intimate illusions and learning how to spell the meaning of life-experiences backwards, some of us discover how the scattered syllables form a single phrase. Those who know that this life of ours takes place in a world that is not all to be explained in human terms; that every moment is a carefully concealed act of His creation, cannot but ask: is there anything wherein His voice is not suppressed? Is there anything wherein His creation is not concealed?

Behind the radiant cloud of living, perplexing the unacquainted souls, some men have sensed the sound of *Let There Be,* in the fullness of being. In others not only a song but a voice, lifting the curtain of unknowableness, reached the mind. Those who know that the grace of guidance may be ultimately bestowed upon those who pray for it, that in spite of their unworthiness and lowliness they may be enlightened by a spark that comes unexpectedly but in far-reaching wisdom, undeserved, yet saving, will not feel alien to the minds that perceived not a spark but a flame.

The idea of revelation remains an absurdity as long as we are unable to comprehend the impact with which the realness of God is pursuing man, every man. However, collecting the memories of the sparks of illuminations we have perceived, the installments of insight that have been bestowed upon us throughout the years, we will find it impossible to remain certain of the impossibility of revelation.

It is not historical curiosity that excites our interest in the problem of revelation. As an event of the past which subsequently affected the course of civilization, revelation would not engage the modern mind any more than the Battle of Marathon or the Congress of Vienna. If it concerns us, it is not because of the impact it had upon past generations but as something which may or may not be of perpetual, unabating relevance. In entering this discourse, we do not conjure up the shadow of an archaic phenomenon, but attempt to debate the question whether to believe that there is a voice in the world that pleads with us in the name of God.

Thus, it is not only a personal issue, but one that concerns the history of all men from the beginning of time to the end of days. No one who has, at least once in his life, sensed the terrifying seriousness of human history or the earnestness of individual existence can afford to ignore that problem.

The most serious obstacle which modern men encounter in entering a discussion about revelation does not arise from their doubts as to whether the accounts of the prophets about their experiences are authentic. The most critical vindication of these accounts, even if it were possible, would be of little relevance. The most serious problem is *the absence of the problem.* An answer to be meaningful presupposes the awareness of a question, but the climate in which we live today is not congenial to the continued growth of questions which have taken centuries to cultivate. The Bible is an answer to the supreme question: *what does God demand of us?* Yet the question has gone out of the world. God is portrayed as a mass of vagueness behind a veil of enigmas, and His voice has become alien to our minds, to our hearts, to our souls. We have learned to listen to every "I" except the "I" of God. The man of our time may proudly declare: nothing animal is alien to me but everything divine is. This is the status of the Bible in modern life: it is a sublime answer, but we do not know the question any more. Unless we recover the question, there is no hope of understanding the Bible.

Resistance to revelation in our time came from two diametrically opposed conceptions of man: one maintained that man was too great to be in need of divine guidance, and the other maintained that man was too small to be worthy of divine guidance. The first conception came from social science, and the second from natural science.

Since the days of the Deists, the idea of man's self-sufficiency has been used as an argument to discredit the belief in revelation. The certainty of man's capacity to find peace, perfection, and the meaning of existence, gained increasing momentum with the advancement of technology. Man's fate, we were told, depended solely upon the development of his social awareness and the utilization of his own power. The course of history was regarded as a perpetual progress in cooperation, an increasing harmonization of interests. Man is too good to be in need of supernatural guidance.

The idea of man's self-sufficiency, man's exaggerated consciousness of himself, was based upon a generalization; from the fact that technology could solve some problems it was deduced that technology could solve all problems. This proved to be a fallacy. Social reforms, it was thought, would cure all ills and eliminate all evils from our world. Yet we have finally discovered what prophets and saints have always known: bread and power alone will not save humanity. There is a passion and drive for cruel deeds which only the awe and fear of God can soothe; there is a suffocating selfishness in man which only holiness can ventilate.

Man is meaningless without God, and any attempt to establish a system of values on the basis of the dogma of man's self-sufficiency is doomed to failure.

The advancement in both natural and social sciences has compelled us to realize how insignificantly small man is in relation to the universe and how abortive are his attempts to establish a universally valid system of values. It is in such humility that modern man finds it preposterous to assume that the infinite spirit should come down to commune with the feeble, finite mind of man; that man could be an ear to God. With the concept of the absolute so far removed from the grasp of his mind, man is, at best, bewildered at the claims of the prophets. With his relative sense of values, with his mind conditioned by circumstances and reduced to the grasp of the piecemeal, constantly stumbling in his efforts to establish a system of universally integrated ideas, how can he conceive that man was ever able to grasp the unconditioned?

Man rarely comprehends how dangerously mighty he is. In our own days it is becoming obvious to many of us that unless man attaches himself to a source of spiritual power—a match for the source of energy that he is now able to exploit—a few men may throw all men into final disaster. There is only one source: the will and wisdom of the living God.

The realization of the dangerous greatness of man, of his immense power and ability to destroy all life on earth, must completely change our conception of man's place and role in the divine scheme. If this great world of ours is not a trifle in the eyes of God, if the Creator is at all concerned with His creation, then man—who has the power to devise both culture and crime, but who is also able to be a proxy for divine justice—is important enough to be the recipient of spiritual light at the rare dawns of his history.

Unless history is a vagary of nonsense, there must be a counterpart to the immense power of man to destroy, there must be a voice that says NO to man, a voice not vague, faint and inward, like qualms of conscience, but equal in spiritual might to man's power to destroy.

The voice speaks to the spirit of prophetic men in singular moments of their lives and cries to the masses through the horror of history. The prophets respond, the masses despair.

The Bible, speaking in the name of a Being that combines justice with omnipotence, is the never-ceasing outcry of "No" to humanity. In the midst of our applauding the feats of civilization, the Bible flings itself like a knife slashing our complacency, reminding us that God, too, has a voice in history.

Resistance to revelation came also from the conception of God. Of one thing we seem to be sure: God dwells at an absolute distance from man, abiding in deep silence. Is it meaningful, then, to speak of communication between God and man?

There is such a distance between the sun and a flower. Can a flower, worlds away from the source of energy, attain a perception of its origin? Can a drop of water ever soar to behold, even for a moment, the stream's distant source? In prophecy it is as if the sun communed with the flower, as if the source sent out a current to reach a drop.

Are we, because of the indescribability of revelation, justified in rejecting *a priori* as untrue the assertion of the prophets that, at certain hours in Israel's history, the divine came in touch with a few chosen souls? That the creative source of our own selves addressed itself to man?

If there are moments in which genius speaks for all men, why should we deny that there are moments in which a voice speaks for God? that the source of goodness communicates its way to the human mind?

True, it seems incredible that we should hold in our gaze words containing a breath of God. What we forget is that at this moment we breathe what God is creating, that right in front of us we behold works that reflect His infinite wisdom, His infinite goodness.

The surest way of misunderstanding revelation is to take it literally, to imagine that God spoke to the prophet on a long-distance telephone. Yet most of us succumb to such fancy, forgetting that the cardinal sin in thinking about ultimate issues is *literal-mindedness*.

The error of literal-mindedness is in assuming that things and words have only one meaning. The truth is that things and words stand for different meanings in different situations. Gold means wealth to the merchant, a means of adornment to the jeweler, "a non-rusting malleable ductile metal of high specific gravity" to the engineer, and kindness to the rhetorician ("a golden heart"). Light is a form of energy to the physicist, a medium of loveliness to the artist, an expression of grandeur in the first chapter of the Bible. *Ruah*, the Hebrew word for spirit, signifies also breath, wind, direction. And he who thinks only of breath, forfeits the deeper meaning of the term. God is called father, but he who takes this name physiologically distorts the meaning of God.

The language of faith employs only a few words coined in its own spirit; most of its terms are borrowed from the general sphere of human experience and endowed with new meaning. Consequently, in taking these terms literally we miss the unique connotations which they assumed in the religious usage.

The meaning of words in scientific language must be clear, distinct, unambiguous, conveying the same concept to all people. In poetry, however, words that have only one meaning are considered flat. The right word is often one that evokes a plurality of meanings and one that must be understood on more than one level. What is a virtue in scientific language is a failure in poetic expression.

Is it correct to insist that Biblical words must be understood exclusively according to one literal meaning? It often seems as if the intention of the prophets was to be understood not in one way, on one level, but in many ways, on many levels, according to the situation in which we find ourselves. And if such was their intention, we must not restrict our understanding to one meaning.

It is usually assumed that the Biblical writers had a bent for lofty, swelling language, a preference for extravagant exaggeration of statement. However, pondering about the substance of what they were trying

76

to express, it dawns upon us that what sounds to us as *grand eloquence* is *understatement* and *modesty of expression*. Indeed, their words must not be taken literally, because a literal understanding would be a partial, shallow understanding; because the literal meaning is but a *minimum of meaning*.[1]

"God spoke." Is it to be taken symbolically: He did not speak, yet it was as if He did? The truth is that *what is literally true to us is a metaphor compared with what is metaphysically real to God*. And when applied to Him our mightiest words are feeble understatements. The speech of God is not less but more than literally real. The nature of revelation, being an event in the realm of the ineffable, is something which words cannot spell, which human language will never be able to portray. Our categories are not applicable to that which is both within and beyond the realm of matter and mind. In speaking about revelation, the more descriptive the terms, the less adequate is the description. The words in which the prophets attempted to relate their experiences were not photographs but illustrations, not descriptions but songs. A psychological reconstruction of the prophetic act is, therefore, no more possible than the attempt to paint a photographic likeness of a face on the basis of a song. The word "revelation" is like an exclamation; it is an *indicative* rather than a descriptive term. Like all terms that express the ultimate, it points to its meaning rather than fully rendering it.

We must not try to read chapters in the Bible dealing with the event at Sinai as if they were texts in systematic theology. Its intention is to celebrate the mystery, to introduce us to it rather than to penetrate or to explain it. As a report about revelation the Bible itself is *a midrash*.

To convey what the prophets experienced, the Bible could use either terms of description or terms of indication. Any description of the act of revelation in empirical categories would have produced a caricature. This is why all the Bible does is to state *that* revelation happened; *how* it happened is something they could only convey in words that are evocative and suggestive.

The same word may be used in either way. The sound is the same, but the spirit is different. "And God said: Let there be light" is different in spirit from a statement such as "And Smith said: Let us turn on the light." The second statement conveys a definite meaning; the first statement evokes an inner response to an ineffable meaning. The statement, man speaks, describes a physiological and psychological act; the statement, God speaks, conveys a mystery. It calls upon our sense of wonder and amazement to respond to a mystery that surpasses our power of comprehension.

There are spiritual facts which are wholly irreducible to verbal expression and completely beyond the range of either imagination or definition.

It was not essential that His will be transmitted as sound; it was essential that it be made known to us. The sound or sight is to the transcendent event what a metaphor is to an abstract principle.

For us, therefore, to imagine revelation, namely, to conceive it as if it were a psychic or physical process, is to pervert its essence and to wreck its mystery. It is just as improper to conceive revelation as a psychophysical act as it is to conceive God as a corporeal being. Few of us are able to think in a way which is never crossed by the path of imagination, and it is usually at the crossroads of thought and imagination that the great sweep of the spirit swerves into the blind alley of a parabolic image.

A ḥasid, it is told, after listening to the discourse of one who lectured to him about the lofty concept of God according to the philosophers, said: "If God were the way you imagine Him, I would not believe in Him." However subtle and noble our concepts may be, as soon as they become descriptive, namely, definite, they confine Him and force Him into the triteness of our minds. Never is our mind so inadequate as in trying to describe God. The same applies to the idea of revelation. When defined, described, it completely eludes us.

Unlike the mystic act, revelation is not the result of a quest for esoteric experience. What characterizes the prophet is, on the contrary, an effort to escape such experience. Never does he relish his vision as one relishes the attainment of a goal longed for. Revelation is not an act of his seeking, but of his being sought after, an act in God's search of man. The prophet did not grope for God. God's search of man, not man's quest for God, was conceived to have been the main event in Israel's history. This is at the core of all Biblical thoughts: God is not a being detached from man to be sought after, but a power that seeks, pursues and calls upon man. The way to God is a way of God. Israel's religion originated in the initiative of God rather than in the efforts of man. It was not an invention of man but a creation of God; not a product of civilization, but a realm of its own. Man would not have known Him if He had not approached man. God's relation to man precedes man's relation to Him.

The mystic experience is man's turning toward God; the prophetic act is God's turning toward man. The former is first of all an event in the life of man, contingent on the aspiration and initiative of man; the latter is first of all an event in the life of God, contingent on the pathos and initiative of God. From the mystic experience we may gain an insight of man into the life of God; from the prophetic act we learn of an insight of God into the life of man.

Therefore, to characterize revelation as a prophetic insight or experience is to reduce a reality to a perception. Seen from man's aspect, to receive a revelation is *to witness how God is turning toward man*. It is not an act of gazing at the divine reality, a static and eternal mystery. The prophet is in the midst of a divine event, of an event in the life of God, for in addressing the prophet, God comes out of His imperceptibility to become audible to man. The full intensity of the event is not in the fact that "man hears" but in the "fact" that "God speaks" to man. The mystic experience is an ecstasy of man; revelation is *an ecstasy of God*.

As described by the prophets in terms of time and space, the act of revelation represents the image of a transcendent event as reflected in the restricted terms of human experience. Its indigenous quality is to be found in the creative fact of how the divine was carried into the concrete experience of man. Imbued with a sense of the crushing marvel of God's reality, compared with which mankind appeared to be less than nothingness,[2] the prophets must have been more astounded about their experience than any one of us to whom the transcendence of God is only a vague concept, of which we occasionally become aware in calm speculation.

To sum up, revelation is a moment in which God succeeded in reaching man; an event to God and an event to man. To receive a revelation is to witness how God is turning toward man.

12. RESPONSE THROUGH DEEDS

Where is the presence, where is the glory of God to be found? It is found in the world ("the whole earth is full of His glory"), in the Bible, and in a sacred deed.

Do only the heavens declare the glory of God? It is deeply significant that Psalm 19 begins, "The heavens declare the glory of God," and concludes with a paean to the Torah and to the mitzvot. The world, the word, as well as the sacred deed are full of His glory. God is more immediately found in the Bible as well as in acts of kindness and worship than in the mountains and forests. It is more meaningful for us to believe in the *immanence of God in deeds* than in the immanence of God in nature. Indeed, the concern of Judaism is primarily not how to find the presence of God in the world of things but how to let Him enter the ways

Part I: Ways to His Presence

in which we deal with things; how to be with Him in time, not only in space. This is why the mitzvah is a supreme source of religious insight and experience. The way to God is a way of God, and the mitzvah is a way of God, a way where the self-evidence of the Holy is disclosed. We have few words, but we know how to live in deeds that express God.

God is One, and His glory is One. And oneness means wholeness, indivisibility. His glory is not partly here and partly there; it is all here and all there. But here and now, in this world, the glory is concealed. It becomes revealed in a sacred deed, in a sacred moment, in a sacrificial deed. No one is lonely when doing a mitzvah, for a mitzvah is where God and man meet.

We do not meet Him in the way in which we meet things of space. To meet Him means to come upon an inner certainty of His realness, upon an awareness of His will. Such meeting, such presence, we experience in deeds.

The presence of God is a majestic expectation, to be sensed and retained and, when lost, to be regained and resumed. Time is the presence of God in the world. Every moment is His subtle arrival, and man's task is *to be present*. His presence is retained in moments in which *God is not alone,* in which we try to be present in His presence, to let Him enter our daily deeds, in which we coin our thoughts in the mint of eternity. The presence is not one realm and the sacred deed another; the sacred deed is the divine in disguise.[1]

The destiny of man is to be a partner of God and a mitzvah is an act in which man is present, an act of participation; while sin is an act in which God is alone; an act of alienation.

Such acts of man's revelations of the divine are acts of redemption. The meaning of redemption is to reveal the holy that is concealed, to disclose the divine that is suppressed. Every man is called upon to be a redeemer, and redemption takes place every moment, every day.

The meaning of Jewish law is disclosed when conceived as sacred prosody. The divine sings in our good deeds, the divine is disclosed in our sacred deeds. Our effort is but a counterpoint in the music of His will. In exposing our lives to God we discover the divine within ourselves and its accord with the divine beyond ourselves.

Knowledge of God is knowledge of living with God. Israel's religious existence consists of three inner attitudes: engagement to the living God to whom we are accountable; engagement to Torah where His voice is audible; and engagement to His concern as expressed in mitzvot (commandments).

Engagement to God comes about in acts of the soul. Engagement to

12. Response Through Deeds

Torah is the result of study and communion with its words. Engagement to His concern comes about through attachment to the essentials of worship. Its meaning is disclosed in acts of worship.

If God were a theory, the study of theology would be the way to understand Him. But God is alive and in need of love and worship. This is why thinking of God is related to our worship. In an analogy of artistic understanding, we sing to Him before we are able to understand Him. We have to love in order to know. Unless we learn how to sing, unless we know how to love, we will never learn how to understand Him.

Jewish tradition interprets the words that Israel uttered at Sinai, "all that the Lord has spoken, we shall do and we shall hear" (Exodus 24:7), as a promise to fulfill His commands even before hearing them, as the *precedence of faith over knowledge*. When at Sinai Israel said *we shall do and we shall hear* (instead of saying, we shall hear and we shall do), a heavenly voice went forth and exclaimed, "Who has revealed to My children this *mystery,* which the ministering angels enact, to fulfill His word before they hear the voice."[2]

Do we not always maintain that we must first explore a system before we decide to accept it? This order of inquiry is valid in regard to pure theory, to principles and rules, but it has limitations when applied to realms where thought and fact, the abstract and the concrete, theory and experience are inseparable. It would be futile, for example, to explore the meaning of music and abstain from listening to music. It would be just as futile to explore the Jewish thought from a distance, in self-detachment. Jewish thought is disclosed in Jewish living. This, therefore, is the way of religious existence. We must accept in order to be able to explore. At the beginning is *the commitment, the supreme acquiescence.*

In our response to His will we perceive His presence in our deeds. His will is revealed in our doing. In carrying out a sacred deed we unseal the wells of faith. *As for me, I shall behold Thy face in righteousness* (Psalms 18:15).

There is a way that leads *from piety to faith*. Piety and faith are not necessarily concurrent. There can be acts of piety without faith. Faith is vision, sensitivity and attachment to God; piety is an attempt to attain such sensitivity and attachment. The gates of faith are not ajar, but the mitzvah is a key. By living as Jews we may attain our faith as Jews. We do not have faith because of deeds; we may attain faith through sacred deeds.

A Jew is asked to take a *leap of action* rather than a *leap of thought*. He is asked to surpass his needs, to do more than he understands in order to understand more than he does. In carrying out the word of the Torah he is ushered into the presence of spiritual meaning. Through the ecstasy

81

of deeds he learns to be certain of the hereness of God. Right living is a way to right thinking.

The sense of the ineffable, the participation in Torah and Israel, the leap of action—they all lead to the same goal. Callousness to the mystery of existence, detachment from Torah and Israel, cruelty and profanity of living, alienate the Jew from God. Response to the wonder, participation in Torah and Israel, discipline in daily life, bring us close to Him.

What commitments must precede the experience of such meaning? What convictions must persist to make such insights possible? Our way of living must be compatible with our essence as created in the likeness of God. We must beware lest our likeness be distorted and even forfeited. In our way of living we must remain true not only to our sense of power and beauty but also to our sense of the grandeur and mystery of existence. The true meaning of existence is disclosed in moments of living in the presence of God. The problem we face is: how can we live in a way which is in agreement with such convictions?

How should man, a being created in the likeness of God, live? What way of living is compatible with the grandeur and mystery of living? It is a problem which man has always been anxious to ignore. Upon the pavement of the Roman city of Timgat an inscription was found which reads: "To hunt, to bathe, to gamble, to laugh, that is to live." Judaism is a reminder of the grandeur and earnestness of living.

It is in *deeds* that man becomes aware of what his life really is, of his power to harm and to hurt, to wreck and to ruin; of his ability to derive joy and to bestow it upon others; to relieve and to increase his own and other people's tensions. It is in the employment of his will, not in reflection, that he meets his own self as it is; not as he should like it to be. In his deeds man exposes his immanent as well as his suppressed desires, spelling even that which he cannot apprehend. What he may not dare to think, he often utters in deeds. The heart is revealed in the deeds.

The deed is the test, the trial, and the risk. What we perform may seem slight, but the aftermath is immense. An individual's misdeed can be the beginning of a nation's disaster. The sun goes down, but the deeds go on. Darkness is over all we have done. If man were able to survey at a glance all he has done in the course of his life, what would he feel? He would be terrified at the extent of his own power. Infinite responsibility without infinite wisdom and infinite power is our ultimate embarrassment.

Not things but deeds are the source of our sad perplexities. Confronted with a world of things, man unloosens a tide of deeds. The fabulous fact of man's ability to act, *the wonder of doing,* is no less amazing than the marvel of being. Ontology inquires: what is *being?* What does it mean to be? The religious mind ponders: what is *doing?* What does it mean to do? What is the relation between the doer and the deed? between doing and being? Is there a purpose to fulfill, a task to carry out?

"A man should always regard himself as though he were half guilty and half meritorious; if he performs one good deed, blessed is he for he moves the scale toward merit; if he commits one transgression, woe to him for he moves the scale toward guilt." Not only the individual but the whole world is in balance.

What ought we to do? How ought we to conduct our lives? These are basic questions of ethics. They are also questions of religion. Philosophy of religion must inquire: why do we ask these questions? Are they meaningful? On what grounds do we state them? To ethics, these are man's questions, necessitated by the nature of human existence. To religion, these are God's questions, and our answer to them concerns not only man but God.

"What ought I to do?" is according to Kant the basic question in ethics. Ours, however, is a more radical, a meta-ethical approach. The ethical question refers to particular deeds; the meta-ethical question refers to all deeds. It deals with doing as such; not only what ought we to do, but what is our right to act at all? We are endowed with the ability to conquer and to control the forces of nature. In exercising power, we submit to our will a world that we did not create, invading realms that do not belong to us. Are we the kings of the universe or mere pirates? By whose grace, by what right, do we exploit, consume and enjoy the fruits of the trees, the blessings of the earth? Who is responsible for the power to exploit, for the privilege to consume?

It is not an academic problem but an issue we face at every moment. By the will alone man becomes the most destructive of all beings. This is our predicament: our power may become our undoing. We stand on a razor's edge. It is so easy to hurt, to destroy, to insult, to kill. Giving birth to one child is a mystery; bringing death to millions is but a skill. It is not quite within the power of the human will to generate life; it is quite within the power of the will to destroy life.

In the midst of such anxiety we are confronted with the claim of the Bible. The world is not all danger, and man is not alone. God endowed man with freedom, and He will share in our use of freedom. The earth is the Lord's, and God is in search of man. He endowed man with power to conquer the earth, and His honor is upon our faith. We abused His power, we betrayed His trust. We cannot expect Him to say, Though thou betrayest me, yet will I trust in thee.

Man is responsible for His deeds, and God is responsible for man's responsibility. He who is a life-giver must be a lawgiver. He shares in our responsibility. He is waiting to enter our deeds through our loyalty to His law. He may become a partner to our deeds.

God and man have a task in common as well as a common and mutual responsibility. What is at stake is the meaning of God's creation, not only the meaning of man's existence. Religion is not a concern for man alone but a plea of God and a claim of man, God's expectation and man's aspiration. It is not an effort solely for the sake of man. Religion spells a task within the world of man, but its ends go far beyond. This is why the Bible proclaimed a law not only for man but for both God and man.

For Thou wilt light my lamp (Psalms 18:29). "The Holy One said to man: Thy lamp is in My hand, My lamp in thine. Thy lamp is in Mine —as it is said: *The lamp of the Lord is the soul of man* (Proverbs 20:27). My lamp is in thine hand, to kindle the perpetual lamp. The Holy One said: If thou lightest My lamp, I will light thine."[3]

Just as man is not alone in what he *is,* he is not alone in what he *does.* A mitzvah is an act which God and man *have in common.* We say: "Blessed art Thou, Lord our God, King of the universe, who has sanctified us with *His* mitzvot." They oblige Him as well as us. Their fulfillment is not valued as an act performed in spite of "the evil drive," but as an act of *communion* with Him. The spirit of mitzvah is *togetherness.* We know, He is a partner to our act.

The oldest form of piety is expressed in the Bible as walking *with God.* Enoch, Noah, walked with God (Genesis 5:24; 6:9). "It has been told thee, O man, what is good, and what the Lord doth require of thee: only to do justly, to love mercy and *to walk humbly with thy God"* (6:8). Only the egotist is confined to himself, a spiritual recluse. In carrying out a good deed it is impossible to be or to feel alone. To fulfill a mitzvah is to be a partisan, to enter into fellowship with His Will.

The moral imperative was not disclosed for the first time through Abraham or Sinai. The criminality of murder was known to men before; even the institution to rest on the seventh day was, according to tradition, familiar to Jews when still in Egypt. Nor was the idea of divine justice unknown. What was new was the idea that justice is an obligation to God, *His way* not only His demand;[4] that injustice is not something God scorns when done by others but that which is the very opposite of God; that the rights of man are not legally protected interests of society but the sacred interests of God. He is not only the guardian of moral order, "the Judge of all the earth," but One who cannot act injustly (Genesis 18:25). His favorite was not Nimrod, "the first man on earth to be a hero" (Genesis 10:9), but Abraham: "I have chosen him that he may charge his sons and his household after him to keep the way of the Lord, to do righteousness and justice" (Genesis 18:19). The Torah is primarily

12. Response Through Deeds

divine ways rather than *divine laws*. Moses prayed: "Let me know Thy ways" (Exodus 33:13). All that God asks of man was summarized: "And now, Israel, what doth the Lord thy God require of thee . . . but to walk in all His ways" (Deuteronomy 10:12).

What does it mean, asked Rabbi Ḥama, son of Rabbi Ḥanina, when it is said: "Ye shall walk after thy Lord your God"? (Deuteronomy 13:5). "Is it possible for a human being to walk after the *Schekhinah;* has it not been said: For the Lord thy God is a devouring fire? But the meaning is to walk in the ways of the Lord. As He clothes the naked so do thou also clothe the naked; as He visited the sick, so do thou also visit the sick; as he comforted mourners, so do Thou also comfort mourners" (*Sotah* 14a).

Not particular acts but all acts, life itself, can be established as a link between man and God. But how can we presume that the platitudes of our actions have meaning to Him?

The validity of science is based upon the premise that the structure of events in nature is intelligible, capable of being observed and described in rational terms. Only because of the analogy of the structure of the human mind to the inner structure of the universe is man able to discover the laws that govern its processes. What about events in the inner and moral life of man? Is there any realm to which they correspond? The prophets who knew how to take the divine measure of human deeds, to see the structure of the absolute light in the spectrum of a single event, sensed that correspondence. What a man does in his darkest corner is relevant to the Creator. In other words, as the rationality of natural events is assumed by science, so is the divinity of human deeds assumed by prophecy.

Thus beyond the idea of the imitation of divinity goes the conviction of *the divinity of deeds.* Sacred acts, mitzvot, do not only imitate; they represent the Divine.

The Bible speaks of man as having been created in the likeness of God, establishing the principle of *an analogy of being.* In his very being, man has something in common with God. Beyond the analogy of being, the Bible teaches the principle of *an analogy in acts.* Man may act in the likeness of God. It is this likeness of acts—"to walk in His ways"—that is the link by which man may come close to God. To live in such likeness is the essence of imitation of the Divine.

In other religions, gods, heroes, priests are holy; to the Bible not only God but "the whole community is holy" (Numbers 16:3). "Ye shall be unto me a kingdom of priests, a holy people" (Exodus 19:6), was the reason for Israel's election, the meaning of its distinction. What obtains between man and God is not mere submission to His power or dependence upon His mercy. The plea is not to obey what He wills but to *do* what He *is*.

It is not said: Ye shall be full of awe for I am holy, but: Ye shall be holy, for I the Lord your God am holy (Leviticus 19:2). How does a human being, "dust and ashes," turn holy? Through doing His mitzvot, His commandments. "The Holy God is sanctified through righteousness" (Isaiah 5:16). A man to be holy must fear his mother and father, keep the Sabbath, not turn to idols . . . nor deal falsely nor lie to one another . . . not curse the deaf nor put a stumbling-block before the blind . . . not be guilty of any injustice . . . not be a tale-bearer . . . not stand idly by the blood of your neighbor . . . not hate . . . not take vengeance nor bear any grudge . . . but love thy neighbor as thyself (Leviticus 19:3–18).

We live by the conviction that acts of goodness reflect the hidden light of His holiness. His light is above our minds but not beyond our will. It is within our power to mirror His unending love in deeds of kindness, like brooks that hold the sky.

To fulfill the will of God in deeds means to act *in the name* of God, not only *for the sake* of God; to carry out in acts what is potential to His will. He is in need of the work of man for the fulfillment of His ends in the world.

Human action is not the beginning. At the beginning is God's eternal expectation. There is an eternal cry in the world: *God is beseeching man* to answer, to return, to fulfill. Something is asked of man, of all men, at all times. In every act we either answyer or defy, we either return or move away, we either fulfill or miss the goal. Life consists of endless opportunities to sanctify the profane, opportunities to redeem the power of God from the chain of potentialities, opportunities to serve spiritual ends.

As surely as we are driven to live, we are driven to serve spiritual ends that surpass our own interests. "The good drive" is not invented by society but is something which makes society possible; not an accidental function but of the very essence of man. We may lack a clear perception of its meaning, but we are moved by the horror of its violation. We are not only in need of God but also in need of serving His ends, and these ends are in need of us.

Mitzvot are not ideals, spiritual entities for ever suspended in eternity. They are commandments addressing every one of us. They are the ways in which God confronts us in particular moments. In the infinite world there is a task for me to accomplish. Not a general task, but a task for me, here and now. Mitzvot are *spiritual ends,* points of eternity in the flux of temporality.

Man and spiritual ends stand in a relation of mutuality to each other.

12. Response Through Deeds

The relation in regard to selfish ends is one-sided: man is in need of eating bread, but the bread is not in need of being eaten. The relation is different in regard to spiritual ends: justice is something that ought to be done, justice is in need of man. The sense of obligation expresses a situation, in which an ideal, as it were, is waiting to be attained. Spiritual ends come with a claim upon the person. They are imperative, not only impressive; demands, not abstract ideas. Esthetic values are experienced as objects of enjoyment, while religious acts are experienced as objects of commitments, as answers to the certainty that something is asked of us, expected of us. Religious ends are *in need of our deeds.*

Judaism is not a science of nature but a science of what man ought to do with nature. It is concerned above all with the problem of living. It takes deeds more seriously than things. Jewish law is, in a sense, *a science of deeds.* Its main concern is not only how to worship Him at certain times but how to live with Him at all times. Every deed is a problem; there is a unique task at every moment. All of life at all moments is the problem and the task,

Part II

The God of the Prophets

13. THE WORSHIP OF NATURE

No one is without a sense of awe, a need to adore, an urge to worship. The question only is what to adore, or more specifically, what object is worthy of our supreme worship. "The starry heavens above . . . fill the mind with ever new and increasing admiration and awe." Indeed, it is hard to live under a sky full of stars and not be struck by its mystery. The sun is endowed with power and beauty, for all eyes to see. Who could refrain from extolling its grandeur? Who could go beyond the realization: nature is the ultimate mystery; and mystery is the end?

The Greeks regarded the elemental powers of nature as holy. Expressions such as "the holy rain" or "the holy light" are characteristic of their attitude.[1] "O Nature, how we worship thee even against our wills," Seneca confesses.[2] In *King Lear* Edmund exclaims, "Thou, nature, art my goddess; to thy law my services are bound."[3] Belarius says, "Stoop boys: this gate instructs you how to *adore the heavens,* and bows you to a morning's holy office."[4]

The religion of nature, the worship of the grandeur of the given, has always had its votaries. Despite the injunction, "Beware lest you lift up your eyes to heaven, and when you see the sun and the moon and the stars, all the host of heaven, you be drawn away and worship them" (Deuteronomy 4:19), there were, even in the times of the Babylonian Exile, those who turned their faces to the east and worshiped the sun.[5]

Indeed, the beauty of nature may become a menace to our spiritual understanding; there is a deadly risk of being enchanted by its power.

> If I have looked at the sun when it shone,
> Or the moon moving in splendor,
> And my heart has been secretly enticed,
> And my mouth has kissed my hand;
> This also would be an iniquity to be punished by the judges,
> For I should have been false to God above.
>
> (Job 31:26–28)

It was in the romantic movement that a new religious enthusiasm for nature began, which lingers on in many minds to this very day. Nature assumed ultimate significance and became the supreme object of adoration, the only source of comfort and salvation, and the final arbiter of values. To love her, to hold communion with her, to expose oneself to her

91

healing sympathy was the highest form of religious experience. The god Pan was resurrected. But soon he died again, when the post-romantic man discovered that nature could not save him; nature is herself in need of salvation. Pitiless is the silence of the sky. Nature is deaf to our cries and indifferent to our values. Her laws know no mercy, no forbearance. They are inexorable, implacable, ruthless.

"To commune with the heart of Nature—this has been the accredited mode since the days of Wordsworth. Nature, Coleridge assures us, has ministrations by which she heals her erring and distempered child. . . ."[6]

The gradual decline of naturalism in contemporary art and philosophy is in a sense a movement of spiritual iconoclasm. At the same time, nature, once the object of ultimate adoration, threatens to become a source of ultimate despair. To Judaism, the adoration of nature is as absurd as the alienation from nature is unnecessary.

Biblical thinking succeeded in subduing the universal tendency of ancient man to endow nature with a mysterious potency like mana and orenda by stressing the indication in all nature of the wisdom and goodness of the Creator.

One of the great achievements of the prophets was the repudiation of nature as an object of adoration. They tried to teach us that neither nature's beauty nor grandeur, neither power nor the state, neither money nor things of space are worthy of our supreme adoration, love, sacrifice, or self-dedication. Yet the *desanctification of nature* did not in any way bring about an alienation of nature. It brought man together with all things in a fellowship of praise. The Biblical man could say that he was "in league with the stones of the field" (Job 5:23).

What then is the ultimate? What object is worthy of our supreme worship? These questions are involved in all problems which man continues to struggle with to this very day. The Western man must choose between the worship of God and the worship of nature. The Bible asserts that for all her power and preciousness, beauty and grandeur, nature is not everything. It calls upon us to remember that what is given is not the ultimate. It calls upon us not to let the world stand as a wall between us and God.

To the Greek mind the universe is the sum and substance of all there is; even the gods are a part of, rather than the cause of the universe. "The world (cosmos), the same for all, was not made by any god or man but was always, and is, and shall be."[7] The universe to Plato is "a visible living being . . . a perceptible god . . . the greatest, best, fairest, most perfect."[8] "O Nature, from thee are all things, in thee are all things, to thee all things return."[9]

In contrast, the Biblical mind is deeply aware that the ultimate, God, is beyond the given. What is given is not ultimate but created by Him Who is not given. Nowhere in the Bible is the reality of the universe questioned, but at the same time a certainty prevails that for all its greatness the universe is as nothing compared with its Maker. "The heaven is My throne, and the earth is My footstool" (Isaiah 66:1). "All the nations are as nothing before Him; they are accounted by Him as things of nought, and vanity" (Isaiah 40:17).

To the Greeks as to many other peoples, the earth is generally known as *Mother Earth*. She is the mother who sends up fruits, the giver of children, and to her men return at death. Greek poetry and drama exalt the divinity of the earth, and according to Plutarch, "The name of *Ge* is dear and precious to every Hellene, and it is our tradition to honor her like any other god." The adoration of the beauty and abundance of the earth in Greek literature is tinged with a sense of gratefulness to the earth for her gifts to man.

Such a concept is alien to the Biblical man. He recognizes only one parent: God as his father. The earth is his sister rather than his mother. Man and earth are equally the creations of God. The prophets and the Psalmist do not honor or exalt the earth, though dwelling upon her grandeur and abundance. They uttter praise to Him who created her.

To the Biblical man, the power of God is behind all phenomena,[10] and he is more concerned to know the will of God who governed nature than to know the order of nature itself. Important and impressive as nature is to him, God is vastly more so. That is why Psalm 104 is a hymn to God rather than an ode to the cosmos.

The idea of the cosmos is one of the outstanding contributions of Greek philosophy, and we can well understand why a similar conception did not emerge in Hebrew thinking. For the idea of a cosmos, of a totality of things, complete in itself, implies the concept of an immanent norm of nature, of an order which has its foundation in nature.

But what are the foundations of nature? To the Greeks who take the world for granted Nature, Order is the answer. To the Biblical mind in its radical amazement nature, order are not an answer but a problem: why is there order, being, at all?

What are the foundations of the earth? There are no natural foundations. The foundations of the world are not of this world. The earth continues to exist because of Him "That sits above the circle of the earth" (Isaiah 40:22).

Now the Biblical man, of course, is conscious of an order of nature which could be relied upon in daily life. But that order is one which was invested in nature by the will of God and remains constantly dependent upon Him. It is not an immanent law but a divine decree that dominates everything. God had given His decree to the sea; He had appointed the foundations of the earth (Proverbs 8:29); and He continued to rule the world from without. Nature is the object of His perpetual care, but this very dependence of nature on divine care is an expression of its contingency. Biblical man does not take anything for granted, and to him the laws of nature are as much in need of derivation as the processes ruled by these laws. The continued existence of the world is guaranteed by God's faithfulness to this covenant. "Thus says the Lord: if My covenant be not with day and night . . ." (Jeremiah 33:25). The world is not an ontological necessity. Indeed, heaven and earth may not last for ever: "They shall perish, but Thou shalt endure" (Psalms 102:27).

The world is not the *all* to the Bible, and so the *all* could never come to denote the world. Biblical man is not enchanted by the given. He realizes the alternative, namely the annihilation of the given. He is not enchanted by the order, because he has a vision of a new order. He is not lost to the here and now, nor to the beyond. He senses the non-given with the given, the past and future with the present. He is taught that "the mountains may depart, the hills be removed, but My kindness shall not depart from thee . . ." (Isaiah 54:10). The Hebrew conception has been rightly characterized by A. N. Whitehead as the doctrine of the *imposed* law, as contrasted with the doctrine of the *immanent* law developed in Greek philosophy. According to the doctrine of the *imposed* law, there is imposed on each existent the necessity of entering into relationships with the other constituents of nature. These imposed behavior patterns are the laws of nature.

The doctrine of the imposed law leads to the monotheistic conception of God as essentially transcendent and only accidentally immanent; while the doctrine of the immanent law leads to the pantheistic doctrine of God as essentially immanent and in no way transcendent. "Subsequent speculation," Whitehead points out, "wavers between these two extremes, seeking their reconciliation. In this, as in most other matters, the history of Western thought consists in the attempted fusion of ideas which in their origin are predominantly Hellenic, with ideas which in their origin are predominantly Semitic."[11]

In a profound sense, the question: what is reality? what is the world to the Biblical man? is best answered by another question: what is the world to God? To him the subject matter of the question—the world—is too wondrous to be fully comprehended in relation to man. The world in its ultimate significance must be understood in relation to God, and the answer to the question is: all things are His servants.

The prophets attacked what may be called the fallacy of isolation. Things and events, man and the world, cannot be treated apart from the

13. The Worship of Nature

will of God but only as inseparable parts of an occasion in which the divine is at stake. Paraphrasing the verse, "that thou canst not stir a flower without troubling a star," a prophet might say, "thou canst not offend a human being without affecting the living God." We are taught to believe that where man loves man His name is sanctified; that in the harmony of husband and wife dwells the presence of God.

To the Biblical man, the sublime is but a form in which the presence of God strikes forth. Things do not always stand still. The stars sing; the mountains tremble in His presence. To think of God man must hear the world. Man is not alone in celebrating God. To praise Him is to join all things in their song to Him. Our kinship with nature is a kinship of praise. All beings praise God. We live in a community of praise.

To the Biblical man, the beauty of the world issued from the grandeur of God; His majesty towered beyond the breathtaking mystery of the universe. Rather than being crushed by the mystery, he was inspired to praise the majesty. And rather than praise the world for its beauty, he called upon the world to praise its Creator.

Modern man dwells upon the order and power of nature; the prophets dwell upon the grandeur and creation of nature. The former directs his attention to the manageable and intelligible aspect of the universe; the latter to its mystery and marvel. What the prophets sense in nature is not a direct reflection of God but an allusion to Him. Nature is not a part of God but rather a fulfillment of His will.

Lift up your eyes on high and see who created these. There is a higher form of seeing. We must learn how to lift up our eyes on high in order to see that the world is more a question than an answer. The world's beauty and power are as naught compared to Him. The grandeur of nature is only the beginning. *Beyond the grandeur is God.*

The Biblical man does not see nature in isolation but in relation to God. "At the beginning God created heaven and earth"—these few words set forth the contingency and absolute dependence of all of reality. What, then, is reality? To the Western man, it is *a thing in itself;* to the Biblical Man, it is *a thing through God.* Looking at a thing his eyes see not so much form, color, force, and motion as an act of God. The world is a gate, not a wall.

Greek philosophy began in a world without God. To most Greek philosophers the natural world was the starting point of speculation. The goal was to develop the idea of a supreme principle—Anaximander's *apeiron* (the Boundless), the *ens perfectissimum* of Aristotle, the world-forming fire of the Stoics—of which they then asserted, "This must be the Divine." The phrase *the Divine* as applied to the first principle, current since the time of Anaximander, and "of epoch-making importance to

Greek philosophy,"[12] illustrates a procedure adopted by philosophers in subsequent ages. It is always a principle first, to which qualities of personal existence are subsequently attributed. Such attribution represents a concession either to one's personal religiosity or to popular religious beliefs. It is a God whose personality is derivative; an adjective transformed into a noun.

Plato could not accept the gods or the example of their conduct. He had to break with the gods and to ask: What is good? Thus the problem of values was born. And it was the idea of values that took the place of God. Plato lets Socrates ask: What is good? But Moses' question was: What does God require of thee?

There is no word in Biblical Hebrew for doubt; there are many expressions of wonder. Just as in dealing with judgments our starting point is doubt, wonder is the Biblical starting point in facing reality. The Biblical man's sense for the mind-surpassing grandeur of reality prevented the power of doubt from setting up its own independent dynasty. Doubt is an act in which the mind inspects its own ideas; wonder is an act in which the mind confronts the universe.

And so the Biblical man never asks: Is there a God? To ask such a question, in which doubt is expressed as to which of two possible attitudes is true, means to accept the power and validity of a third attitude, namely the attitude of doubt. The Bible does not know doubt as an absolute attitude. For there is no doubt in which faith is not involved. The questions advanced in the Bible are of a different kind.

Lift up your eyes on high and see, Who created these?

This does not reflect a process of thinking that is neatly arranged in the order of doubt first, and faith second; first the question, then the answer. It reflects a situation in which the mind stands *face to face* with the mystery rather than with its own concepts.

A question is an interrogative sentence calling for either a positive or a negative answer. But the sentence *Who created these?* is a question that contains the impossibility of giving a negative answer; it is an answer in disguise; *a question of amazement,* not of curiosity. This, then, is the prophet's thesis: there is a way of asking the great question which can only elicit an affirmative answer. What is the way?

"At the end of the days, I, Nebuchadnezzar, lifted my eyes to heaven, and my power of knowledge returned to me." This confession of the king of Babylon reported in the Book of Daniel (4:31), gives us an inkling of how to recover one's ability to ask the ultimate question: *to lift the eyes to heaven.*

14. HOW TO IDENTIFY THE DIVINE

How do we identify the divine? In order to recognize what it is, we would have to know it. But if our knowledge were contingent upon acts of a divine communication, we might never be able to identify such a communication as divine.

Moreover, an idea does not become valid or credible by virtue of the circumstances in which it enters our mind. Any message that claims to be divine must stand on its own and be saturated with a unique meaningfulness which would identify it as divine. If a person should appear among us and proclaim an idea communicated to him in a miraculous manner, and our critical examinations should even confirm the miraculous manner of his experience, would we for that matter feel obliged to accept his idea as valid and true?

Nor should our own inner experiences fare better. We must be in possession of an *a priori* idea of the divine, of a quality or relation representing to us the ultimate, by which we would be able to identify it when given to us in such acts.

Compellingness is not a mark of the highest nor is our feeling or being in a state of absolute dependence an index of His presence. Physical force or inner obsessions may overpower us with irresistible compellingness and, as has often been pointed out, a survivor of a wrecked ship embracing a floating board is in a state of absolute dependence upon the board.

No inquiry can get under way without some presupposition or perspective to start from. The scientist in formulating a problem must anticipate, in some measure, the content of the solution he is aiming at, for otherwise he would neither know what he asks about nor be able to judge whether the solutions he will find will be relevant to his problem. Philosophy has been defined as a science with a minimum of presuppositions, for there is no way of proceeding in our thoughts without any perspective, without any initial assumption.

Such an initial assumption lies at the beginning of all speculation about God. To the speculative mind God is the most perfect being, and it is the attribute of perfection and its implication of wisdom which serve as a starting point for the inquiries into the existence and nature of God.

The notion of God as a perfect being is not of Biblical extraction. It is

97

the product not of prophetic religion but of Greek philosophy; a postulate of reason rather than a direct, compelling, initial answer of man to His reality. In the Decalogue, God does not speak of His being perfect but of His having made free men out of slaves. Signifying a state of being without defect and lack, perfection is a term of praise which we may utter in pouring forth our emotion; yet for man to utter it as a name for His essence would mean to evaluate and to endorse Him.

We were never told: "Hear, O Israel, God is perfect!" It is an attribution which is strikingly absent in both the Biblical and rabbinic literature.

There is, however, one idea that carries our thoughts beyond the horizon of our island; an idea which addresses itself to all minds and is tacitly accepted as an axiom by science and as a dogma by monotheistic religion. It is the idea of the one. All knowledge and understanding rest upon its validity. In spite of the profound differences in what it describes and means in the various realms of human thought, there is much that is common and much that is of mutual importance.

The perspective on which we depend in science and philosophy, notwithstanding all specialization and meticulousness in studying the details, is a view of the whole, without which our knowledge would be like a book composed exclusively of iotas. Accordingly, all sciences and philosophies have one axiom in common—the axiom of *unity* of all that is, was and will be. They all assume that things are not entirely divorced from and indifferent to each other, but subject to universal laws, and that they form, by their interaction with one another or, as Lotze put it, by their "sympathetic rapport," a universe. However, the possibility of their interaction with each other is conditioned upon a unity that pervades all of them. The world could not exist at all except as one; deprived of unity, it would not be a cosmos but chaos, an agglomeration of countless possibilities.

The exponents of pluralism, asserting that "reality is made up of a number of relatively independent entities, each of which exists, at any rate to some extent, in its own right," seem to deny the fundamental unity and wholeness of the universe. Yet, while questioning whether that unity is absolute and all-pervading to a degree that would exclude chance and indeterminations, they are bound to supplement the pluralistic hypothesis by a principle of unity, in order to explain the interaction of the independent entities, and to account for that which makes reality a world.[1]

Nor does the theory of relativity contradict the doctrine of constancy and unity of nature. Showing that the simultaneity of two processes is relative and that magnitudes are determined by the system of reference in which they are measured, its aim is to find new invariants by describing reality in a way which would be independent of the choice of the system of reference. It does not discard the principle of unity, but, on the contrary, strives to "satisfy a new and more strict demand for unity."[2]

While it is impossible to trace back the way in which the great secret of the all-embracing unity reached our minds, it certainly was not attained by mere sense perception or by a mind that thought in installments, through a series of distinct steps, each logically dependent on those which preceded. What the idea of the universe refers to surpasses the scope of perception or the extension of any possible premise, embracing things known and unknown, origins and ends, facts and possibilities, the prehistoric past and the far-stretching future, phenomena which Newton described as well as those which will be observed a thousand years from now. The idea of the universe is a metaphysical insight.

The intuition of that all-pervading unity has often inspired man with a sense of living in cosmic brotherhood with all beings. Out of the awareness of the oneness of nature comes often an emotion of being one with nature.

> I am the eye with which the Universe
> Beholds itself and knows itself divine.
> (Shelley, "Hymn of Apollo," vi. 1f)

There is deep philosophical significance to such cosmic piety. Knowledge is at all possible because of the kinship of the knower and the known, because man's intelligence seems to correspond to the world's intelligibility. But over and above that there is another kinship: the kinship of being. We are all—men, stars, flowers, birds—assigned to the same cast, rehearsing for the same inexplicable drama. We all have a mystery in common—the mystery of being.

But we are all *one* in purpose? True, we all have being, even suffering and a struggle for existence in common; but do we have strivings, commitments in common? Man's position in nature is too distinct to justify the idea that his vocation is to conform to her ways or to be one with her essence.

The idea of unity, from which cosmic piety draws its inspiration, is a half-truth. For while the things of nature may constitute a unit, the realm of values seems to be torn between good and evil and in many other directions. History is no less our abode than nature, and the conflicts that rage within it look more like perennial warfare between two hostile principles than like a sphere of harmony.

It is, indeed, a spiritual temptation to meditate on the cosmic fellowship of all beings or to surrender once and for all to the spirit of the whole. It is suspiciously easier to feel one with nature than to feel one with every man: with the savage, with the leper, with the slave. Those who know that to be one with the whole means to be for the sake of every part of the whole will seek to love not only humanity but also the individual man, to regard any man as if he were all men. Once we decide to serve here and now, we discover that the vision of abstract unity goes out of sight like lightning, and what remains is the gloom of a drizzly night, where we must in toil and tears strike the darkness to beget a gleam, to light a torch.

Polytheists are blind to the unity that transcends a world of multiplicity, while monists overlook the multiplicity of a world, the abundance and discord of which encounter us wherever we turn. Monism is a loom for weaving an illusion. Life is tangled, fierce, fickle. We cannot remain in agreement with all goals. We are constantly compelled to make a choice, and the choice of one goal means the forsaking of another.

Even granted its validity, the idea of universal harmony in nature, of a general concord in the relations of the part to the whole is destitute of significance to the immediate problems of living. However intricate, wise and prodigal of beauty nature is, we in our human confusions are unable to translate its general laws into the language of individual decisions, for to decide means to transcend rather than follow the pattern of natural laws. The norms of spiritual living are a challenge to nature not a part of nature. There is a discrepancy between being and spirit, between facts and norms, between that which is and that which ought to be. Nature shows little regard for spiritual norms and is often callous, if not hostile to our moral endeavors.

Man is more than reason. Man is life. In facing the all-embracing question, he faces that which is more than a principle, more than a theoretical problem. A principle is something he may conceive or convert into an object of his mind, but in facing the ultimate question man finds himself called upon and challenged beyond words to the depth of his existence. It is not a question that he comprehends but the fact of his being exposed to a knowledge that comprehends him. God is one, but one is not God. Some of us are inclined to deify the one supreme force or law that regulates all phenomena of nature, in the same manner in which primitive peoples once deified the stars. Yet, to refer to the supreme law of nature as God or to say that the world came into being by virtue of its own energy is to beg the question.

For the cardinal question is not what is the law that would explain the interaction of phenomena in the universe, but why is there a law, a universe at all. The content and operation of the universal law may be conceived and described, but the fact that there is such a law does not lose its ineffable character by the knowledge we may acquire about the scope of its operation.

As noted above, it is not nature's order and wisdom which are manifest in time and space, but the indicativeness within all order and wisdom of that which surpasses them, of that which is beyond time and space which communicates to us an awareness of the ultimate questions.

The ultimate problem is not a problem of syntax, of trying to learn how the various parts of nature are collocated and arranged in their relations to one another. The problem is: What does reality, what does unity stand for? Universal laws one attempts to describe by relations within the given, within the known, but in facing our ultimate question we are carried beyond the known, to the presence of the divine.

From the empirical plurality of facts and values, we could not infer *one* design which would dominate both the realm of facts and the realm of norms, nature and history. It is only in the mirror of a divine unity, in which we may behold the unity of all: of necessity and freedom, of law and love. It alone gives us an insight into the unity that transcends all conflicts, the brotherhood of hope and grief, of joy and fear, of tower and grave, of good and evil. Unity as a scientific concept is only a reflection of a transcendent idea, embracing not only time and space but also being and value, the known and the mystery, the here and the beyond.

God cannot be distilled to a well-defined idea. All concepts fade when applied to His essence. To the pious man knowledge of God is not a thought within his grasp, but a form of thinking in which he tries to comprehend all reality. Over and against the split between man and nature, self and thought, time and timelessness, the pious man is able to sense the interweaving of all, the holding together of what is apart.

How do we identify the divine?

Divine is a message that discloses unity where we see diversity, that discloses peace when we are involved in discord. God is He who holds our fitful lives together, who reveals to us that what is empirically diverse in color, in interest, in creeds—races, classes, nations—is one in His eyes and one in essence.

God means: No one is ever alone; the essence of the temporal is the eternal; the moment is an image of eternity in an infinite mosaic. God means: *Togetherness of all beings in holy otherness.*

When God becomes our form of thinking we begin to sense all men in one man, the whole world in a grain of sand, eternity in a moment. To worldly ethics one human being is less than two human beings, to the religious mind if a man has caused a single soul to perish, it is as though he had caused a whole world to perish, and if he has saved a single soul, it is as though he had saved a whole world.[3]

If in the afterglow of a religious insight I can see a way to gather up my scattered life, to unite what lies in strife; a way that is good for all men as it is for me—I will know it is His way.

15. ONE GOD

Monotheism, to this day, is at variance with vulgar thinking; it is something against which popular instinct continues to rebel. Polytheism seems to be more compatible with emotional moods and imagination than uncompromising monotheism, and great poets have often felt drawn to pagan gods. The world over, polytheism exercises an almost hypnotic appeal, stirring up powerful, latent yearnings for pagan forms; for it is obviously easier to an average mind to worship under polytheistic than under monotheistic thought.

Yet, while popular and even poetic imagination is fascinated by a vision of ultimate pluralism, metaphysical thought as well as scientific reflection is drawn to the concept of unity.

It is impossible to ignore the patent fact that unity is that which the uninterrupted advance of knowledge and experience leads us to, whether or not we are consciously striving for it. In our own age we have been forced into the realization that, in terms of human relations, there will be either one world or no world. But political and moral unity as a goal presupposes unity as a source; the brotherhood of men would be an empty dream without the fatherhood of God.

Eternity is another word for unity. In it, past and future are not apart; here is everywhere, and now goes on forever. The opposite of eternity is diffusion not time. Eternity does not begin when time is at its end. Time is eternity broken in space, like a ray of light refracted in the water.

The vision of the unbroken ray above the water, the craving for unity and coherence, is the predominant feature of a mature mind. All science, all philosophy, all art are a search after it. But unity is a task, not a condition. The world lies in strife, in discord, in divergence. Unity is beyond, not within, reality.* We all crave it. We are all animated by a passionate will to endure; and to endure means to be *one*.

The world is *not* one with God, and this is why His power does not surge unhampered throughout all stages of being. Creature is detached from the Creator, and the universe is in a state of spiritual disorder. Yet God has not withdrawn entirely from this world. The spirit of this unity hovers over the face of all plurality, and the major trend of all our thinking and striving is its mighty intimation. The goal of all efforts is to bring about the restitution of the unity of God and world. The restoration of that unity is a constant process and its accomplishment will be the essence of Messianic redemption.

Xenophanes, looking at the universe, said: "All is one." Parmenides, in taking the one seriously, was bound to deny the reality of everything else. Moses, however, did not say: "All is one," but: "God is One." Within the world there is the stubborn fact of plurality, divergence and conflict: "See, I have set before thee this day life and good, death and evil" (Deuteronomy 30:15). But God is the origin of all:

> I am the Lord, and there is none else;
> Beside Me there is no God . . .
> I am the Lord, and there is none else;
> I form the light, and create darkness;
> I make peace, and create evil;
> I am the Lord, that doeth all these things.
> (Isaiah 45:5–7)

The vision of the One, upon which we stake our effort and our ultimate hope, is not to be found in contemplations about nature or history. It is a vision of Him who transcends the scenes of both, subdued yet present everywhere, giving us the power to aid in bringing about ultimate unification.

> Whither shall I go from Thy spirit?
> Or whither shall I flee from Thy presence?
> If I ascend up into heaven, Thou art there;
> If I make my bed in the netherworld, behold, Thou art there . . .
> And if I say: Surely the darkness shall envelop me,
> And the light about me shall be night,
> Even the darkness is not too dark for Thee . . .
> (Psalms 139:7–12)

Mythopoeic thought is drawn to the beauty of the sparkling waves, their relentless surge and tantalizing rhythm. Abiding in the fragment, it

---

* "Thou art He who ties them together and unites them; and aside from Thee there is no unity either above or below" (Second Introduction to *Tikkune Zohar*).

Part II: The God of the Prophets

accepts the instrumental as the final, it has an image, an expression that corresponds to its experience. In contrast, he who takes the ineffable seriously is not infatuated with the fraction. To his mind there is no power in the world which could bear the air of divinity.

Nothing we can count, divide or surpass—a fraction or plurality—can be taken as the ultimate. Beyond two is one. Plurality is incompatible with the sense of the ineffable. You cannot ask in regard to the divine: Which one? There is only one synonym for God: One.

To the speculative mind the oneness of God is an idea inferred from the idea of the ultimate perfection of God; to the sense of the ineffable the oneness of God is self-evident.

Nothing in Jewish life is more hallowed than the saying of the Shema: "Hear, O Israel, the Lord is our God, the Lord is One." All over the world "the people acclaim His Oneness evening and morning, twice every day, and with tender affection recite the Shema" (Kedushah of Musaf on the Sabbath). The voice that calls: "Hear, He is One," is recalled, revived. It is the climax of devotion at the close of the Day of Atonement. It is the last word to come from the lips of the dying Jew and from the lips of those who are present at that moment.

Yet, ask an average Jew what the adjective "one" means, and he will tell you its negative meaning—it denies the existence of many deities. But is such a negation worth the price of martyrdom which Israel was so often willing to pay for it? Is there no positive content in it to justify the unsurpassed dignity which the idea of One God has attained in Jewish history? Furthermore, doubts have been raised whether the term "one" is at all meaningful when applied to God. For how can we designate Him by a number? A number is one of a series of symbols used in arranging quantities, in order to set them in a relation to one another. Since God is not in time or space, not a part of a series, "the term 'one' is just as inapplicable to God as the term 'many'; for both unity and plurality are categories of quantity, and are, therefore, as inapplicable to God as crooked and straight in reference to sweetness, or salted and insipid in reference to a voice" (Maimonides, The Guide of the Perplexed, I, 57).

The boldness of coming out against all deities, against the sanctities of all nations, had more behind it than the abstraction: "One, not many." Behind that revolutionary statement: "All the gods of the nations are vanities," was a new insight into the relation of the divine to nature: "but He made the heavens" (Psalms 96:5). In paganism the deity was a part of nature, and worship was an element in man's relation to nature. Man and his deities were both subjects of nature. Monotheism in teaching that God is the Creator, that nature and man are both fellow-creatures of

104

God, redeemed man from exclusive allegiance to nature. The earth is our sister, not our mother.

The heavens are not God, they are His witnesses: they declare His glory.

Monotheism was not attained by means of numerical reduction, by bringing down the multitude of deities to the smallest possible number. One means *unique.*

The minimum of knowledge is the knowledge of God's uniqueness.[1] His being unique is an aspect of His being ineffable.

To say He is more than the universe would be like saying that eternity is more than a day.

He is not only superior, He is incomparable. There is no equivalent of the divine. He is not "an aspect of nature," not an additional reality, existing along with this world, but a reality that is over and above the universe.

> With whom will ye compare Me
> That I should be similar?
> Saith the Holy One.
> (Isaiah 40:25)

God is one means He alone is truly real. One means exclusively, no one else, no one besides, alone, only. In I Kings 4:19, as well as in other Biblical passages, *ehad* means "only." Significantly the etymology of the English word "only" is one-ly.

"One" signifies "the same." This is the true meaning of "God is One." He is a being who is both beyond and here, both in nature and in history, both love and power, near and far, known and unknown, Father and Eternal. The true concept of unity is attained only in knowing that there is one being who is both Creator and Redeemer; "I am the Lord, thy God, who brought thee out of the land of Egypt" (Exodus 20:2). It is this declaration of the *sameness,* of the identity of the Creator and the Redeemer, with which the Decalogue begins.[2]

> They depicted Thee in countless visions;
> Despite all comparisons Thou art One.
> (*The Hymn of Glory*)

His is only a single way: His power is His love, His justice is His mercy. What is divergent to us is one in Him. This is a thought to which we may apply the words of Ibn Gabirol:

> Thou art One

And none can penetrate . . .
The mystery of Thy unfathomable unity . . .
(Ibn Gabirol, *Keter Malkhut*)

Moral sentiments do not originate in reason as such. A most learned man may be wicked, while a plain unlettered man may be righteous. Moral sentiments originate in man's sense of unity, in his appreciation of what is common to men. Perhaps the most fundamental statement of ethics is contained in the words of the last prophet of Israel: "Have we not all one Father? Has not one God made us? Then why do we break faith with one another, every man with his fellow, by dishonouring our time-honoured troth?" (Malachi 2:10). The ultimate principle of ethics is not an imperative but an ontological fact. While it is true that what distinguishes a moral attitude is the consciousness of obligation to do it, yet an act is not good because we feel obliged to do it; it is rather that we feel obliged to do it because it is good.

Seen from God, the good is identical with life and organic to the world; wickedness is a disease, and evil identical with death. For evil is *divergence*, confusion, that which *alienates* man from man, man from God, while good is *convergence*, togetherness, *union*. Good and evil are not qualities of the mind but relations within reality. Evil is division, contest, lack of unity, and as the unity of all being is prior to the plurality of things, so is the good prior to evil.

Good and evil persist regardless of whether or not we pay attention to them. We are not born into a vacuum, but stand, *nolens volens*, in relations to all men and to one God. Just as we do not create the dimensions of space in order to construct geometrical figures, so we do not create the moral and the spiritual relations; they are given with existence. All we do is try to find our way in them. The good does not begin in the consciousness of man. It is being realized in the natural co-operation of all beings, in what they are for each other.

Neither stars nor stones, neither atoms nor waves, but their belonging together, their interaction, the relation of all things to one another constitutes the universe. No cell could exist alone, all bodies are interdependent, affect and serve one another.

Rabbi Moshe of Kobryn said once to his disciples: "Do you want to know where God is?" He took a piece of bread from the table, showed it to everybody and said: "Here is God."[3]

In saying God is everywhere, we do not intend to say He is like the air, the parts of which are found in countless places. One in a metaphyical sense means wholeness, indivisibility. God is not partly here and partly there; He is all here and all there.

15. One God

Lord, where shall I find thee?
High and hidden is thy place;
And where shall I not find thee?
The world is full of thy glory.
                    (Jehudah Halevi)

"Can any hide himself in secret places that I shall not see him? saith the Lord. Do not I fill heaven and earth? saith the Lord" (Jeremiah 23:24).

God is within all things, not only in the life of man. "Why did God speak to Moses from the thornbush?" was a question a pagan asked of a rabbi. To the pagan mind He should have appeared upon a lofty mountain or in the majesty of a thunderstorm. And the rabbi answered: "To teach you that there is no place on earth where the Shekhinah is not, not even a humble thornbush" (*Exodus Rabbah* 2:9; cf. *Song of Songs Rabbah* 3:16). Just as the soul fills the body, so God fills the world. Just as the soul carries the body so God carries the world.[4]

The natural and the supernatural are not two different spheres, detached from one another as heaven from earth. God is not beyond but right here; not only close to my thoughts but also to my body. This is why man is taught to be aware of His presence, not only by prayer, study and meditation but also in his physical demeanor, by how and what to eat and drink, by keeping the body free from whatever sullies and defiles.

"An idol is near and far; God is far and near" (*Deuteronomy Rabbah* 2:6). "God is far, and yet nothing is closer than He." "He is near with every kind of nearness" (Jerushalmi Berakhot 13a).

It is His otherness, ineffable and immediate as the air we breathe and do not see, which enables us to sense His distant nearness. "For thus saith the high and lofty One that inhabiteth eternity, whose name *is* Holy; I dwell in the high and holy place, with him also that is of a contrite and humble spirit, to revive the spirit of the humble, and to revive the heart of the contrite ones" (Isaiah 57:15).

Unity of God is power for unity of God with all things. He is one in Himself and striving to be one with the world. Rabbi Samuel ben Ammi remarked that the Biblical narrative of creation proclaims: "One day . . . a second day . . . a third day," and so on. If it is a matter of time reckoning, we would expect the Bible to say: "One day . . . two days . . . three days" or: "The first day . . . the second day . . . the third day," but surely not "one, second, third!"

Yom eḥad, one day, really means the day which God desired to be *one* with man. "From the beginning of creation the Holy One, blessed be He, longed to enter into partnership with the terrestrial world."[5] The unity of God is a concern for the unity of the world.

16.   THE DIVINE CONCERN

In their eagerness to avoid the possibility of ascribing anthropomorphic features to God, philosophers have traditionally adopted the procedure prevalent in general ontology, in which the notion of existence that served as a subject matter of analysis was derived from the realm of inanimate rather than from the realm of animate and personal existence. The subsequent efforts to fill the ontological shell with spiritual or moral content have encountered insurmountable difficulties, primarily because of the disparity of inanimate, animate and spiritual existence.

A pencil, a pigeon, and a poet have being in common; not only their essence but their existence is not the same. The difference between the existence of a human being and the existence of a pencil is as radical and intrinsic as the difference between the existence of the pencil and the nonexistence of the Flying Dutchman. This becomes apparent when we compare a living man with a corpse. They both contain the same chemical elements in exactly the same proportions, at least immediately after death. Yet a man who is dead is nonexistent as a man, as a human or social being, although he is still existent as a corpse.

Temporality and uninterruptedness express the relation of existence to time, a passive relation. What distinguishes organic from inorganic existence is the fact that the plant or the animal stands in an active and defensive relation to temporality. All finite existence, a stone or a dog, is constantly on the verge of nonexistence: any moment it may cease to exist. But unlike the stone, the dog is endowed to a degree with the ability to fight or avoid the ills of life.

Life, we know from biology, is not a passive state of indifference and inertia. The essence of life is intense care and concern. For example, the life of the cell depends upon its power to manufacture and to retain certain substances that are necessary to its survival. These substances are prevented from diffusing out, because the outer surface of the cell is impermeable to them. At the same time, this surface, owing to the selective permeability of the protoplasm, allows other favorable substances to penetrate into the cell from the outside, while refusing admission to substances that are unfavorable. Every cell behaves like an accordion, contracting when brought into contact with something destructive. On the

108

basis of these observations the following biological principle may be established: every living organism abhors its own destruction.

We may, therefore, say that just as the peculiar quality of inorganic existence is necessity and inertia, the peculiar asset of organic existence, or life, is concern. Life *is* concern.

Such concern is reflexive: it refers to one's own self and is rooted in the anxiety of the self about its own future. If man paid no attention to the future, if he were indifferent to that which may or may not come, he would not know any anxiety. The past is gone, at present he is alive, it is only the time to come of which he is apprehensive.

A man entirely unconcerned with his self is dead; a man exclusively concerned with his self is a beast. The mark of distinction from the beast as well as the index of maturity is the tridimensionality of man's concern. The child becomes human, not by discovering the environment which includes things and other selves, but by becoming sensitive to the interests of other selves. Human is he who is concerned with other selves. Man is a being that can never be self-sufficient, not only by what he must take in but also by what he must give out. A stone is self-sufficient, man is self-surpassing. Always in need of other beings to give himself to, man cannot even be in accord with his own self unless he serves something beyond himself. The peace of mind attainable in solitude is not the result of ignoring that which is not the self or escaping from it, but of reconciliation with it. The range of needs increases with the rise of the form of existence: a stone is more self-sufficient than a plant, and a horse requires more for its survival than a tree. A vital requirement of human life is transitive concern, a regard for others, in addition to a reflexive concern, an intense regard for itself.

At first the other selves are considered as means to attain the fulfillment of his own needs. The shift from the animal to the human dimension takes place when, as a result of various events, such as observing other people's suffering, falling in love or by being morally educated, he begins to acknowledge the other selves as ends, to respond to their needs even regardless of personal expediency. It is an act of *de jure* or even *de facto* recognition of other human beings as equals, as a result of which he becomes concerned with their concern; what is of importance to them becomes vital to him. Cain when asked about the whereabouts of his brother, gave answer: "Am I my brother's keeper?" (Genesis 4:9). Abraham, unasked, unsolicited, pleaded for Sodom, the city of wickedness.

It is not a mechanical, lateral extension of the concern for oneself that brings about the concern for others. The concern for others often demands the price of self-denial. How could self-denial or even self-extinction be explained as a self-extension? Consequently, we cannot say that the concern for others lies on the same level as the concern for oneself, consisting merely in substituting another self for one's own. The motivation of our transitive concern may be selfish. The fact of our transitive concern is not.

The concern for others is not an extension in breadth but an ascension, a rise. Man reaches a new vertical dimension, the dimension of the holy, when he grows beyond his self-interests, when that which is of interest to others becomes vital to him, and it is only in this dimension, in the understanding of its perennial validity, that the concern for other human beings and the devotion to ideals may reach the degree of self-denial. Distant ends, religious, moral and artistic interests, may become as relevant to man as his concern for food. The self, the fellow-man and the dimension of the holy are the *three* dimensions of a mature human concern.

God's existence—what may it mean? Being eternal, temporality does not apply to Him. May reflexive concern be predicated of Him? He does not have to be concerned about Himself, since there is no need of His being on guard against danger to His existence. The only concern that may be ascribed to Him is a transitive concern, one which is implied in the very concept of creation. For if creation is conceived as a voluntary activity of the Supreme Being, it implies a concern with that which is coming into being. Since God's existence is continuous, His concern or care for His creatures must be abiding. While man's concern for others is often tainted with concern for his own self and characterized as a lack of self-sufficiency and a requirement for the perpetuation of his own existence, God's care for His creatures is a pure concern.

According to Cicero: "The gods are careful about great things and neglect small ones" (*De Natura Deorum*, Book ii, ch. 66, 167). According to the prophets of Israel, from Moses to Malachi, God is concerned with small matters. What the prophets tried to convey to man was not a conception of an eternal harmony, of an unchangeable rhythm of wisdom, but the perception of God's concern with concrete situations. Disclosing the pattern of history, in which the human is interwoven with the divine, they breathed a divine earnestness into the world of man.

In mythology the deities are thought of as self-seeking, as concerned with their own selves. Immortal, superior to man in power and wisdom, they are often inferior to man in morality. "Homer and Hesiod have ascribed to the gods all the things that are a shame and a disgrace among mortals, stealings and adulteries and deceivings of one another" (Xenophanes).

16. The Divine Concern

The Bible tells us nothing about God in Himself; all its sayings refer to His relations to man. His own life and essence are neither told nor disclosed. We hear of no reflexive concern, of no passions, except a passion for justice. The only events in the life of God the Bible knows of are acts done for the sake of man: acts of creation, acts of redemption (from Ur, from Egypt, from Babylon), or acts of revelation.

Zeus is passionately interested in pretty female deities and becomes inflamed with rage against those who incite his jealousy. The God of Israel is passionately interested in widows and orphans.

Divine concern means His taking interest in the fate of man; it means that the moral and spiritual state of man engages His attention. It is true that His concern is, to most of us, one of the most baffling mysteries, but it is just as true that to those whose life is open to God His care and love are a constant experience.

In ascribing a transitive concern to God, we employ neither an anthropomorphic nor an anthropopathic concept but an idea that we should like to characterize as an *anthropopneumism (anthropos + pneuma)*. We ascribe to Him not a psychic but a spiritual characteristic, not an emotional but a moral attitude. Those who refuse to ascribe a transitive concern to God are unknowingly compelled to conceive His existence, if it should mean anything at all, after the analogy of physical being and to think of Him in terms of "physiomorphism."

Creation in the language of the Bible is an act of expression. God said: "Let there be"; and it was. And creation is not an act that happened once, but a continuous process. The word *Yehi,* "Let there be," stands forever in the universe. If it were not for the presence of that word, there would be no world, there would be no finite being (compare Midrash Tehillim, ed. Buber, p. 498).

When we say that He is present within all being, we do not mean that He inheres in them as a component or ingredient of their physical structure. *God in the universe is a spirit of concern for life. What is a thing to us is a concern to God; what is a part of the physical world of being is also a part of a divine world of meaning. To be is to stand for,* to stand for a divine concern.

God is present in His continuous expression. He is immanent in all beings in the way in which a person is immanent in a cry that he utters: He stands for what he says. He is concerned with what he says. All beings are replete with the divine word which only leaves when our viciousness profanes and overbears His silent, patient presence.

We usually forget where He is, forget that our own self-concern is a cupful drawn from the spirit of divine concern. There is, however, a way of keeping ourselves open to the presence of that spirit. There are

111

moments in which we feel the challenge of a power that, not born of our will nor installed by it, robs us of independence by its judgment of the rectitude or depravity of our actions, by its gnawing at our heart when we offend against its injunctions. It is as if there were no privacy within ourselves, no possibility of either retreat or escape, no place in us in which to bury the remains of our guilt feelings. There is a voice that reaches everywhere, knowing no mercy, digging in the burial places of charitable forgetfulness.

God is not all in all. He is in all beings but He is *not* all beings. He is within the darkness but He is not the darkness. His one concern permeates all beings: He is all there, but the absence of the divine is also there. His ends are concealed in the cold facts of nature.

The impenetrable fog in which the world is clad is God's disguise. To know God means to sense display in His disguise and to be aware of the disguise in His most magnificent display.

God is within the world, present and concealed in the essence of things, If not for His presence, there would be no essence; if not for His concealment, there would be no appearance.

If the universe were explainable as a robot, we could assume that God is separated from it and His relation to it would be like that of a watchmaker to a clock. But the ineffable cries out of all things. It is only the idea of a divine presence hidden within the rational order of nature which is compatible with our scientific view of nature and in accord with our sense of the ineffable.

The soul dwells within, yet the spirit is always hovering above reality. God's infinite concern is present in the world, His essence is transcendent. He includes the universe, but, to quote Solomon's prayer in dedicating the Temple: "Behold, the heaven, and the heaven of heavens, cannot contain Thee" (I Kings 8:27).

The Bible is primarily not man's vision of God but God's vision of man. The Bible is not man's theology but God's anthropology, dealing with man and what He asks of him rather than with the nature of God. God did not reveal to the prophets eternal mysteries but His knowledge and love of man. It was not the aspiration of Israel to know the Absolute but to ascertain what He asks of man; to commune with His will rather than with His essence.

In the depth of our trembling, all that we can utter is the awareness of our being known to God. Man cannot see God, but man can be seen by God. He is not the object of a discovery but the subject of revelation.

There are no concepts which we could appoint to designate the greatness of God or to represent Him to our minds. He is not a being, whose existence could be either confirmed or described by our thoughts. He is a reality, in the face of which, when becoming alive to its meaning, we are overtaken with a feeling of infinite unworthiness.

Accustomed to thinking in categories of space, we conceive of God as being vis-à-vis ourselves, as if we were here and He were there. We think of Him in the likeness of things, as if He were a thing among things, a being among beings.

Entering the meditation about the ultimate, we must rid ourselves of the intellectual habit of converting reality into an object of our minds. Thinking of God is totally different from thinking about all other matters. We often fail in trying to understand Him, not because we do not know how to extend our concepts far enough, but because we do not know how to begin close enough. To think of God is not to find Him as an object in our minds, but to find ourselves in Him. Religion begins where experience ends, and the end of experience is a perception of our being perceived.

To have knowledge of a thing is to have its concept at our mind's disposal. Since concept and thing, definition and essence belong to different realms, we are able to conquer and to own a thing theoretically, while the thing itself may be away from us, as is the case, for example, in our knowledge of stellar nebulae.

God is neither a thing nor an idea; He is within and beyond all things and all ideas. Thinking of God is not beyond but within Him. The thought of Him would not be in front of us, if God were not behind it.

The thought of God has no façade. We are all in it as soon as it is all in us. To conceive it is to be absorbed by it, like the present in the past, in a past that never dies.

Our knowing Him and His reality are not apart. To think of Him is to open our minds to His all-pervading presence, to our being replete with His presence. To think of things means to have a concept within the mind, while to think of Him is like walking under a canopy of thought, like being surrounded by thought. He remains beyond our reach as long as we do not know that our reach is within Him; that He is the Knower and we are the known; that to be means to be thought of by Him.

Thinking of God is made possible by His being the *subject* and by our being His *object*. To think of God is to expose ourselves to Him, to conceive ourselves as a reflection of His reality. He cannot be limited to a thought. To think means to set aside or to separate an object from the thinking subject. But in setting Him apart, we gain an idea and lose Him. Since He is not away from us and we are not beyond Him, He can never become the mere object of our thought. As, in thinking about ourselves, the object cannot be detached from the subject, so in thinking of God the subject cannot be detached from the object. *In thinking of Him, we realize that it is through Him that we think of Him. Thus, we must think of Him as the subject of all, as the life of our life, as the mind of our mind.*

If an idea had ability to think and to transcend itself, it would be aware of its being at this moment a thought of my mind. The religious man has such an awareness of being known by God, as if he were an object, a thought in His mind.

To the philosopher God is an *object,* to men at prayer He is the *subject.* Their aim is not to possess Him as a concept of knowledge, to be informed about Him, as if He were a fact among facts. What they crave for is to be wholly possessed by Him, to be an object of His knowledge and to sense it. The task is not to know the unknown but to be penetrated with it; *not to know* but *to be known* to Him, to expose ourselves to Him rather than Him to us; not to judge and to assert but to listen and to be judged by Him.

His knowledge of man precedes man's knowledge of Him, while man's knowledge of Him comprehends only what God asks of man. This is the essential content of prophetic revelation.

17. PROCESS AND EVENT

Prophetic inspiration must be understood as *an event,* not as *a process.* What is the difference between process and event? A process happens regularly, following a relatively permanent pattern; an event is extraordinary, irregular. A process may be continuous, steady, uniform; events happen suddenly, intermittently, occasionally. Processes are typical; events are unique. A process follows a law, events create a precedent.

A process occurs in the physical order. But not all events are reducible to physical terms. The life of Beethoven left music behind; yet valued in physical terms its effects on the world were felt less than the effect of a normal rain storm or an earthquake.

Man lives in an order of events, not only in an order of processes. It is a spiritual order. Moments of insight, moments of decision, moments of prayer—may be insignificant in the world of space, yet they put life into focus.

Nature is made up of processes—organic life, for example, may be described as consisting of the processes of birth, growth, maturity and decay; history consists primarily of events. What lends human, historical character to the life of Pericles or Aristotle are not the organic processes through which they went but the extraordinary, surprising and unpredictable acts, achievements or events which distinguished them from all other human beings.

An event is a happening that cannot be reduced to a part of a process. It is something we can neither predict nor fully explain. To speak of events is to imply that there are happenings *in the world* that are beyond the reach of our explanations. What the consciousness of events implies, the belief in revelation claims explicitly, namely, that a voice of God *enters the world* which pleads with man to do His will.

What do we mean by "the world"? If we mean an ultimate, closed, fixed and self-sufficient system of phenomena behaving in accord with the laws known to us, then such a concept would exclude the possibility of admitting any super-mundane intervention or penetration by a voice not accounted for by these laws. Indeed, if the world as described by natural science is regarded as the ultimate, then there is no sense in searching for the Divine which is by definition the ultimate. How could there be one ultimate within the other?

The claim of the Bible is absurd, unless we are ready to comprehend that the world as scrutinized and depicted by science is but a thin surface of the profoundly unknown. Order is only one of the aspects of nature; its reality is a mystery given but not known. Countless relations that determine our life in history are neither known nor predictable. What history does with the laws of nature cannot be expressed by a law of nature.

To assume that the entire complex of natural laws is transcended by the freedom of God would presuppose the metaphysical understanding that the laws of nature are derived not from a blind necessity but from freedom, that the ultimate is not fate but God. Revelation is not an act of interfering with the normal course of natural processes but the act of instilling a new creative moment into the course of history. A process has no future. It becomes obsolete and is always replaced by its own effects. We do not ponder about last year's snow. An event, on the other hand, retains its significance even after it has passed; it remains as a lasting motive because and regardless of its effects. Great events, just as great works of art, are significant in themselves. Our interest in them endures long after they are gone.

It is, indeed, one of the peculiar features of human existence that the past does not altogether vanish, that some events of hoary antiquity may hold us in their spell to this very day. Events which are dead, things which are gone, can neither be sensed nor told. There is a liberation from what is definitely past. On the other hand, there are events which never become past. Sacred history may be described as an attempt to overcome the dividing line of past and present, as an attempt *to see the past in the present tense.*

Such understanding of time is not peculiar to historians. It is shared unknowingly by all men and is essential to civilized living.

18. THE DIVINE PATHOS

The prophets did not see the world as a superficial succession of causes and effects in the world; they saw it rather as a meaningful relation among events. History revealed the work of God and therefore needed interpretation. To the prophet God is never an object; He is always a person, a subject. The prophet does not think of God as of something absolute in the sense of unrelated; he thinks of Him primarily as of One who takes a direct part in the events of the world.

The prophets never ask: *"What is God?"* They are interested only in His activity and influence in human affairs. Even their views of what we would call basic principles took the form of concrete aims and tasks. It is from this point of view that we must try to answer the questions: What is typically prophetic theology like? What attitude to God defines the meaning of prophecy? Which aspect of the monotheism they affirmed had the most decisive influence upon their thought and feeling?

Prophecy consists in the inspired communication of divine attitudes to the prophetic consciousness. The divine *pathos* is the ground-tone of all these attitudes. Echoed in almost every prophetic statement, *pathos* is the central category of the prophetic understanding of God.

To the prophet, God does not reveal himself in an abstract absoluteness, but in a specific and unique way—in a personal and intimate relation to the world. God does not simply command and expect obedience; He is also moved and affected by what happens in the world and he reacts accordingly. Events and human actions arouse in Him joy or sorrow, pleasure or wrath. He is not conceived as judging facts, so to speak, "objectively," in detached impassibility. He reacts in an intimate and subjective manner, and thus determines the value of events. Quite obviously in the Biblical view, man's deeds can move Him, affect Him,

18. The Divine Pathos

grieve Him, or, on the other hand, gladden and please Him. This notion that God can be intimately affected, that he possesses not merely intelligence and will, but also feeling and *pathos,* basically defines the prophetic consciousness of God.

How then did the prophets conceive of divine pathos? As is clear from detailed descriptions of *pathos,* the latter was not understood as a passion such as may powerfully grip a human being. By passion we mean drunkenness of the mind, an agitation of the soul devoid of reasoned purpose, operating blindly "either in the choice of its end, or, even if the end has been dictated by reason, in the fulfilment of it, for it is an emotional convulsion which excludes a free consideration of principles and the determination of conduct in accordance with them."[1]

Pathos is not, however, to be understood as mere feeling. *Pathos* is an act formed with intention, depending on free will, the result of decision and determination. The divine *pathos* is the theme of the prophetic mission. The aim of the prophet is to reorient the people by communicating to them the divine *pathos* which, by impelling the people to "return," is itself transformed. Even "in the moment of anger" (Jeremiah 18:7), what God intends is not that His anger should be executed, but that it should be appeased and annulled by the people's repentance.

To the prophets, the divine *pathos* is not an absolute force which exists regardless of man, something ultimate or eternal. It is rather a reaction to human history, an attitude called forth by man's conduct; an effect, not a cause. Man is in a sense an agent, not only the recipient. It is within his power to deserve either the *pathos* of love or the *pathos* of anger.

The divine *pathos* is not merely intentional; it is also *transitive.* The gods of mythology are self-centered, egotistic. Their passions—erotic love, jealousy, envy—are determined by considerations of self. Zeus is "hit by the dart of desire and is inflamed with passion" for Io, with whom he desires "to enjoy the pleasures of Cypris," so that his "eye may be eased of its desire."[2]

Pathos, on the other hand, is not a self-centered and self-contained state; it is always, in prophetic thinking, directed outward; it always expresses a relation to man. It is therefore not one of God's attributes as such. It has not a reflexive, but rather a transitive character. Hence, whereas in the mythological genealogy of the gods man plays no part, the "history" of God cannot be separated from the history of the People Israel: the history of the divine *pathos* is embedded in human affairs.

In primitive religion, God's anger is something arbitrary, and unrelated to any conditions. The prophetic thought that human actions bring about divine *pathos,* emphasizes the unique position that man occupies in his relation to God. The divine *pathos* rooted though it is in God's free will, emerges in the context of conditions which are quite clearly human conditions.

The prophets know two different kinds of divine *pathos:* from the point of view of man, the *pathos* of redemption and that of affliction; from the point of view of God, the *pathos* of sympathy and that of rejection. But the fact that rejection seems to occur more frequently in the Biblical account should not be taken to prove that wrath is inherently one of God's chief attributes. On the contrary, prophecy aims at the annulment of the *pathos* of affliction and rejection. The prophets experience God's wrath as suffering which He receives at the hand of man. It is the incredible disloyalty of His people which arouses in Him the *pathos* which afflicts. God's word comes as an appeal and a warning to His people not to arouse His anger.

The basic features emerging from the above analysis indicate that the divine *pathos* is not conceived as an essential attribute of God. The *pathos* is not felt as something objective, as a finality with which man is confronted, but as an expression of God's will; it is a functional rather than a substantial reality. The prophets never identify God's *pathos* with His essence, because it is for them not something absolute, but a form of relation. Indeed, prophecy would be impossible were the divine *pathos* in its particular structure a necessary attribute of God. If the structure of the *pathos* were immutable and remained unchanged even after the people had "turned," prophecy would lose its function, which is precisely so to influence men as to bring about a change in the divine pathos of rejection and affliction.

God's *pathos* was not thought of as a sort of fever of the mind which, disregarding the standards of justice, culminates in irrational and irresponsible action. There is justice in all His ways, the Bible does not tire of insisting.

There is no dichotomy of *pathos* and *ethos,* of motive and norm. They do not exist side by side opposing each other; they involve and presuppose each other. It is because God is the source of goodness, that His *pathos* is ethical; and it is because God is absolutely personal—devoid of anything impersonal—that this *ethos* is full of *pathos.*

Pathos, then, is not an attitude taken arbitrarily. Its inner law is the moral law; *ethos* is inherent in *pathos.* God is concerned about the world and shares in its fate. Indeed, this is the essence of God's moral nature: His willingness to be intimately involved in the history of man.

There are two pitfalls in our religious understanding: the humanization of God and the anesthetization of God. Both threaten our understanding of the ethical integrity of God's will. Humanization leads to the conception of God as the ally of the people; whether it does right or wrong God would not fail His people. The idea of the divine anger shatters such horrible complacency.

The anesthetization of God would reduce Him to a mystery, Whose will is unknown, Who has nothing to say to man. Such indifference was refuted by the prophets' own experiences of being addressed by Him and called upon to convey His word to the people.

A comparison with other theological systems can help to reveal the uniqueness of the prophetic idea of God. The Stoics considered *pathos* to be unreasonable and unnatural emotion, whereas apathy—the subduing and the overcoming of the emotions—was taken to be the supreme moral task. Spinoza held feeling to be "confused ideas." Laotse's *Tao* (the "divine way") is the eternal silence, the everlasting calm and the unchangeable law of the cosmic order. In accordance with *Tao*, man is to rid himself of desire and sympathy, greed and passion, and humbly and quietly become like *Tao*. Zeal and unrest are to be avoided. To live according to *Tao* means to live passively. The God of the prophets, however, is not the Law, but the Lawgiver. The order emanating from Him is not a rigid, unchangeable structure, but a historic-dynamical reality. Aristotle's god ever rests in itself. Things long for it and thus are set into motion; it is in this sense the "prime mover," but is itself immovable. Aristotle's God knows no feeling or suffering; it is simply pure thought thinking itself. The prophet's God is concerned with the world, and His thoughts are about it. He is the God of the fathers, the God of the covenant. The divine *pathos* expresses itself in the relation between God and His people. God is the "Holy One of Israel."

Many civilizations, too, know an inescapable, unyielding power standing above the gods. Fate is supreme; it cannot be evaded. The divine *pathos*, on the other hand, strives at overcoming destiny. Its dynamic character, which makes every decision provisional, conquers fate. In Greek theology, the highest power does not need man. Events are a monologue. But Jewish religion starts with the covenant: God *and* man. An apathetical, immobile conception of God could not possibly fit into prophetic religion.

The divine *pathos*, though it is rooted in His freedom, is not simply will. God as pure will is found in Islam. In the Koran, Allah is represented as a will removed from all considerations, working without any relation to actuality. Since everything is rigorously determined, the dialogue is again reduced to a monologue. Central is not the relation between Allah and man, but simply Allah himself. The prophets explicitly fought against the idea, widespread even in Palestine, that God was the

Creator of the world but did not interfere with the course of nature and history. This essentially deistic notion has no place for the divine *pathos* because it has no place for any genuine connection between God and the world.

The decisive importance of the idea of divine *pathos* emerges clearly when we consider the possible forms in which God's relation to the world may present itself. A purely ethical monotheism in which God, the guardian of the moral order, keeps the world subject to the law, would restrict the scope of God's knowledge and concern to what is of ethical significance. God's relation to man would, in general, run along the lines of a universal principle. The divine *pathos* alone is able to break through this rigidity and create new dimensions for the unique, the specific, and the particular.

The idea of divine *pathos* throws light on many types of relation between God and man unknown in apathetic religion. The covenant between God and Israel is an example. The category of divine *pathos* leads to the basic affirmation that God is interested in human history, that every deed and event in the world concerns Him and arouses His reaction. What is characteristic of the prophets is not foreknowledge of the future but insight into the present *pathos* of God.

The idea of divine *pathos* has also its anthropological significance. Man has his relation to God. A religion without man is as impossible as a religion without God. That God takes man seriously is shown by his concern for human existence. It finds its deepest expression in the fact that God can actually suffer. At the heart of the prophetic affirmation is the certainty that God is concerned about the world to the point of suffering.

In sum, the divine *pathos* is the unity of the eternal and the temporal, of the rational and the irrational, of the metaphysical and the historical. It is the real basis of the relation between God and man, of the correlation of Creator and creation, of the dialogue between the Holy One of Israel and His people.

The meaning of the divine *pathos* was often misunderstood by Jewish as well as by Christian and Islamic religious philosophy, which tended to overlook its specific form and content and to interpret it as simply an aspect of anthropomorphism, or to be more precise, of anthropopathism.

Marcion, the gnostic leader, bitterly assailed anthropopathism. In the polemics of Jews and Christians against heathenism, the emotions of the pagan gods formed a favorite target of attack. In more modern times, too, exception was frequently taken to God's wrath, which was held to be incompatible with His justice and love. But, of course, God's wrath is not something in itself but is part of the entire structure of the divine *pathos*. God's anger is conditioned by God's will and aroused by man's sins; it can be dissipated by the "return" of the people. Divine wrath is not opposed to love, but rather its counterpart. It is the very evidence of God's love. Only because God loves His people is He capable of being kindled with anger against them. God's love, justice, and wrath are part of the same structure of divine *pathos*.

Embarrassment over the "emotional" and irrational features of the Biblical account of God induced the so-called historical school of Bible criticism to assume an evolutionary development. In ancient times, it was alleged, Israel knew only the awe-inspiring God; in later times, however, they came to think of God as a kind and loving God. This view is neither true to fact nor in line with the fundamental Biblical outlook. It likewise ignores the crucial polarity—love and anger, justice and mercy—which characterizes the divine *pathos*.

Whether philosophical or historical, the objections to anthropopathism have generally prevailed. Why? What has been the strength of this opposition to the idea of divine *pathos?* It seems to us to be due to a combination of various tendencies which have their origin in Greek classical philosophy. The Eleatics taught that whatever exists is unchangeable. This ontological view was very soon put to use to determine the nature of God. Xenophanes, Anaxagoras, Plato, and Aristotle followed in much the same line. The principle that mutuability cannot be attributed to God is thus an ontological dogma, and as such it has become the common property of religious philosophers.

It is easy to see how on the basis of the ontological view of the Eleatics there emerged a static conception of God. According to Greek thinking, impassivity and immobility are characteristic of the divine. Now since in Greek psychology, affects or feelings are described as emotions (movements) of the soul, it is obvious that they cannot be brought into harmony with the idea of God. The ontological basis of this system of thought may, of course, be challenged by another ontological system which sees in changeability the very sign of real being. Such a system will lead to a dynamic rather than static idea of God.

Since Plato, we have become familiar with the distinction between a rational immortal component of the human soul and one that is irrational and mortal. The rational component is believed to be indivisible, whereas the irrational one is usually subdivided into a noble and a less noble part, the former comprising the passions, the latter the evil desires. In medieval philosophy, the three elements are reduced to two, but in either case the life of the emotions is separated from the realm of the rational. The dualism of values thus engendered has deeply penetrated Western thinking.

To the degree that theology has subscribed to this dualism of values, it has attributed to God the power of thinking, but excluded the emotions. But this dualism is utterly foreign to Biblical thinking. The emotions are part of the entire spiritual structure, and Scripture never demeans them.

The wisdom of the Greek exalted reason above the passions. Zeno even demanded the complete extinction of the feelings on moral grounds. All the other schools of Greek ethics acknowledged the inferior character of the irrational emotions as against the rational part of the soul. This opinion was projected into theology. The ideal of the sage was made to find its realization in God. Plato constantly stressed the notion that the gods are without emotions, desires, or needs.

The Greek word *"pathos"* implies suffering, and in the Greek view, *pathos* is necessarily passive; in the state of pathos, a person is affected and directed by an agent outside himself. The person who is thus affected finds himself in a relation of dependence upon the agent, comparable to the relation of cause and effect. From very early times, it was felt that God could not be affected in such a way. God, the Supreme Cause, could not possibly suffer from or be affected by something which is effected by Himself. Passivity was held to be incompatible with the dignity of the Divine. It was on these grounds—the conception of a First Cause and its dignity—that *pathos* was rejected.

Such a line of reasoning may be applicable to a God derived from abstraction. A God of abstraction is a high and mighty First Cause, which, dwelling in lonely splendor of eternity, will never submit to human prayer, and it will be beneath its dignity to be affected by anything which it has itself caused to come into being. But it is a dogmatic sort of dignity which insists upon God's pride rather than love, upon His decorum rather than mercy.

The God of the prophets continues to be involved in human history and to be affected by human acts. It is a paradox beyond compare that the Eternal God is concerned with what is happening in time. "For thus says the high and lofty One who inhabits eternity, whose name is Holy: I dwell in the high and holy place, with him also who is of a contrite and humble spirit, to revive the spirit of the humble, and to revive the heart of the contrite ones" (Isaiah 57:15).

Authentic Jewish thought evaluates the emotions in a manner diametrically opposed to the Greek view. The emotions have often been regarded as inspirations from God, as the reflection of a higher power. Neither in the legal nor in the moral parts of the Bible is there a suggestion that the desires and the passions are to be negated. Asceticism was not the ideal of Biblical man. Since the feelings were considered valuable, there was no reason to eliminate them from the conception of God.

Is it more compatible with our conception of the grandeur of God to claim that He is emotionally blind to the misery of man rather than profoundly moved? To conceive of God not as an onlooker but as a participant, to conceive of man not as an idea in the mind of God but as a concern—the category of divine pathos is an indispensable implication. To the Biblical mind the conception of God as cold, detached and unemotional is totally alien.

An apathetic and ascetic God would have struck Biblical man with a sense not of dignity and grandeur but rather of poverty and emptiness. Only through arbitrary allegorizing was later religious philosophy able to find an apathetic God in the Bible.

Recognizing the motives lying behind the Greek rejection of anthropopathism helps us get an insight into the meaning of the teaching itself. We can see how very questionable are the presuppositions in terms of which anthropopathism was for centuries repudiated by religious philosophy. Present-day philosophy has abandoned many of these axioms taken over from ancient Greek philosophy and it will also have to revise its attitude towards anthropopathism.

The mystic strives to experience God as something final, immediate. In mythical thinking, too, God Himself is the object of the imagination. For the aborigines, indeed, God dwells in the visible symbol. Once religious thinking proclaimed God to be invisible and different from man, there would seem to be no escaping agnosticism. The prophets overcame this dilemma by separating essence and expression. They were not out to experience God Himself, but rather His expressions in the image of vision, in the word of inspiration, in the acts of history. Prophetic revelation, indeed, does not reveal anything about God's essence. What the prophet knows about God is God's *pathos,* but this is not experienced as a part of the divine essence. Not God Himself is the object of understanding, but only His relation to Israel and to the world. Hence revelation means not that God makes Himself known, but that He makes His will known. In the separation of essence and relation the prophetic knowledge of God becomes possible.

The prophets are familiar with various forms of the divine *pathos:* love and anger, mercy and indignation, kindness and wrath. But what is, so to speak, the intrinsic property of the divine *pathos?*

In every one of its forms, the divine *pathos* points to a connection between God and man—a connection which originates with God. God "looks at" the world and its events. He experiences and judges them; this means that He is concerned with man and is somehow related to His people. The basic feature of the divine *pathos* is God's transcendental attention to man.

Yet even here we must not think that we reach God's essence. God's transcendental attention merely defines the limits of the prophet's understanding of God. The prophet never speculates about God's real being. In the divine *pathos,* which is a manifestation of God's transcendental attention, he finds the answer to the events of life. For in it is implied God's interest in the world and His concern for it.

The world is looked upon by God. God knows us. God can be experienced by us only if and when we are aware of His attention to us, of His being concerned with us. The prophet is impressed by God's concern with the world. This is the ultimate reality for prophetic spirituality.

God's transcendental attention engenders in man the sense of being the object of the divine subject. In all that the prophets knew about God, they never found in Him a desire which did not bear upon man. God is not the object of religious discovery, but the sovereign subject of revelation. He is the supreme subject.

19. PROPHETIC SYMPATHY

The nature of man's response to the divine corresponds to the content of his apprehension of the divine. When the divine is sensed as mysterious perfection, the response is one of fear and trembling; when sensed as absolute Will the response is one of unconditional obedience; when sensed as *pathos* the response is one of *sympathy.*

Such a classification must not be taken in an absolute sense, as if the awareness of one aspect of the divine either excluded or obscured the awareness of any other aspect. However, no reality or subject can be apprehended simultaneously and wholeheartedly in all its aspects. To the prophet the *pathos* was the predominant and staggering aspect of the divine. Even if in the first place the people's practical compliance with the divine demand was the purpose of his mission, the inner personal identification of the prophet with the divine *pathos* was, as we have shown, the central feature of his own life. Not the word and the law in themselves, but the fact of divine passibility was the focal point in his religious consciousness. The divine pathos is reflected in his attitudes, hopes, and prayers. He was dominated by an intimate concern for the divine concern. Sympathy, then, is the essential mode in which the prophet responds to the divine situation. It is the way of fulfilling personally the demand addressed to him in moments of revelation.

It is no mere listening to, and conveying a divine message which distinguishes his personal life. The prophet not only hears and apprehends the divine *pathos;* he is convulsed by it to the depths of his soul. His service of the divine word is not carried out through mental appropriation but through the harmony of his being with its fundamental intention and emotional content.

Any other attitude is impossible to the prophet whose mission is to proclaim the *pathos* to the people. How could he remain indifferent, unmoved? *Epochē* in the face of divine pathos would be callousness to the divine.

For the Biblical man who has an awareness of the unity of the psychical life, and for whom the passions form an integral part of the human spiritual structure, an unemotional sobriety could not be the form of religious consciousness. An emotional religion of sympathy is more compatible with his mentality than a cold self-detached religion of obedience. Man is expected to love his God with all his heart, with all his soul, with all his might.

In contrast to the Stoic sage who is a *homo apathetikos,* the prophet may be characterized as a *homo sympathetikos.* For the phenomenology of religion the prophet represents a type *sui generis.* The *pathos* of God is upon him. It moves him. It breaks out in him like a storm in the soul, overwhelming his inner life, his thoughts, feelings, wishes, and hopes. It takes possession of his heart and mind, giving him the courage to act against the world.

The words of the prophet are often like thunders; they sound as if he were in a state of hysteria. But what appears to us as wild emotionalism must have seemed like restraint to him who has to convey the emotion of the Almighty in the feeble language of man. His sympathy is an overflow of powerful emotion which comes in response to what he sensed in divinity.

Like a scream in the night is the prophet's word. The world is at ease and asleep, while the prophet is hit by a blast from heaven. No one seems to hear the distress in the world; no one seems to care when the poor is suppressed. But God is distressed, and the prophet has pity for God who cares for the distressed.

A single crime—to us it is slight, but to the prophet—a disaster. The prophet's scream which sounds hysterical to us is like a subdued sigh to him. Exaggeration to us is understatement to him.

The unique feature of religious sympathy is not self-conquest but self-dedication; not the suppression of emotion but its redirection; not silent subordination, but active co-operation with God; not love which aspires to the Being of God in Himself, but harmony of the soul with the concern of God. To be a prophet means to identify one's concern with the concern of God.

Sympathy is an act in which a person is open to the presence of another person. It is a feeling which feels the feeling to which it reacts; the opposite of emotional solitariness. In prophetic sympathy, man is open to the presence and emotion of the transcendent Subject. He carries within himself the awareness of what is happening to God.

Sympathy was not an end in itself. Nothing is further from the prophetic mind than to inculcate or to live out a life of feeling, a religion of sentimentality. Not mere feeling but action will mitigate the world's misery, society's injustice, or the people's alienation from God. Only action will relieve the tension between God and man. Both *pathos* and *sympathy* are, from the perspective of the total situation, demands rather than fulfillments. Prophetic sympathy is no delight; unlike ecstasy it is not a goal but a sense of challenge and a commitment.

Part III

Man and His Needs

20.   THE PROBLEM OF NEEDS

The Bible is an answer to the question, What does God require of man? But to modern man, this question is suppressed by another one, namely, What does man demand of God? Modern man continues to ponder: What will I get out of life? What escapes his attention is the fundamental, yet forgotten question: What will life get out of me?

The alarming fact is that man is becoming "a fighter for needs" rather than "a fighter for ends," as defined by William James.

Absorbed in the struggle for the emancipation of the individual, we have concentrated our attention upon the idea of human rights and over-looked the importance of human obligations. More and more the sense of commitment, which is so essential a component of human existence, was lost in the melting pot of conceit and sophistication. Oblivious to the fact of his receiving infinitely more than he is able to return, man began to consider his self as the only end. Caring only for his needs rather than for his being needed, he is hardly able to realize that rights are anything more than legalized interests.

Needs are looked upon today as if they were holy, as if they contained the totality of existence. Needs are our gods, and we toil and spare no effort to gratify them. Suppression of a desire is considered a sacrilege that must inevitably avenge itself in the form of some mental disorder. We worship not one but a whole pantheon of needs and have come to look upon moral and spiritual norms as nothing but personal desires in disguise.

Specifically, need denotes the absence or shortage of something indispensable to the well-being of a person, evoking the urgent desire for satisfaction. The term "need" is generally used in two ways: one denoting the actual lack, an objective condition, and the other denoting the awareness of such a lack. It is in the second sense, in which need is synonymous with interest, namely "an unsatisfied capacity corresponding to an unrealized condition," that the term is used here.

Every human being is a cluster of needs, yet these needs are not the same in all men nor unalterable in any one man. There is a fixed minimum of needs for all men, but no fixed maximum for any man. Unlike animals, man is the playground for the unpredictable emergence and multiplication of needs and interests, some of which are indigenous to his

129

nature, while others are induced by advertisement, fashion, envy, or come about as miscarriages of authentic needs. We usually fail to discern between authentic and artificial needs and, misjudging a whim for an aspiration, we are thrown into ugly tensions. Most obsessions are the perpetuation of such misjudgments. In fact, more people die in the epidemics of needs than in the epidemics of disease. To stem the expansion of man's needs, which in turn is brought about by technological and social advancement, would mean to halt the stream on which civilization is riding. Yet the stream unchecked may sweep away civilization itself, since the pressure of needs turned into aggressive interests is the constant cause of wars and increases in direct proportion to technological progress.

We cannot make our judgments, decisions, and directions for action dependent upon our needs. The fact is that man who has found out so much about so many things knows neither his own heart nor his own voice. Many of the interests and needs we cherish are imposed on us by conventions of society; they are not indigenous to our essence. While some of them are necessities, others, as I said before, are fictitious, and adopted as a result of convention, advertisement, or sheer envy.

The contemporary man believes he has found the philosopher's stone in the concept of needs. But who knows his true needs? How are we going to discern authentic from fictitious needs, necessities from make-believes?

Having absorbed an enormous amount of needs and having been taught to cherish the high values, such as justice, liberty, faith, as private or national interests, we are beginning to wonder whether needs and interests should be relied upon. While it is true that there are interests which all men have in common, most of our private and national interests, as asserted in daily living, divide and antagonize rather than unite us.

Interest is a subjective, dividing principle. It is the excitement of feeling, accompanying special attention paid to some object. But do we pay sufficient attention to the demands for universal justice? In fact, the interest in universal welfare is usually blocked by the interest in personal welfare, particularly when it is to be achieved at the price of renouncing one's vested interests. It is just because the power of interests is tyrannizing our lives, determining our views and actions, that we lose sight of the values that count most.

Short is the way from need to greed. Evil conditions make us seethe with evil needs, with mad dreams. Can we afford to pursue all our innate needs, even our will for power?

In the tragic confusion of interests, in which every one of us is caught, no distinction seems to be as indispensable as the distinction between right and wrong interests. Yet the concepts of right and wrong, to be standards in our dealing with interests, cannot themselves be interests.

20. The Problem of Needs

Determined as they are by temperament, bias, background, and environment of every individual and group, needs are our problems rather than our norms. They are in need of, rather than the origins of, standards.

He who sets out to employ the realities of life as means for satisfying his own desires will soon forfeit his freedom and be degraded to a mere tool. Acquiring things, he becomes enslaved to them; in subduing others, he loses his own soul. It is as if unchecked covetousness were double-faced; a sneer and subtle vengeance behind a captivating smile. We can ill afford to set up needs, an unknown, variable, vacillating, and eventually degrading factor, as a universal standard, as a supreme, abiding rule or pattern for living.

We feel jailed in the confinement of personal needs. The more we indulge in satisfactions, the deeper is our feeling of oppressiveness. To be an iconoclast of idolized needs, to defy our own immoral interests, though they seem to be vital and have long been cherished, we must be able to say *no* to ourselves in the name of a higher *yes*. Yet our minds are late, slow and erratic. What can give us the power to curb the deference to wrong needs, to detect spiritual fallacies, to ward off false ideals, and to wrestle with inattentiveness to the unseemly and holy?

This, indeed, is the purpose of our religious traditions: to keep alive the higher "yes" as well as the power of man to say "Here I am"; to teach our minds to understand the true demand and to teach our conscience to be present. Too often, we misunderstand the demand; too often the call goes forth, and history records our conscience as absent.

Religion has adjusted itself to the modern temper by proclaiming that it too is the satisfaction of a need. This conception, which is surely diametrically opposed to the prophetic attitude, has richly contributed to the misunderstanding and sterilization of religious thinking. To define religion primarily as a quest for personal satisfaction, as the satisfaction of a human need, is to make of it a refined sort of magic. Did the thunderous voice at Sinai proclaim the ten Words in order to satisfy a need? The people felt a need for a graven image, but that need was condemned. The people were homesick for the fleshpots of Egypt. They asked: Give us flesh. And the Lord gave them spirit, not only flesh.

To understand the problem of needs, we must face the problem of man, the subject of needs. Man is animated by more needs than any other being. They seem to lie beneath his will and are independent of his volition. They are the source rather than the product of desire. Consequently, we shall only be able to judge needs if we succeed in understanding the meaning of existence.

21. THE ILLUSION OF HUMAN SELF-SUFFICIENCY

Animals are content when their needs are satisfied; man insists not only on being satisfied but also on being able to satisfy, on *being a need*, not only on *having needs*. Personal needs come and go, but one anxiety remains: *Am I needed?* There is no man who has not been moved by that anxiety.

It is a most significant fact that man is not sufficient to himself, that life is not meaningful to him unless it is serving an end beyond itself, unless it is of value to someone else. The self may have the highest rate of exchange, yet men do not live by currency alone, but by the good attainable in expending it. To hoard the self is to grow a colossal sense for the futility of living.

Man is not an all-inclusive end to himself. The second maxim of Kant, never to use human beings merely as means but to regard them also as ends, only suggests how a person ought to be treated by other people, not how he ought to treat himself. For if a person thinks that he is an end to himself, then he will use others as means. Moreover, if the idea of man being an end is to be taken as a true estimate of his worth, he cannot be expected to sacrifice his life or his interests for the good of someone else or even of a group. He must treat himself the way he expects others to treat him. Why should even a group or a whole people be worth the sacrifice of one's life? To a person who regards himself as an absolute end a thousand lives will not be worth more than his own life.

Sophisticated thinking may enable man to feign his being sufficient to himself. Yet the way to insanity is paved with such illusions. The feeling of futility that comes with the sense of being useless, of not being needed in the world, is the most common cause of psychoneurosis. The only way to avoid despair is *to be a need* rather than an end. *Happiness,* in fact, may be defined as the *certainty of being needed.* But *who* is in need of man?

The first answer that comes to mind is a social one—man's purpose is to serve society or mankind. The ultimate worth of a person would then be determined by his usefulness to others, by the efficiency of his social work. Yet, in spite of his instrumentalist attitude, man expects others to take him not for what he may mean to them but as a being valuable in himself.

132

21. The Illusion of Human Self-Sufficiency

Even he who does not regard himself as an absolute end, rebels against being treated as a means to an end, as subservient to other men. The rich, the men of the world, want to be loved for their own sake, for their essence, whatever it may mean, not for their achievements or possessions. Nor do the old and sick expect help because of what they may give us in return. Who needs the old, the incurably sick, the maintenance of whom is a drain on the treasury of the state? It is, moreover, obvious that such service does not claim all of one's life and can therefore not be the ultimate answer to his quest of meaning for life as a whole. Man has more to give than what other men are able or willing to accept.

There are alleys in the soul where man walks alone, ways that do not lead to society, a world of privacy that shrinks from the public eye. Life comprises not only arable, productive land, but also mountains of dreams, an underground of sorrow, towers of yearning, which can hardly be utilized to the last for the good of society, unless man be converted into a machine in which every screw must serve a function or be removed. It is a profiteering state which, trying to exploit the individual, asks all of man for itself.

And if society as embodied in the state should prove to be corrupt and my effort to cure its evil unavailing, would my life as an individual have been totally void of meaning? If society should decide to reject my services and even place me in solitary confinement, so that I will surely die without being able to bequeath any influence to the world I love, will I then feel compelled to end my life?

Human existence cannot derive its ultimate meaning from society, because society itself is in need of meaning. It is as legitimate to ask: Is mankind needed?—as it is to ask: Am I needed?

Humanity begins in the individual man, just as history takes its rise from a singular event. It is always one man at a time whom we keep in mind when we pledge: "with malice toward none, with charity for all," or when trying to fulfill: "Love thy neighbor as thyself." The term "mankind," which in biology denotes the human species, has an entirely different meaning in the realm of ethics and religion. Here mankind is not conceived as a species, as an abstract concept, stripped from its concrete reality, but as an abundance of specific individuals; as a community of persons rather than as a herd of a multitude of nondescripts.

While it is true that the good of all counts more than the good of one, it is the concrete individual who lends meaning to the human race. We do not think that a human being is valuable because he is a member of the race; it is rather the opposite: the human race is valuable because it is composed of human beings.

There is not a soul on this earth which, however vaguely or rarely, has

133

not realized that life is dismal if not mirrored in something which is lasting. We are all in search of a conviction that there is something which is worth the toil of living. There is not a soul which has not felt a craving to know of something that outlasts life, strife and agony.

Man's quest for a meaning of existence is essentially a quest for the lasting, a quest for abidingness. In a sense, human life is often a race against time, going through efforts to perpetuate experiences, attaching itself to values or establishing relations that do not perish at once. His quest is not a product of desire but an essential element of his nature, characteristic not only of his mind but also of his very existence.

Man is continuous both with the rest of organic nature and with the infinite outpouring of the spirit of God. A minority in the realm of being, he stands somewhere between God and the beasts. Unable to live alone, he must commune with either of the two.

Both Adam and the beasts were blessed by the Lord, but man was also charged with conquering the earth and dominating the beast. Man is always faced with the choice of listening either to God or to the snake. It is always easier to envy the beast, to worship a totem and be dominated by it, than to hearken to the Voice.

Our existence seesaws between animality and divinity, between that which is more and that which is less than humanity: below is evanescence, futility, and above is the open door of the divine exchequer where we lay up the sterling coin of piety and spirit, the immortal remains of our dying lives. We are constantly in the mills of death, but we are also the contemporaries of God.

Man is "a little lower than the angels" (Psalms 8:5) and a little higher than the beasts. Like a pendulum he swings to and fro under the combined action of gravity and momentum, of the gravitation of selfishness and the momentum of the divine, of a vision beheld by God in the darkness of flesh and blood. We fail to understand the meaning of our existence when we disregard our commitments to that vision.

If man is not more than human, then he is less than human. Man is but a short, critical stage between the animal and the spiritual. His state is one of constant wavering, of soaring or descending. Undeviating humanity is nonexistent. The emancipated man is yet to emerge.

Man is more than what he is to himself. In his reason he may be limited, in his will he may be wicked, yet he stands in a relation to God which he may betray but not sever and which constitutes the essential meaning of his life. He is the knot in which heaven and earth are interlaced.

When carried away by the joy of acting as we please, adopting any desire, accepting any opportunity for action if the body welcomes it, we feel perfectly satisfied to walk on all fours. Yet there are moments in every one's life when he begins to wonder whether the pleasures of the body or the interests of the self should serve as the perspective from which all decisions should be made.

In spite of the delights that are within our reach, we refuse to barter our souls for selfish rewards and to live without a conscience on the proceeds. Even those who have forfeited the ability for compassion have not forfeited the ability to be horrified at their inability to feel compassion. Time and again every one of us tries to sit in judgment over his life. Even those who have gambled away the vision of virtue are not deprived of the horror of crime. There is only one way to fumigate the obnoxious air of our world—to live beyond our own needs and interests.

The possibility of eliminating self-regard ultimately depends on the nature of the self; it is a metaphysical rather than a psychological issue. If the self exists for its own sake, such independence would be neither possible nor desirable. It is only in assuming that the self is not the hub but a spoke, neither its own beginning nor its own end, that such possibility could be affirmed.

All our experiences are needs, dissolving when the needs are fulfilled. But the truth is, our existence, too, is a need. We are such stuff as needs are made of, and our little life is rounded by a will. *Lasting* in our life is neither passion nor delight, neither joy nor pain, but the answer to a need. The lasting in us is not our will to live. There is a need for our lives, and in living we satisfy it. Lasting is not our desire, but our answer to that need, an agreement not an impulse. Our needs are temporal, while our being needed is lasting.

We have started our inquiry with the question of the individual man— what is the meaning of the individual man?—and established his uniqueness in his being pregnant with immense potentialities, of which he becomes aware in his experience of needs. We have also pointed out that he finds no happiness in utilizing his potentialities for the satisfaction of his own needs, that his destiny is to be a need.

But who is in need of man? Nature? Do the mountains stand in need of our poems? Would the stars fade away if astronomers ceased to exist? The earth can get along without the aid of the human species. Nature is replete with opportunity to satisfy all our needs except one—the need of being needed.

Unlike all other needs, the need of being needed is a striving to give rather than to obtain satisfaction. It is a desire to satisfy a transcendent desire, a craving to satisfy a craving.

All needs are one-sided. When hungry we are in need of food, yet food is *not* in need of being consumed. Things of beauty attract our minds; we feel the need of perceiving them, yet they are not in need of being perceived by us. It is in such one-sidedness, that most of living is imprisoned. Examine an average mind, and you will find that it is dominated by an effort to cut reality to the measure of the ego, as if the world existed for the sake of pleasing one's ego. Every one of us entertains more relations with things than with people, and even in dealings with people we behave toward them as if they were things, tools, means to be used for our own selfish ends. How rarely do we face a person as a person. We are all dominated by the desire to appropriate and to own. Only a free person knows that the true meaning of existence is experienced in giving, in endowing, in meeting a person face to face, in fulfilling other people's needs.

When realizing the surplus of what we see over what we feel, the mind is evasive, even the heart is incomplete. Why are we discontent with mere living for the sake of living? Who has made us thirsty for what is more than existence?

Religion begins with the certainty that something is asked of us, that there are ends which are in need of us. Unlike all other values, moral and religious ends evoke in us a sense of obligation. They present themselves as tasks rather than as objects of perception. Thus, religious living consists in serving ends which are in need of us.

Man is not an innocent bystander in the cosmic drama. There is in us more kinship with the divine than we are able to believe. The souls of men are candles of the Lord, lit on the cosmic way, rather than fireworks produced by the combustion of nature's explosive compositions, and every soul is indispensable to Him. Man is needed, he is *a need of God*.

22. NEEDS AND ENDS

Ends are requirements which are often independent of needs. Just as our sense perception does not create but only registers the perceived things, so is a feeling of need merely an inner response to an objective end. Feelings, perceptions are ours; ends, things are the world's; and the world is the Lord's.

Morality and religion do not begin as feelings within man but as responses to goals and situations outside of man. It is always in regard to an objective situation that we judge and assert it is right or wrong; and it is in answer to what is beyond the ineffable that man says yes to God.

136

22. Needs and Ends

A free man does not look upon himself as if he were a repository of fixed needs, but regards his life as an orientation toward ends. To have a goal before one's eyes, to pursue it and to keep on extending it, seems to be the way of civilized living. It is typical of the debauchee to adjust his ends to his selfish needs. He is always ready to conform to his needs. Indeed, anybody can be taught to have needs and to indulge in costly food, dress or anything which satisfies the appetites or tastes. Yet, free men are not blind in obeying needs but, weighing and comparing their relative merits, they will seek to satisfy those which contribute to the enhancement and enrichment of higher values. In other words, they would approve only of those needs that serve the attainment of good ends. They do not say: "Needs justify the ends," but on the contrary: "Ends justify the needs." To be able to forego the gratification of one need for the sake of another, or for the sake of moral, esthetic or religious principles, they must be, to some degree, independent of needs.

Psychological fatalism which maintains that there is only one way, an animal way, is a paralyzing fallacy to which the spirit of man will never surrender. The mind is not a repository of fixed ideas but rather an orientation toward or a perspective from which the world is apprehended.

Just as in the Middle Ages sciences were regarded as *ancillae theologiae,* it is claimed today that the problems of metaphysics, religion, ethics, and the arts are essentially problems of psychology. There is a tendency which we should like to call *pan-psychology.* It proclaims psychology as capable of explaining the origin and development of the laws, principles and values of logic, religion, and ethics by reducing both form and content of thought and conduct to subjective psychical processes, to impulses and functions of psychical development.

The error of this view lies in its confounding values, laws, or principles with the psychical setting in which they come to our attention. It is fallacious to identify the content of knowledge with the emotional reactions which accompany its acquisition, or concepts with mental functions. Our affirming or denying a conclusion, our saying yes or no to an idea, is an act in which we claim to assert the truth on the basis of either logical cogency or intuitive certainty. It is precisely the immunity to emotion that enables us to entertain a claim to knowing the truth.

Such a claim is entertained by the pan-psychologist himself. Laws must be applied by him to the vague, manifold and chaotic psychological processes if they are to be classified, interpreted and made intelligible. But such laws, to be universally valid, must be capable of being logically and epistemologically defended; they must be categories, not psychical processes themselves. Otherwise they would be merely additional subject

137

matter for psychological analysis without any cognitive value. Are we not, then, compelled to admit that there are cognitive acts the validity of which is independent of impulses?

From the point of view of pan-psychology we would have to deny it. Yet we have no more right to say that logical categories are the offspring of impulses than to say that impulses are the offspring of categories. Categories are facts of human consciousness which are just as undeniably given as impulses. We seem, in fact, to be more dependent on categories in trying to understand impulses than we are in need of impulses in developing our categories.

Good and evil are not psychological concepts, although the ways in which they are understood are affected by the psychological conditions of the human personality, just as the particular forms in which they are realized are often determined by historical, political, and social conditions. However, good and evil as such do not denote functions of the soul or society but goals and ends and are, in their essence, independent of the psychical chain of causation.

In his consciousness of good and evil or in complying with religious precepts even at the price of frustrating personal interests, man does not regard his attitude as a mere expression of a feeling: he is sure of reflecting objective *requiredness*, of striving for a goal which is valid regardless of his own liking. Should we, against the empirical fact of such consciousness, condemn it as wishful thinking or rather say that our theories about the relativity of all moral goals result from a time-conditioned decline of attentiveness to ultimate goals?

Man's consciousness of requiredness is, of course, no proof that the particular forms in which he tries to attain his moral or religious ends are absolutely valid. However, the fact of such consciousness may serve as an index of his being committed to striving for valid ends. Man's conception of these ends is subject to change; his being committed endures forever.

Moral actions may, of course, be explained on selfish grounds. As a social being the welfare of an individual depends upon the welfare of all other members of the group. Any service, therefore, that extends beyond the confines of my direct needs would be an investment in my own personal welfare. Altruism would be egoism in disguise, and moral deeds not different from the generous service any intelligent merchant extends to his customers. Sacrificing my own interests for the sake of another man would be merely another example of the kind of self-denial I exercise in regard to my own interests, denying to myself the satisfaction of some needs in order to attain the satisfaction of others. To adjust my conduct to the interests of other people as far as it would ultimately suit me would be all I am morally bound to do.

Yet what constitutes the consciousness of good and evil, of right and wrong is the requiredness to act not for my own sake, to do the right even if no advantage would accrue to myself. The expediency of a good deed may serve as an incentive to carry out a moral obligation, yet it is certainly not identical with it.

Man's life is not only driven by a centripetal force revolving around the ego, but is also impelled by centrifugal forces outward from the ego-center. His acts are not only self-regarding but also self-surpassing.

Even in the pursuit of private ends, man is often compelled to establish or to advance universal values. It is as if man stood under a command to employ his abilities for unselfish stakes, a command which he is obliged to listen to and suffers for disregarding. That command is not the product but the origin of civilization. Civilized living is the result of that urge, of that drive to proceed in our efforts beyond immediate needs, beyond individual, tribal, or national goals.

The urge to build a family, to serve society or dedicate oneself to art and science, may often originate in the desire to satisfy one's own appetite or ambition. Yet, seen from the watchtower of history, the selfish usefulness of required deeds, the possibility of regarding them as instrumental to the attainment of one's own selfish goals, is God's secret weapon in His struggle with man's callousness.

Life is tridimensional, every act can be evaluated by two co-ordinate axes, the abscissa is man, the ordinate is God. Whatever man does to man, he also does to God. To those who are attentive to Him who is beyond the ineffable, God's relation to the world is an actuality, an absolute implication of being, the ultimate in reality, obtaining even if at this moment it is not perceived or acknowledged by anybody; those who reject or betray it do not diminish its validity.

The right or the morally good is an end that surpasses our experience of needs. It is beyond the power of an emotion to sense adequately the supreme grandeur of the moral end; our efforts to express it are conditioned by the limitations of our nature. And still the vision of that absolute grandeur is not always lost. In studying the history of man's attempts to implement the moral end, we must not confound his vision with his interpretation. Man's understanding of *what* is right and wrong has often varied throughout the ages; yet the consciousness *that* there is a distinction between right and wrong is permanent and universal. In formulating laws, he often fumbles and fails to find adequate ways of implementing justice or to preserve all the time a clear grasp of its meaning. Yet even when forfeiting his vision, he does not quite lose an awareness of what was once in his sight. He knows that justice is a standard to which his laws must conform in order to deserve the name of justice. We know of no tribe, of no code that would insist that it is good to hate or that it is right to injure each other. Justice is something which all men are able to esteem.

In order to retain that vision alive, we must try to preserve and augment the sense of the ineffable, to remember constantly the superiority of our task to our will and to keep aflame our awareness of living in the great fellowship of all beings, in which we are all equal before the ultimate. Conformity to the ego is no longer our exclusive concern, for we become concerned with another problem—how to fulfill what is asked of us.

Man is neither the lord of the universe nor even the master of his own destiny. Our life is not our own property but a possession of God. And it is this divine ownership that makes life a sacred thing.

23. GOD IS IN NEED OF MAN

There is only one way to define Jewish religion. It is the *awareness of God's interest in man,* the awareness of a *covenant,* of a responsibility that lies on Him as well as on us. Our task is to concur with His interest, to carry out His vision of our task. *God is in need of man for the attainment of His ends, and religion, as Jewish tradition understands it, is a way of serving these ends, of which we are in need, even though we may not be aware of them, ends which we must learn to feel the need of.*

Life is a *partnership* of God and man; God is not detached from or indifferent to our joys and griefs. Authentic vital needs of man's body and soul are a divine concern. This is why human life is holy. God is a partner and a partisan in man's struggle for justice, peace and holiness, and it is because of His being in need of man that He entered a *covenant* with him for all time, a mutual bond embracing God and man, a relationship to which God, not only man, is committed.

This day you have avowed the Lord to be your God, promising to walk in His ways, to obey His rules and commandments, and to hearken to His voice; And this day the Lord has avowed you to be His very own people, as He has promised you, and to obey His commandments. (Deuteronomy 26:17–18)

23. God Is in Need of Man

Some people think that religion comes about as a perception of an answer to a prayer, while in truth it comes about in our knowing that God shares our prayer. The essence of Judaism is the awareness of the *reciprocity* of God and man, of man's *togetherness* with Him who abides in eternal otherness. For the task of living is His and ours, and so is the responsibility. We have rights, not only obligations; our ultimate commitment is our ultimate privilege.

His need is a self-imposed concern. God is now in need of man, because He freely made him a partner in His enterprise, "a partner in the work of creation." "From the first day of creation the Holy One, blessed be He, longed to enter into *partnership* with the terrestrial world" to dwell *with* His creatures within the terrestrial world. (*Numbers Rabbah,* ch. 13, 6; compare *Genesis Rabbah* ch. 3,9). Expounding the verse in Genesis 17:1, the Midrash remarked: "In the view of Rabbi Johanan we need His honor; in the view of Rabbi Simeon ben Lakish He needs our honor" (*Genesis Rabbah,* ch. 30; unlike Theodor, p. 277).

"When Israel performs the will of the Omnipresent, they add strength to the heavenly power; as it is said: 'To God we render strength' (Psalms 60:14). When, however, Israel does not perform the will of the Omnipresent, they weaken—if it is possible to say so—the great power of Him who is above; as it is written, 'Thou didst weaken the Rock that begot Thee.'" (Pesikta, ed. Buber, XXVI, 166b; compare the two versions.)

Man's relationship to God is not one of passive reliance upon His Omnipotence but one of active assistance. "The impious rely on their gods . . . the righteous are the support of God." (*Genesis Rabbah* ch. 69,3.)

The Patriarchs are therefore called "the chariot of the Lord." (*Genesis Rabbah,* ch. 47,6; 82,6.)

> He glories in me, He delights in me;
> My crown of beauty He shall be.
> His glory rests on me, and mine on Him;
> He is near to me, when I call on Him.
> *(The Hymn of Glory)*

The extreme boldness of this paradox was expressed in a Tannaitic interpretation of Isaiah 43:12: "Ye are my witnesses, saith the Lord, and I am God"—when you are my witnesses I am God, and when you are not my witnesses I am not God.[1]

For thousands of years the deity and darkness were thought to be the same: a being, self-attached and full of blind desires; a being whom man revered but did not trust; that would reveal itself to the mad but not to the meek. For thousands of years it was accepted as a fact that the ultimate deity was hostile to man and could only be appeased by offerings of blood, until the prophets came who could not bear any more to see the defeat of God at the hands of fear, and proclaimed that darkness was His abode, not His essence; that as bright as midday's sun was His voice giving an answer to the question: What does God desire?

Is it music?

> Take away from me the noise of your songs,
> And to the melody of your lyres I will not listen.
>
> (Amos 5:23)

Is it prayer?

> When you spread out your hands,
> I will hide my eyes from you;
> Though you make many a prayer,
> I will not listen.
> Your hands are full of bloodshed—
>
> (Isaiah 1:15)

Is it sacrifice?

Does the Lord delight in burnt-offerings and sacrifices as much as in obedience to the voice of the Lord?

> (I Samuel 15:22)

And now, O Israel, what does the Lord your God require of you but to stand in awe of the Lord your God, walk in His ways, love Him, serve the Lord your God with all your mind and heart, and keep the commands of the Lord and His statutes that I am commanding you today, for your good?

> (Deuteronomy 10:12)

To satisfy nonreligious needs we seek to exploit the forces of nature to our advantage. But do we seek to exploit anything in order to satisfy our religious needs? What, then, is the way of satisfying the religious need? What are the ends man is striving to attain in religion?

There is, indeed, in every human being an unquenchable need for the lasting, an urge to worship and to revere. Divergence begins in the object and manner of worship. Yet that unquenchable need is often miscarried into self-aggrandizement or a desire to find a guarantee for personal immortality. Judaism shows it to be a need *to be needed by God*. It teaches us that every man is in need of God because God is in need of man. Our need of Him is but an echo of His need of us.

There is, of course, the constant danger of believing what we wish rather than wishing what we believe, of cherishing our need as God rather than adopting God as our need. This is why we must always appraise our needs in the light of divine ends.

23. God Is in Need of Man

It is natural and common to care for personal and national goals. But is it as natural and common to care for other people's needs or to be concerned with universal ends? Conventional needs like pleasure are easily assimilated by social osmosis. Spiritual needs have to be implanted, cherished and cultivated by the vision of their ends. We do not have to rise above ourselves in order to dream of being strong, brave, rich, of being rulers of an empire or "a kingdom of soldiers." But we have to be inspired in order to dream God's dream: "You shall be holy, for I your God am holy." . . . "You shall be unto Me a kingdom of priests, a holy people."

It is God who teaches us our ultimate ends. Abraham may not have felt the need for abandoning home and country, nor were the people of Israel eager to give up the flesh-pots of Egypt for the prospect of going into the wilderness.

Analyzing man's potentialities, it becomes evident that his uniqueness and essential meaning lie in his ability to satisfy ends that go beyond his ego, while his natural concern is: What may others do for my ego? Religion teaches him to ponder about what he may do for others and to realize that no man's ego is worthy of being the ultimate end.

There is an ancient hymn with which we conclude our daily prayers and which gives expression to our conception of ultimate ends. It is a hymn which may be regarded as the national anthem of the Jewish people.

We hope therefore, Lord our God, soon to behold thy majestic glory, when the abominations shall be removed from the earth, and the false gods exterminated; when the world shall be perfected under the reign of the Almighty, and all mankind will call upon thy name, and all the wicked of the earth will be turned to thee. May all the inhabitants of the world realize and know that to thee every knee must bend, every tongue must vow allegiance. May they bend the knee and prostrate themselves before thee, Lord our God, and give honor to thy glorious name; may they all accept the yoke of thy kingdom, and do thou reign over them speedily forever and ever. For the kingdom is thine, and to all eternity thou wilt reign in glory, as it is written in thy Torah: "The Lord shall be King forever and ever." And it is said: "The Lord shall be King over all the earth; on that day the Lord shall be One, and his name One."

Jewish religious education consists in converting ends into personal needs rather than in converting needs into ends, so that, for example, the end to have regard for other people's lives becomes my concern. Yet, if those ends are not assimilated as needs but remain mere duties, uncongenial to the heart, incumbent but not enjoyed, then there is a state of tension between the self and the task. The perfectly moral act bears a seed within its flower: the sense of objective requiredness within the subjective concern. Thus, justice is good not because we feel the need of it; rather we ought to feel the need of justice because it is good.

Religions may be classified as those of self-satisfaction, of self-annihilation or of fellowship. In the first worship is a quest for satisfaction of personal needs like salvation or desire for immortality. In the second all personal needs are discarded, and man seeks to dedicate his life to God at the price of annihilating all desire, believing that human sacrifice or at least complete self-denial is the only true form of worship. The third form of religion, while shunning the idea of considering God a means for attaining personal ends, insists that there is a partnership of God and man, that human needs are God's concern and that divine ends ought to become human needs. It rejects the idea that the good should be done in self-detachment, that the satisfaction felt in doing the good would taint the purity of the act. Judaism demands the full participation of the person in the service of the Lord; the heart rather than boycotting the acts of the will ought to respond in joy and undivided delight.

Pleasure, though not the spring, may and ought to be the by-product of moral or religious action. The good or the holy is not necessarily that which I do not desire, and the feeling of pleasure or gratification does not divest a good deed of its quality of goodness. The heart and the mind are rivals but not irreconcilable enemies, and their reconciliation is a major end in striving for integrity. It is true that the idea of justice and the will to justice are not twin-born. But a moral person is a partisan who loves the love of good. It is not true that love and obedience cannot live together, that the good never springs from the heart. To be free of selfish interests does not mean to be neutral, indifferent, or to be devoid of interests, but, on the contrary, to be a partisan of the self-surpassing. God does not dwell beyond the sky. He dwells, we believe, in every heart that is willing to let Him in.

The sense of moral obligation remains impotent unless it is stronger than all other obligations, stronger than the stubborn power of selfish interests. To compete with selfish inclinations the moral obligation must be allied with the highest passion of the spirit.

To be stronger than evil, the moral imperative must be more powerful than the passion for evil. An abstract norm, an ethereal idea, is no match for the gravitation of the ego. Passion can only be subdued by stronger passion.

From the fact that an end is adopted and cherished as a personal interest, it does not follow that the end was of psychological origin, just as our utilization of the quantum theory does not prove that it came about as the result of utilitarian motives. Thus, the fact of God becoming a human need does not vitiate the objectivity and validity of the idea of God.

The solution to the problem of needs lies not in fostering a need to end all needs but in fostering a need to calm all other needs. There is a breath of God in every man, a force lying deeper than the stratum of will, and which may be stirred to become an aspiration strong enough to give direction and even to run counter to all winds.

24. NEEDS AS SPIRITUAL OPPORTUNITIES

Throughout the ages two extreme views have most frequently been voiced—one deifying desire, the other vilifying it. There were those who, overwhelmed by the dark power of passion, believed that they sensed in its raving a manifestation of the gods and celebrated its gratification as a sacred ritual. Dionysian orgies, fertility rites, sacred prostitution are extreme examples of a view that subconsciously has never died out.

The exponents of the other extreme, frightened by the destructive power of unbridled passion, have taught man to see ugliness in desire, Satan in the rapture of the flesh. Their advice was to repress the appetites, and their ideal, self-renunciation and asceticism. Some Greeks said: "Passion is a god, Eros"; Buddhists say: "Desire is evil."

To the Jewish mind, being neither enticed nor horrified by the powers of passion, desires are neither benign nor pernicious but, like fire, they do not agree with straw. They should be neither quenched nor supplied with fuel. Rather than worship fire and be consumed by it, we should let a light come out of the flames. *Needs are spiritual opportunities.*

Allegiance to Judaism does not imply defiance of legitimate needs, a tyranny of the spirit. Prosperity is a worthy goal of aspiration and a promised reward for good living. Although there is no celebration of our animal nature, recognition of its right and role is never missing. There is an earnest care for its welfare, needs, and limitations.

Judaism does not despise the carnal. It does not urge us to desert the flesh but to control and to counsel it; to please the natural needs of the flesh so that the spirit should not be molested by unnatural frustrations. We are not commanded to be pyromaniacs of the soul. On the contrary, a need that serves the enhancement of life, without causing injury to anyone else, is the work of the Creator, and the wanton or ignorant destruc-

145

tion or defacement of His creation is vandalism. "It is indeed God's gift to man, that he should eat and drink and be happy as he toils" (Ecclesiastes 3:13).

Good living obviously implies control and the relative conquest of passions, but not the renunciation of all satisfaction. Decisive is not the act of conquest but how the victory is utilized. Our ideal is not ruthless conquest but careful alteration of needs. Passion is a many-headed monster, and the goal is achieved through painstaking metamorphosis rather than by amputation or mutilation.

Judaism is not committed to a doctrine of original sin and knows nothing of the inherent depravity of human nature. The word "flesh" did not assume in its vocabulary the odor of sinfulness; carnal needs were not thought of as being rooted in evil. Nowhere in the Bible is found any indication of the idea that the soul is imprisoned in a corrupt body, that to seek satisfaction in this world means to lose one's soul or to forfeit the covenant with God, that the allegiance to God demands renunciation of worldly goods.

Our flesh is not evil but material for applying the spirit. The carnal is something to be surpassed rather than annihilated. Heaven and earth are equally His creation. Nothing in creation may be discarded or abused. The enemy is not in the flesh; it is in the heart, in the ego.

To the Bible good is equated with life. Being is intrinsically good. "God saw it was good." The Torah is conceived as a "Tree of Life," advancing the equation of life and goodness; "In the way of righteousness is life" (Proverbs 12:28).

There is no conflict between God and man, no hostility between spirit and body, no wedge between the holy and the secular. Man does not exist apart from God. The human is the borderline of the divine.

Life passes on in proximity to the sacred, and it is this proximity that endows existence with ultimate significance. In our relation to the immediate we touch upon the most distant. Even the satisfaction of physical needs can be a sacred act. Perhaps the essential message of Judaism is that in doing the finite we may perceive the infinite. It is incumbent on us to obtain the perception of the impossible in the possible, the perception of life eternal in everyday deeds.

God is not hiding in a temple. The Torah came to tell inattentive man: "You are not alone, you live constantly in holy neighborhood; remember: 'Love thy neighbor—God—as thyself.'" We are not asked to abandon life and to say farewell to this world, but to keep the spark within aflame, and to suffer His light to reflect in our face. Let our greed not rise like a barrier to this neighborhood. God is waiting on every road that leads from intention to action, from desire to satisfaction.

146

24. Needs as Spiritual Opportunities

Man is endowed with the ability of being superior to his own self. He does not have to feel helpless in the face of the "evil inclination." He is capable of conquering evil; "God made man upright." If you ask: "Why did He create the 'evil inclination'?" . . . Says the Lord: "You turn it evil."

One can serve God with the body, with his passions even with "the evil impulse" (*Sifre Deuteronomy,* § 32) ; one must only be able to distinguish between the dross and the gold. This world acquires flavor only when a little of the other world is mingled with it. Without nobility of spirit, the flesh may, indeed, become a focus of darkness.

The road to the sacred leads through the secular. The spiritual rests upon the carnal, like "the spirit that hovers over the face of the water." Jewish living means living according to a system of checks and balances.

Holiness does not signify an air that prevails in the solemn atmosphere of a sanctuary, a quality reserved for supreme acts, an adverb of the spiritual, the distinction of hermits and priests. In his great Code, Maimonides, unlike the editor of the Mishnah, named the section dealing with the laws of the Temple cult The Book of Service, while the section dealing with the laws of chastity and diet he named The Book of Holiness. The strength of holiness lies underground, in the somatic. It is primarily in the way in which we gratify physical needs that the seed of holiness is planted. Originally the holy (*kadosh*) meant that which is set apart, isolated, segregated. In Jewish piety it assumed a new meaning, denoting a quality that is involved, immersed in common and earthly endeavors; carried primarily by individual, private, simple deeds rather than public ceremonies. "Man should always regard himself as if the Holy dwelled within his body, for it is written: 'The Holy One is within you' (Hosea 11:9), therefore one should not mortify his body" (Taanit 11b).

Man is the source and the initiator of holiness in this world. "If a man will sanctify himself a little, God will sanctify him more and more; if he sanctified himself below, he will be sanctified from above" (Yoma 39a).

Judaism teaches us how even the gratification of animal needs can be an act of sanctification. The enjoyment of food may be a way of purification. Something of my soul may be drowned in a glass of water, when its content is gulped down as if nothing in the world mattered except my thirst. But we can come a bit closer to God, when remembering Him still more in excitement and passion.

Sanctification is not an unearthly concept. There is no dualism of the earthly and the sublime. All things are sublime. They were all created by God and their continuous being, their blind adherence to the laws of necessity are, as noted above, a way of obedience to the Creator. The existence of things throughout the universe is a supreme ritual.

147

A man alive, a flower blooming in the spring, is a fulfillment of God's command: "Let there be!" In living we are directly doing the will of God, in a way which is beyond choice or decision. This is why our very existence is contact with His will; why life is holy and a responsibility of God as well as man.

The giver of life did not ask us to despise our brief and poor life but to ennoble it, not to sacrifice but to sanctify it.

To the votaries of the ancient orgiastic cults .wine was an intoxicant used to stimulate frenzy, "that which makes man delirious" (Herodotus 4.79). To ascetics wine is pernicious, a source of evil. To the Jews wine is more than anything else associated with the term and act of sanctification (Kiddush). Over wine and bread we invoke the sanctity of the Sabbath. "Sanctify thyself in things that are permitted to you" (Yevamot 20a), not only in ritual, in ways prescribed by the Torah." "In all thy ways know Him" (Proverbs 3:6).

Sanctification as a reason for walking in His ways is not a concept of religious pragmatism—the theory according to which the tangible effects would serve as the criteria for the validity of commandments. The good is to be done for God's sake, not for the furtherance of man's perfection.

We are taught that man is needed, that our authentic needs are divine requirements, symbols of cosmic needs. God is the subject of all subjects. Life is His and ours. He has not thrown us out into the world and abandoned us. He shares in our toil; He is partner to our anxieties. A man in need is not the exclusive and ultimate subject of need: God is in need with him. Becoming conscious of a need, one has to ask himself: Is God in need with me? To have God as a partner to one's actions is to remember that our problems are not exclusively our own. Jewish existence is living shared with God.

25. FREEDOM

We have said that the grand premise of religion is that man is able to surpass himself. Such ability is the essence of freedom.

Who is to be regarded as free? Free is not always he whose actions are dominated by his own will, since the will is not an ultimate and isolated entity but rather determined in its motivations by forces which are beyond its control. Nor is he free who *is* what he wants to be, since what a person wants to be is obviously determined by factors outside him. Is he who does good for its own sake to be considered free? But how is it possible to do good for its own sake?

Man lives in bondage to his natural environment, to society, and to his own "character"; he is enslaved to needs, interests, and selfish desires. Yet to be free means to transcend nature, society, "character," needs, interests, desires. How then is freedom conceivable?

The reality of freedom, of the ability to think, to will, or to make decisions beyond physiological and psychological causation is only conceivable if we assume that human life embraces both *process and event*.[1] If man is treated as a process, if his future determinations are regarded as calculable, then freedom must be denied. Freedom means that man is capable of expressing himself in events beyond his being involved in the natural processes of living.

To believe in freedom is to believe in events, namely to maintain that man is able to escape the bonds of the processes in which he is involved and to act in a way not necessitated by antecedent factors. Freedom is the state of going out of the self, an act of *spiritual ecstasy*, in the original sense of the term.

Who, then, is free? The creative man who is not carried away by the streams of necessity, who is not enchained by processes, who is not enslaved to circumstances.

We are free at rare moments. Most of the time we are driven by a process; we submit to the power of inherited character qualities or to the force of external circumstances. Freedom is not a continual state of man, "a permanent attitude of the conscious subject." It *is* not, it *happens*. Freedom is an act, an event. We all are endowed with the potentiality of freedom. In actuality, however, we only act freely in rare creative moments.

Man's ability to transcend the self, to rise above all natural ties and bonds, presupposes further that every man lives in a realm governed by law and necessity as well as in a realm of creative possibilities. It presupposes his belonging to a dimension that is higher than nature, society, and the self, and accepts the reality of such a dimension beyond the natural order. Freedom does not mean the right to live as we please. It means the power to live spiritually, to rise to a higher level of existence.

Freedom is not, as is often maintained, a principle of uncertainty, the ability to act without motive. Such a view confounds freedom with chaos, free will with a freak of unmotivated volition, with subrational action.

Nor is freedom the same as the ability to choose between motives. Freedom includes an act of choice, but its root is in the realization that the self is no sovereign, in the discontent with the tyranny of the ego. Freedom comes about in the moment of transcending the self, thus rising above the habit of regarding the self as its own end. *Freedom is an act of self-engagement of the spirit, a spiritual event.*

Integrity is the fruit of freedom. The slave will always ask: What will serve my interests? It is the free man who is able to transcend the causality of interest and deed, of act and the desire for personal reward. It is the free man who asks: Why should I be interested in my interests? What are the values I ought to feel in need of serving?

But inner freedom is *spiritual ecstasy,* the state of being beyond all interests and selfishness. Inner freedom is a miracle of the soul. How could such a miracle be achieved?

The course in which human life moves is, like the orbit of heavenly bodies, an ellipse, not a circle. We are attached to two centers: to the focus of our self and to the focus of God. Driven by two forces, we have both the impulse to acquire, to enjoy, to possess and the urge to respond, to yield, to give.

It is the dedication of the heart and mind to the fact of our being present at a concern of God, the knowledge of being a part of an eternal spiritual movement that conjures power out of a weary conscience, that, striking the bottom out of conceit, tears selfishness to shreds. It is the sense of the ineffable that leads us beyond the horizon of personal interests, helping us to realize the absurdity of regarding the ego as an end.

The basic issue of freedom is how we can be sure that the so-called events are not disguised aspects of a process, or that creative acts are not brought upon by natural developments of which we are not aware. The idea of creative possibilities and the possibility of living spiritually depend upon the idea of creation and man's being more than the product of nature.

The ultimate concept in Greek philosophy is the idea of cosmos, of order; the first teaching in the Bible is the idea of *creation.* Translated into eternal principles, cosmos means fate, while creation means freedom. The essential meaning of creation is not the idea that the universe was created at a particular moment in time. The essential meaning of creation is, as Maimonides explained, the idea that the universe did not come about by necessity but as a result of freedom.

Man is free to act in freedom and free to forfeit freedom. In choosing evil he surrenders his attachment to the spirit and foregoes the opportunity to let freedom happen. Thus we may be free in employing or in ignoring freedom; we are not free in having freedom. We are free to choose between good and evil; we are not free in having to choose. We are in fact compelled to choose. Thus all freedom is a situation of God's waiting for man to choose.

The decisive thought in the message of the prophets is not the presence of God to man but rather the presence of man to God. The prophets speak not so much of man's concern for God as of God's concern for man. At the beginning is God's concern. It is because of His concern for man that man may have a concern for Him, that we are able to search for Him.

In Jewish thinking, the problem of being can never be treated in isolation but only in relation to God. The supreme categories in such ontology are not being and becoming but law and love (justice and compassion, order and pathos). Being, as well as all beings, stands in a polarity of divine justice and divine compassion.

To most of us, the abstract static principle of order and necessity is an ultimate category and one which is inherent in the very concept of being (or of our consciousness of being). To the Jewish mind, order or necessity is not an ultimate category but an aspect of the dynamic attribute of divine judgment. Jewish thinking, furthermore, claims that being is constituted (created) and maintained not only by necessity but also by freedom, by God's free and personal concern for being.

The divine concern is not a theological afterthought but a fundamental category of ontology. Reality seems to be maintained by the necessity of its laws. Yet, when we inquire: why is necessity necessary? there is only one answer: the divine freedom, the divine concern.

The question may be asked: Is it plausible to believe that the eternal should be concerned with the trivial? Should we not rather assume that man is too insignificant to be an object for His concern? The truth, however, is that nothing is trivial. What seems infinitely small in our eyes is infinitely great in the eyes of the infinite God. Because the finite is never isolated; it is involved in countless ways in the course of infinite events. And the higher the level of spiritual awareness, the greater is the degree of sensibility to, and concern for, others.

We must continue to ask: what is man that God should care for him? And we must continue to remember that it is precisely God's care for man that constitutes the greatness of man. To *be* is to *stand for,* and what man stands for is the great mystery of being His partner. *God is in need of man.*

Part IV

Religious Observance

26. RELIGION AND LAW

The claim of Judaism that religions and law are inseparable is difficult for many of us to comprehend. The difficulty may be explained by modern man's conception of the essence of religion. To the modern mind, religion is a state of the soul, inwardness; feeling rather than obedience, faith rather than action, spiritual rather than concrete. To Judaism, religion is not a feeling for something that is, but *an answer* to Him who is asking us to live in a certain way. It is in its very origin a consciousness of total commitment; a realization that all of life is not only man's but also God's sphere of interest.

"God asks for the heart."[1] Yet does he ask for the heart only? Is the right intention enough? Some doctrines insist that love is the sole condition for salvation (Sufi,[2] Bhakti-marga), stressing the importance of inwardness, of love, or faith, to the exclusion of good works.

Paul waged a passionate battle against the power of law and proclaimed instead the religion of grace. Law, he claimed, cannot conquer sin, nor can righteousness be attained through works of law. A man is justified "by faith without the deeds of the law."[3]

That salvation is attained by faith alone was Luther's central thesis. The antinomian tendency resulted in the overemphasis of love and faith to the exclusion of good works.

The Formula of Concord of 1580, still valid in Protestantism, condemns the statement that good works are necessary to salvation and rejects the doctrine that they are harmful to salvation. According to Ritschl, the doctrine of the merit of good deeds is an intruder in the domain of Christian theology; the only way of salvation is justification by faith. Barth, following Kierkegaard, voices Lutheran thoughts, when he claims that man's deeds are too sinful to be good. There are fundamentally no human deeds, which, because of their significance in this world, find favor in God's eyes. God can be approached through God alone.

Those who have only paid attention to the relation of man to the ideals, disregarding the relation of the ideals to man, have in their theories seen only the motive but not the purpose of either religion or morality. Echoing the Paulinian doctrine that man is saved by faith alone, Kant and his disciples taught that the essence of religion or morality would consist in an absolute quality of the soul or the will, regardless of the actions that

155

may come out of it or the ends that may be attained. Accordingly, the value of a religious act would be determined wholly by the intensity of one's faith or by the rectitude of one's inner disposition. The intention, not the deed, the *how*, not the *what* of one's conduct, would be essential, and no motive other than the sense of duty would be of any moral value. Thus acts of kindness, when not dictated by the sense of duty, are no better than cruelty, and compassion or regard for human happiness as such is looked upon as an ulterior motive. "I would not break my word even to save mankind!" exclaimed Fichte. His salvation and righteousness were apparently so much more important to him than the fate of all men that he would have destroyed mankind to save himself. Does not such an attitude illustrate the truth of the proverb, "The road to hell is paved with good intentions"? Should we not say that a concern with one's own salvation and righteousness that outweighs the regard for the welfare of other human beings cannot be qualified as a good intention?

The dichotomy of faith and works which presented such an important problem in Christian theology was never a problem in Judaism. To us, the basic problem is neither what is the right action nor what is the right intention. The basic problem is: what is right living? And life is indivisible. The inner sphere is never isolated from outward activities. Deed and thought are bound into one. All a person thinks and feels enters everything he does, and all he does is involved in everything he thinks and feels.

Spiritual aspirations are doomed to failure when we try to cultivate deeds at the expense of thoughts or thoughts at the expense of deeds. Is it the artist's inner vision or his wrestling with the stone that brings about a work of sculpture? Right living is like a work of art, the product of a vision and of a wrestling with concrete situations.

Judaism is averse to generalities, averse to looking for meaning in life detached from doing, as if the meaning were a separate entity. Its tendency is to make ideas convertible into deeds, to interpret metaphysical insights as patterns for action, to endow the most sublime principles with bearing upon everyday conduct. In its tradition, the abstract became concrete, the absolute historic. By enacting the holy on the stage of concrete living, we perceive our kinship with the divine, the presence of the divine. What cannot be grasped in reflection, we comprehend in deeds.

The world needs more than the secret holiness of individual inwardness. It needs more than sacred sentiments and good intentions. God asks for the heart because He needs the lives. It is by lives that the world will be redeemed, by lives that beat in concordance with God, by deeds that outbeat the finite charity of the human heart.

Man's power of action is less vague than his power of intention. And an action has intrinsic meaning; its value to the world is independent of what it means to the person performing it. The act of giving food to a helpless child is meaningful regardless of whether or not the moral intention is present. God asks for the heart, and we must spell our answer in terms of deeds.

It would be a device of conceit, if not presumption, to insist that purity of the heart is the exclusive test of piety. Perfect purity is something we rarely know how to obtain or how to retain. No one can claim to have purged all the dross even from his finest desire. The self is finite, but selfishness is infinite.

God asks for the heart, but the heart is oppressed with uncertainty in its own twilight. God asks for faith, and the heart is not sure of its own faith. It is good that there is a dawn of decision for the night of the heart; deeds to objectify faith, definite forms to verify belief.

The heart is often a lonely voice in the marketplace of living. Man may entertain lofty ideals and behave like the ass that, as the saying goes, "carries gold and eats thistles." The problem of the soul is how to live nobly in an animal environment; how to persuade and train the tongue and the senses to behave in agreement with the insights of the soul.

The integrity of life is not exclusively a thing of the heart; it implies more than consciousness of the moral law. The innermost chamber must be guarded at the uttermost outposts. Religion is not the same as spiritualism; what man does in his concrete, physical existence is directly relevant to the divine. Spirituality is the goal, not the way of man. In this world music is played on physical instruments, and to the Jew the mitzvot are the instruments on which the holy is carried out. If man were only mind, worship in thought would be the form in which to commune with God. But man is body and soul, and his goal is so to live that both "his heart and his flesh should sing to the living God."

But how do we know what the right deeds are? Is the knowledge of right and wrong derived by reason and conscience alone?

There are those who are ready to discard the message of the divine commands and call upon us to rely on our conscience. Man, we are told, is only under obligation to act in conformity with his reason and conscience, and must not be subjected to any laws except those which he imposes upon himself. Moral laws are attainable by reason and conscience, and there is no need for a lawgiver. God is necessary merely as a guarantee for the ultimate triumph of the moral effort.

The fallacy of the doctrine of autonomy is in equating man with "the good drive," and all of his nature with reason and conscience. Man's capacity for love and self-denial ("the good drive") does not constitute the totality of his nature. He is also inclined to love success, to adore the victors and to despite the vanquished. Those who call upon us to rely on our inner voice fail to realize that there is more than one voice within us, that the power of selfishness may easily subdue the pangs of conscience. The conscience, moreover, is often celebrated for what is beyond its ability. The conscience is not a legislative power, capable of teaching us what we ought to do but rather a preventive agency; a brake, not a guide; a fence, not a way. It raises its voice after a wrong deed has been committed, but often fails to give us direction in advance of our actions.

The individual's insight alone is unable to cope with all the problems of living. It is the guidance of tradition on which we must rely, and whose norms we must learn to interpret and to apply. We must learn not only the ends but also the means by which to realize the ends; not only the general laws but also the particular forms.

Judaism calls upon us to listen *not only* to the voice of the conscience but also to the norms of a heteronomous law. The good is not an abstract idea but a commandment, and the ultimate meaning of its fulfillment is in its being *an answer* to God.

Man had to be expelled from the Garden of Eden; he had to witness the murder of half of the human species by Cain out of envy; experience the catastrophe of the Flood; the confusion of the languages; slavery in Egypt and the wonder of the Exodus, to be ready to accept the law.

We believe that the Jew is committed to a divine law; that the ultimate standards are beyond man rather than within man. We believe that there is a law, the essence of which is derived from prophetic events, and the interpretation of which is in the hands of the sages.

We are taught that God gave man not only life but also a law. The supreme imperative is not merely to believe in God but to do the will of God. The classical code, *Turim,* begins with the words of Judah ben Tema: "Be bold as a leopard, light as an eagle, swift as a deer, and strong as a lion *to do* the will of your Father who is in heaven."[4]

What is *law?* A way of dealing with the most difficult of all problems: life. The law is a problem to him who thinks that life is a commonplace. *The law is an answer* to him who knows that *life is a problem.*

In Judaism allegiance to God involves a commitment to Jewish law, to a discipline, to specific obligations. These terms, against which modern man seems to feel an aversion, are in fact a part of civilized living. Every one of us who acknowledges allegiance to the state of which he is a citizen is committed to its law, and accepts the obligations it imposes upon him. His loyalty will on occasion prompt him to do even more than mere allegiance would demand. Indeed, the word "loyalty" is derived from the same root as "legal," *ligo,* which means "to be bound." Similarly, the word "obligation" comes from the Latin *obligo,* to bind, and denotes the state of being bound by a legal or moral tie.

The object of the prophets was to guide and to demand, not only to console and to reassure. Judaism is meaningless as an optional attitude to be assumed at our convenience. To the Jewish mind life is a complex of obligations, and the fundamental category of Judaism is *a demand* rather than *a dogma,* a *commitment* rather than a feeling. *God's will* stands higher than *man's creed.* Reverence for the authority of the law is an expression of our love for God.

However, beyond His will is His love. The Torah was given to Israel as a sign of His love. To reciprocate that love we strive to attain *ahavat Torah* [love of the Torah].

A degree of self-control is the prerequiste for creative living. Does not a work of art represent the triumph of form over inchoate matter? Emotion controlled by an idea? We suffer from the illusion of being mature as well as from a tendency to overestimate the degree of human perfectibility. No one is mature unless he has learned to be engaged in pursuits which require discipline and self-control, and human perfectibility is contingent upon the capacity for self-control.

There are positive as well as negative mitzvot, actions as well as abstentions. Indeed, the sense for the holy is often expressed in terms of restrictions, just as the mystery of God is conveyed *via negationis,* in *negative theology* which claims we can never say what He is; we can only say what He is not. Inadequate would be our service if it consisted only of rituals and positive deeds which are so faulty and often abortive. Precious as positive deeds are, there are times when the silence of sacred abstentions is more articulate than the language of deeds.[5]

There is a sure way of missing the meaning of the law by either atomization or generalization, by seeing the parts without the whole or by seeing the whole without the parts.

It is impossible to understand the significance of single acts, detached from the total character of a life in which they are set. Acts are components of a whole and derive their character from the structure of the whole. There is an intimate relation between all acts and experiences of a person. Yet just as the parts are determined by the whole, the whole is determined by the parts. Consequently, the amputation of one part may affect the integrity of the entire structure, unless that part has outlived its vital role in the organic body of the whole.

Some people are so occupied collecting shreds and patches of the law, that they hardly think of weaving the pattern of the whole; others are so enchanted by the glamor of generalities, by the image of ideals, that while their eyes fly up, their actions remain below.

What we must try to avoid is not only the failure to observe a single mitzvah, but the loss of the whole, the loss of belonging to the spiritual order of Jewish living. The order of Jewish living is meant to be, not a set of rituals but an order of all man's existence, shaping all his traits, interests, and dispositions; not so much the performance of single acts, the taking of a step now and then, as the pursuit of a way, being on the way; not so much the acts of fulfilling as the state of being committed to the task, the belonging to an order in which single deeds, aggregates of religious feeling, sporadic sentiments, moral episodes become a part of a complete pattern.[6]

It is a distortion to reduce Judaism to a cult or system of ceremonies. The Torah is both the detail and the whole. As time and space are presupposed in any perception, so is the totality of life implied in every act of piety. There is an objective coherence that holds all episodes together. A man may commit a crime now and teach mathematics effortlessly an hour later. But when a man prays, all he has done in his life enters his prayer.

Jewish tradition does not maintain that every iota of the law was revealed to Moses at Sinai. This is an unwarranted extension of the rabbinic conception of revelation. "Could Moses have learned the whole Torah? Of the Torah it is said, *Its measure is longer than the earth and broader than the sea* (Job 11:9) ; could then Moses have learned it in forty days? No, it was only the principles thereof (*kelalim*) which God taught Moses."[7]

The Rabbis maintain that "things not revealed to Moses were revealed to Rabbi Akiba and his colleagues."[8] The role of the sages in interpreting the word of the Bible and their power to issue new ordinances are basic elements of Jewish belief, and something for which our sages found sanction in Deuteronomy 17:11. The Torah was compared to "a fountain which continually sends forth water, giving forth more than it absorbs. In the same sense, you can teach (or say) more Torah than you received at Sinai."[9]

In their intention to inspire greater joy and love of God, the Rabbis expanded the scope of the law, imposing more and more restrictions and prohibitions. "There is no generation in which the Rabbis do not add to the law."[10] In the time of Moses, only what he had explicitly received at Sinai [the written law] was binding, plus several ordinances which he added for whatever reasons he saw fit. [However] the prophets, the Tannaim, and the rabbis of every generation [have continued to multiply these restrictions].[11]

The industrial civilization has profoundly affected the condition of man, and vast numbers of Jews loyal to Jewish law feel that many of the rabbinic restrictions tend to impede rather than to inspire greater joy and love of God.

In their zeal to carry out the ancient injunction, "make a hedge about the Torah," many rabbis failed to heed the warning, "Do not consider the hedge more important than the vineyard." Excessive regard for the hedge may spell ruin for the vineyard.[12] The vineyard is being trodden down. It is all but laid waste. Is this the time to insist upon the sanctity of the hedges? "Were the Torah given as a rigid immutable code of laws, Israel could not survive. . . . Moses exclaimed: Lord of the universe, let me know what is the law. And the Lord said: Rule by the principle of majority. . . . The law will be explained, now one way, now another, according to the perception of the majority of the *sages*."[13]

27. LAW AND LIFE

Does Judaism glorify outward action, regardless of intention and motive? Is it action it calls for rather than devotion? Is a person to be judged by what he *does* rather than by what he *is?* Is conduct alone important? Have the mitzvot nothing to say to the soul? Has the soul nothing to say through the mitzvot? We are commanded to carry out specific rituals, such as reciting twice a day "Hear O Israel . . ." or setting of the *tefillin* on arm and head. Are we merely commanded *to recite "Hear* O Israel . . . God is One," and not *to hear?* Is one's setting of the *tefillin* on head and arm merely a matter of external performance?

No religious act is properly fulfilled unless it is done with a willing heart and a craving soul. You cannot worship Him with your body, if you do not know how to worship Him in your soul.[1] The relationship between deed and inner devotion must be understood, as we shall see, in terms of polarity.

Observance must not be reduced to external compliance with the law. Agreement of the heart with the spirit, not only with the letter of the law, is itself a requirement of the law. The goal is to live beyond the dictates of the law; to fulfill the eternal suddenly; to create goodness out of nothing, as it were.

The law, stiff with formality, is *a cry for creativity;* a call for nobility concealed in the form of commandments. It is not designed to be a yoke, a curb, a strait jacket for human action. Above all, the Torah asks for *love: thou shalt love thy God; thou shalt love thy neighbor.* All observance is training in the art of love. To forget that love is the purpose of all *mitzvot* is to vitiate their meaning. "Those who think that the performance is the main thing are mistaken. The main thing is the heart; what we do and what we say has only one purpose: to evoke the devotion of the heart. This is the essence and purpose of all mitzvot: to love Him wholeheartedly."[2]

"All ye do should be done out of love."[3] The end of our readiness to obey is the ability to love. The law is given to be cherished, not merely to be complied with.

Jewish observance, it must be stressed, takes place on two levels. It consists of acts performed by the body in a clearly defined and tangible manner, and of acts of the soul carried out in a manner that is neither definable nor ostensible; of the right intention and of putting the right intention into action. Both body and soul must participate in carrying out a ritual, a law, an imperative, a mitzvah. Thoughts, feelings ensconced in the inwardness of man, deeds performed in the absence of the soul, are incomplete.

Judaism stresses the importance of a fixed pattern of deeds as well as that of spontaneity of devotion, quantity as well as quality of religious living, action as well as kavvanah. A good deed consists not only in *what* but also in *how* we do it. Even those mitzvot which require for their fulfillment a concrete object and an external act call for inner acknowledgement, participation, understanding and the freedom of the heart.

It is true that the law speaks always of external performance and rarely of inner devotion. It does not rigorously insist upon kavvanah. There is wisdom in this reticence. The rabbis knew that man may be commanded to act in a certain way, but not to feel in a certain way; that the actions of man may be regulated, but not his thoughts or emotions.

There are, therefore, no detailed laws of kavvanah, and kavvanah may, indeed, run dry in the mere halakhah. To maintain the flow of kavvanah we must keep alive the sense of the ineffable, that which lies beyond kavvanah.

Jewish observance may be divided into two classes: into duties that call for both external performance and an act of the soul, and into duties that call only for an act of the soul. Thus the mind and the heart are never exempted from being engaged in the service of God. The number of precepts which call for external performance as well as for an act of the soul is limited; whereas the number of precepts which are exclusively duties of the heart to be carried out in the soul is endless.

We exalt the deed; we do not idolize external performance. The outward performance is but an aspect of the totality of a deed. Jewish literature dilates on the idea that every act of man hinges and rests on the intention and hidden sentiments of the heart, that the duties of the heart take precedence over the duties to fulfill the practical precepts. They are binding upon us "at all seasons, in all places, every hour, every moment, under all circumstances, as long as we have life and reason."[4]

No other area of observance required such strict adherence to formalities as the ritual at the Temple in Jerusalem. The description of the rules and customs according to which the ceremonies of sacrifice were conducted occupies almost a whole section of the Mishnah. Significantly, however, the two main tractates of that section begin with a statement about the inner attitude of the priest, stressing the principle that the validity of the ceremony depends first of all upon what goes on in the mind of the priest. Having set forth all the minutiae of the priest's performance, the editor of the Mishnah resumes the original principle and concludes the second tractate with a statement that almost sounds like a proclamation: "It amounts to the same, whether one offers much or little—provided one directs his heart to heaven." The good Lord may pardon every one that directed his heart to seek God . . . though he was not cleansed according to the purification of the sanctuary. (II Chronicles 30:18–19.)

To the ancient rabbis the pursuit of learning, of Torah, was one of the highest goals.[5] Did that conception imply that in the eyes of God the scholar in the house of learning stood higher than the peasant in the field? It was a favorite saying of the scholars in Yavneh:

> I am a creature of God,
> My neighbor is also a creature of God;
> My work is in the city,
> His work is in the field;
> I rise early to my work,
> He rises early to his.
> Just as he is not overbearing in his calling,
> So am I not overbearing in my calling.
> Perhaps thou sayest:
> I do great things and he does small things!
> We have learnt:
> It matters not whether one does much or little,
> If only he directs his heart to heaven.[6]

"God asks for the heart," not only for deeds; for insight, not only for obedience; for understanding and knowledge of God, not only for acceptance.

The main function of observance is not in imposing a discipline but in keeping us spiritually perceptive. Judaism is not interested in automatons. In its essence obedience is a form of imitating God. *That* we observe is obedience; *what* we observe is imitation of God.[7] If a deed is good in itself, why should it be considered imperfect if done without the participation of the soul? Why is kavvanah necessary?

A moral deed unwittingly done may be relevant to the world because of the aid it renders unto others. Yet a deed without devotion, for all its effects on the lives of others, will leave the life of the doer unaffected. The true goal for man is *to be* what he *does*. The worth of a religion is the worth of the individuals living it. A mitzvah, therefore, is not mere doing but an act that embraces both the doer and the deed. The means may be external, but the end is personal. Your deeds be pure, so that ye shall be holy.

A hero is he who is greater than his feats, and a pious man is he who is greater than his rituals. The deed is definite, yet the task is infinite.

It is a distortion to say that Judaism consists exclusively of performing ritual or moral deeds, and to forget that the goal of all performing is in *transforming* the soul. Even before Israel was told in the Ten Commandments what *to do* it was told what *to be: a holy people*. To perform deeds of holiness is to absorb the holiness of deeds. We must learn how to be one with what we do. This is why in addition to halakhah, *the science of deeds*, there is agadah, *the art of being*.

Man is not for the sake of good deeds; the good deeds are for the sake of man. Judaism asks for more than works, for more than the *opus operatum*. The goal is not that a ceremony be *performed;* the goal is that man be *transformed;* to worship the Holy in order to be holy. The purpose to the mitzvot is *to sanctify* man.

The more we do for His sake, the more we receive for our sake. What ultimately counts most is not the scope of one's deeds but their impact upon the life of the soul. "He who does a mitzvah lights a lamp before God and endows his soul with more life."[8]

Man is more than what he does. What he does is spiritually a minimum of what he is. Deeds are outpourings, not the essence of the self. They may reflect or refine the self, but they remain the functions, not the substance of inner life. It is the inner life, however, which is our most urgent problem.

The Torah has no glory if man remains apart. The goal is for man to be an incarnation of the Torah;[9] for the Torah to be in man, in his soul and in his deeds.

28. KAVVANAH

What is meant by the term "kavvanah"? In its verbal form the original meaning seems to be: to straighten, to place in a straight line, to direct. From this it came to mean to direct the mind, to pay attention, to do a thing with an intention. The noun kavvanah denotes meaning, purpose, motive, and intention.

To have kavvanah means, according to a classical formulation, "to direct the heart to the Father in heaven." The phrasing does not say direct the heart to the "text" or to the "content of the prayer." Kavvanah, then, is more than paying attention to the text of the liturgy or to the performance of the mitzvah. Kavvanah is attentiveness to God. Its purpose is to direct the heart rather than the tongue or the arms. It is not an act of the mind that serves to guide the external action, but one that has meaning in itself.

"Mitzvah" means commandment. In doing a mitzvah our primary awareness is the thought of carrying out that which He commanded us to do, and it is such awareness which places our action in the direction of the divine. Kavvanah in this sense is not the awareness of being commanded but the awareness of Him who commands; not of a yoke we carry but of the Will we remember; the awareness of God rather than the awareness of duty. Such awareness is more than an attitude of the mind; it is an act of valuation or *appreciation* of being commanded, of living in a covenant, of the opportunity to act in agreement with God.

Appreciation is not the same as reflection. It is an attitude of the whole person. It is one's being drawn to the preciousness of an object or a situation. To sense the preciousness of being able to listen to an imperative of God; to be perceptive of the unique worth of doing a mitzvah, is the beginning of higher kavvanah.

It is in such appreciation that we realize that to *perform* is to lend *form* to a divine theme; that our task is to set forth the divine in acts, to express the spirit in tangible forms. For a mitzvah is like a musical score, and its performance is not a mechanical accomplishment but an artistic act.

The music in a score is open only to him who has music in his soul. It is not enough to play the notes; one must *be* what he *plays*. It is not

165

enough to do the mitzvah; one must *live* what he *does*. The goal is to find access to the sacred deed. But the holiness in the mitzvah is only open to him who knows how to discover the holiness in his own soul. To do a mitzvah is one thing; to partake of its inspiration another. And in order to partake we must learn how to bestow.

Those who dwell exclusively on the technicalities of performance fail to be sensitive to the essence of the task. When the soul is dull, the mitzvah is a shell. "The dead cannot praise God" (Psalms 115:17). The mitzvot do not always shine by their own light. When we open our inner life to a mitzvah, songs rise up in our souls.

The presence of God demands more than the presence of mind. Kavvanah is direction to God and requires the redirection of the whole person. It is the act of bringing together the scattered forces of the self; the participation of heart and soul, not only of will and mind; the integration of the soul with the theme of the mitzvah.

It is one thing to be *for* a cause and another thing to be *in* a cause. It is not enough to help thy neighbor; "Thou shalt love thy neighbor." It is not enough to serve thy God; you are asked "to serve Him with all your heart and with all your soul" (Deuteronomy 11:13). It is not enough to love Him: "thou shalt love . . . with all thy heart, and with all thy soul, and with all thy might" (Deuteronomy 6:5–6).

What we feel primarily is our inability to feel adequately. Human inadequacy is not an inference of humility; it is the truth of existence. A mitzvah is neither a substitute for thought nor an expression of kavvanah. A mitzvah is an act in which we go beyond the scope of our thought and intention. He who plants a tree rises beyond the level of his own intention. He who does a mitzvah plants a tree in the divine garden of eternity.

With a sacred deed goes a cry of the soul, inarticulate at times, that is more expressive of what we witness, of what we sense, than words.

A pious man is usually pictured as a sort of bookworm, a person who thrives among the pages of ancient tomes, and to whom life with its longing, sadness, and tensions, is but a footnote in a scholarly commentary on the Bible. The truth is that a religious man is like a salamander, that legendary animal that originates from a fire of myrtlewood kept burning for seven years.

Religion is born of fire, of a flame, in which the dross of the mind and soul is melted away. Religion can only thrive on fire. "The Lord spoke unto Moses. . . . This they shall give . . . half a shekel for an offering to the Lord" (Exodus 30:13). Said Rabbi Meir: "The Lord showed unto Moses a coin of fire, saying: This is what they shall give."[1] A life of religion is an altar. "Fire shall be kept burning upon the altar continually; it shall not go out" (Leviticus 6:6).

Man cannot live without acts of exaltation, without moments of trembling and revering, without being transported by grandeur. For weeks and months he may be confined to the routine of sensible interests, until an hour arrives when all his habits burst under the strain. Common sense may sign a decree that life be kept under the lock of average conceptions, but much in our lives is made to be burned up in a holy flame or it will rot in monstrous deeds, in evil thoughts. To satisfy his need for exaltation, man will plunge into rage, wage wars; he will set the city of Rome afire.

When superimposed as a yoke, as a dogma, as a fear, religion tends to violate rather than to nurture the spirit of man. Religion must be an altar upon which the fire of the soul may be kindled in holiness.

29. RELIGIOUS BEHAVIORISM

It is important that we analyze a popular misunderstanding of Judaism which may be called "religious behaviorism." It signifies an attitude toward the law as well as a philosophy of Judaism as a whole. As an attitude toward the law, it stresses the external compliance with the law and disregards the importance of inner devotion. It maintains that, according to Judaism, there is only one way in which the will of God need be fulfilled, namely, outward action; that inner devotion is not indigenous to Judaism; that Judaism is concerned with deeds, not with ideas; that all it asks for is obedience to the law. It is a Judaism that consists of laws, deeds, things; it has two dimensions; depth, the personal dimension, is missing. Accordingly, religious behaviorists speak of discipline, tradition, observance, but never of religious experience, of religious ideas. You do not have to believe, but you must observe the law; as if all that mattered is how men behaved in physical terms; as if God were not concerned with the inner life; as if faith were not indigenous to Judaism, but *orthopraxis* were. Such a conception reduces Judaism to a sort of sacred physics, with no sense for the imponderable, the introspective, the metaphysical.

As a personal attitude religious behaviorism usually reflects a widely held theology in which the supreme article of faith is *respect for tradition*. People are urged to observe the rituals or to attend services out of deference to what has come down to us from our ancestors. The *theology of respect* pleads for the maintenance of the inherited and transmitted customs and institutions and is characterized by a spirit of conformity, excessive moderation and disrespect of spontaneity.

Wise, important, essential, and pedagogically useful as the principle "respect for tradition" is, it is grotesque and self-defeating to make of it the supreme article of faith. We do not adhere to the specific forms of observance because of their antiquity. Antics of the past are hardly more venerable than vagaries of the present. Is the archaic a mark of vital preference? Is unconditional respect for the past the essence of Judaism? Did not Judaism begin when Abraham broke with tradition and rejected the past? Religious behaviorism is guilty of a total misunderstanding of the nature of man. Is it psychologically true that religious deeds can be performed in a spiritual vacuum, in the absence of the soul? Is respect without reason, ancestral loyalty without faith, or group-consciousness without personal conviction compatible with the life of a free man?

Let us analyze the origin as well as the basic assumptions of religious behaviorism in the light of Jewish thinking.

The theory of Judaism as a system of religious behaviorism goes back to Spinoza and Moses Mendelssohn.

Spinoza advanced the theory that the Israelites were distinguished from other nations neither in knowledge nor in piety. "Of God and nature they had only very primitive ideas," above which not even the prophets were able to rise.

"Scriptural doctrine contains no lofty speculations nor philosophic reasoning, but only very simple matters, such as could be understood by the slowest intelligence." "I should be surprised if I found [the prophets] teaching any new speculative doctrine which was not a commonplace to . . . Gentile philosophers." "It, therefore, follows that we must by no means go to the prophets for knowledge, either of natural or spiritual phenomena." "The Israelites knew scarcely anything of God, although he was revealed to them." It is hardly likely that they "should have held any sound notions about the Deity, or that Moses should have taught them anything beyond a rule of right living. . . . Thus the rule of right living, the worship and the love of God, was to them rather a bondage than the true liberty, the gift and grace of the Deity." What the Bible contains is not a religion but a law, the character of which was political rather than religious.[1]

Spinoza's insistence upon the intellectual irrelevance and spiritual inferiority of the Bible has proved to be of momentous importance, and has shaped the minds of subsequent generations in their attitude to the Bible.

Kant, Fichte, Hegel, and the thinkers of the romantic school, even when rejecting his views about metaphysics, adopted his views about the Bible.[2]

It is one of the ironies of Jewish history that Moses Mendelssohn, a zealous opponent of Spinoza's metaphysical theories and profoundly different from him in motivation and intention, has nevertheless embraced Spinoza's view of the essential nature of the Bible.

Mendelssohn believed that ultimate religious verities cannot be communicated from the outside, for our mind would not understand them if they were not already known to us. Ultimate verities have their origin in the mind rather than in revelation. The Jewish belief in one God is not a revelation but part of a natural religion at which all men can arrive by the exercise of reason. With Spinoza, he maintains that Judaism asks for obedience to a law but not acceptance of doctrines. "Judaism is no revealed religion in the usual sense of the term, but only *revealed legislation,* laws, commandments and regulations, which were supernaturally given to the Jews through Moses." It demands no faith, no specific religious attitudes. "The spirit of Judaism is freedom in doctrine and conformity in action."[3]

In the spirit of Spinoza and Moses Mendelssohn, many of those who take the law seriously, as well as those who pay lip service to it, maintain that the science of law is the only authentic expression of Judaism; that agadah—in the strict sense of the non-legal rabbinic literature and in the wider sense of all post-rabbinic attempts to interpret the non-legal ideas and beliefs of our faith—is not "within the mainstream of Judaism." Theology, it is claimed, is alien to Judaism; the law, "an ox who gores a cow," is Jewish theology, for Judaism is law and nothing else. Such *pan-halakhic* "theology" claims that in Judaism religious living consists of complying with a law rather than of striving to attain a goal which is the purpose of the law. It is a view that exalts the Torah only because it discloses the law, not because it discloses a way of finding God in life. It claims that obedience is the substance rather than the form of religious existence; that the law is an end, not a way.

This, indeed, has been the contention of those who attacked Judaism that "the law of Moses commands only right action, and says nothing about purity of heart." Albo rejects this as being the opposite of the truth. "For do we not read, *Circumcise therefore the foreskin of your heart* (Deuteronomy 10:16) ; *And thou shalt love the Lord thy God with all thy heart* (Deuteronomy 6:5) ; *And thou shalt love thy neighbor as thyself* (Leviticus 19:18) ; *But thou shalt fear thy God* (Leviticus 19: 14) ; *Thou shalt not take vengeance, nor bear any grudge against the children of thy people* (Leviticus 19:18). The reason it commands right action is because purity of heart is of no account unless practice is in agreement with it. The most important thing, however, is intention. David says, *Create me a clean heart* (Psalms 51:12).⁴

Judaism is not another word for legalism. The rules of observance are law in form and love in substance. The Torah contains both law and love. Law is what holds the world together; love is what brings the world forward. The law is the means, not the end; the way, not the goal. One of the goals is "Ye shall be holy." The Torah is guidance to an end through a law. It is both a vision and a law. Man created in the likeness of God is called upon to re-create the world in the likeness of the vision of God. Halakhah is neither the ultimate nor the all-embracing term for Jewish learning and living. The Torah is more than a system of laws; only a portion of the Pentateuch deals with law. The prophets, the Psalms, agadic midrashim, are not a part of halakhah. The Torah comprises both halakhah and agadah. Like body and soul, they are mutually dependent, and each is a dimension of its own.

Agadah is usually defined negatively as embracing all non-legal or non-halakhic parts of rabbinic literature,⁵ whether in the form of a tale or an explanation of scripture; an epigram or a homily. Significantly, though the Bible, like rabbinic literature, embraces both legal and non-legal teachings, the distinction between halakhah and agadah was never applied to it.⁶ The fact remains that, central as is law, only a small part of the Bible deals with the law. The narratives of the Bible are as holy as its legal portions.⁷ According to one rabbi, "the conversation of the servants of the patriarchs is more beautiful than even the laws of the later generations."⁸

The preciousness and fundamental importance of agadah is categorically set forth in the following statement of the ancient rabbis: *"If you desire to know Him at whose word the universe came into being, study agadah for hereby will you recognize the Holy One and cleave unto His ways."*⁹ It is by means of agadah that the name of God is sanctified in the world.¹⁰ To those who did not appreciate the value of agadah, the rabbis applied the verse, "They give no heed to the works of the Lord, nor to the acts of His hands."¹¹

In the Tannaitic period, agadah was an organic part of Jewish learning. It was said that just as the written Torah consists of three parts, the Pentateuch, the Prophets, and the Hagiographa, the oral Torah consists of midrash, halakhah, and agadah.¹²

The collections of agadah that have been preserved contain an almost inexhaustible wealth of religious insight and feeling, for in the agadah the religious consciousness with its motivations, difficulties, perplexities, and longings, came to immediate and imaginative expression. And a Jew

170

was commanded to study not only halakhah but also agadah.[13] On the Day of Judgment one would be held accountable for having failed to study agadah.[14] According to a decision of a later authority, one is obliged to devote a third of one's studies to the field of agadah.[15]

Jewish enlightenment, however, showed little appreciation of agadah.[16] In a study on Jewish education in which all aspects of classical Jewish literature were recommended as topics of instruction, the author strongly inveighs against including agadah in the curriculum.[17]

The translators of the Septuagint committed a fatal and momentous error when, for lack of a Greek equivalent, they rendered "Torah" with *"nomos,"* which means *law,* giving rise to a huge and chronic misconception of Judaism and supplying an effective weapon to those who sought to attack the teachings of Judaism. That the Jews considered Scripture as teaching is evidenced by the fact that in the Aramaic translations Torah is rendered with *oraita* which can only mean teaching, never law.

In the Avesta, religion is called law (*daêna*), and the Persians had no way of distinguishing between religion and law. In Judaism even the word *Torah* is not all-inclusive. "A man who has Torah but no *yirat shamayim* (awe and fear of God) is like a treasurer who was given the keys to the inner chamber but not the keys to the outer chamber."[18] Nor does the term *mitzvot,* commandments, express the totality of Judaism. The acceptance of *God* must precede, and is distinguished from, the acceptance of the commandments.[19]

At the head of the Decalogue stand the words, *I am the Lord thy God.* The rabbis offered a parable. "The Emperor extended his reign over a new province. Said his attendants to him: Issue some decrees upon the people. But the emperor replied: Only after they will have accepted my *kingship,* will I issue *decrees.* For if they do not accept my kingship, how will they carry out my decrees? Likewise, God said to Israel, *I am the Lord thy God—Thou shalt have no other gods.* I am He whose kingship you have taken upon yourselves in Egypt. And when they said to Him: Yes, yes, He continued, *Thou shalt have no other gods beside me."*[20]

Through sheer punctiliousness in observing the law one may become oblivious of the living presence and forget that the law is not for its own sake but for the sake of God. Indeed, the essence of observance has, at times, become encrusted with so many customs and conventions that the jewel was lost in the setting. Outward compliance with externalities of the law took the place of the engagement of the whole person to the living God. What is the ultimate objective of observance if not to become sensitive to the spirit of Him, in whose ways the mitzvot are signposts?

Halakhah must not be observed for its own sake but for the sake of God. The law must not be idolized. It is a part, not all, of the Torah. We live and die for the sake of God rather than for the sake of the law.

We are told, *Ye shall keep my Sabbaths, and reverence My sanctuary* (Leviticus 19:30). One might think that we are commanded to pay homage to the sanctuary. The Talmud exhorts us: "Just as one does not revere the Sabbath but Him who commanded the observance of the Sabbath, one is not to revere the sanctuary but Him who gave the commandment concerning the sanctuary."[21]

The glorification of the law and the insistence upon its strict observance did not lead the rabbis to a deification of the law. "The Sabbath is given unto you, not you unto the Sabbath." The ancient rabbis knew that excessive piety may endanger the fulfillment of the essence of the law. "There is nothing more important, according to the Torah, than to preserve human life. . . . Even when there is the slightest possibility that a life may be at stake one may disregard every prohibition of the law." One must sacrifice mitzvot for the sake of man, rather than sacrifice man for the sake of mitzvot. The purpose of the Torah is "to bring life to Israel, in this world and in the world to come."

The ultimate requirement is to act beyond the requirements of the law. Torah is not the same as law, as *din*. To fulfill one's duties is not enough. One may be a *scoundrel* within the limits of the law.[22] Why was Jerusalem destroyed? Because her people acted according to the law, and did not act beyond the requirements of the law.[23]

Halakhah stresses uniformity, agadah represents the principle of inflection and diversity. Rules are generalizations. In actual living, we come upon countless problems for which no general solutions are available. There are many ways of applying a general rule to a concrete situation. There are evil applications of noble rules. Thus the choice of the right way of applying a general rule to a particular situation is "left to the heart,"[24] to the individual, to one's conscience.

It was in the spirit of a radical demand for inner purity that the word of the Psalmist (119:113), *I hate those who are of a divided mind,* was applied to those who serve the Lord out of fear rather than out of love.[25] We must always remember the words of Isaiah 29:13. "This people draw near with their mouth and honor Me with their lips, while their hearts are far from Me, and their fear of Me is a commandment of men learned by rote."

The rendering of "Torah" with *"nomos"* was not done thoughtlessly. It is rather an example of a tendency toward legalism or *pan-halakhism* which regards halakhah as the only authentic source of Jewish thinking and living. Both in the Rabbinic period and in the Middle Ages there were people who took a negative attitude toward agadah and would even "reject and ridicule" some of its statements.

The exponents of religious behaviorism claim that Judaism is a religion of law, not a religion of faith, that faith "was never regarded by Judaism as something meritorious in itself." This, of course, would be valid, if Abraham's willingness to sacrifice his only son, or Job's avowal, "though He slay me, yet will I trust in Him" (13:15), could be disregarded. What if not the power of faith, is the motive behind the injunction of the Mishnah, "A man is obliged to bless God for the evil things that come upon him as he is obliged to bless God for the good things that come to him"?[26] "If there is anything sure, it is that the highest motives which worked through the history of Judaism are the strong belief in God and the unshaken confidence that at last this God, the God of Israel, will be the God of the whole world; or, in other words, Faith and Hope are the two most prominent characteristics of Judaism."[27]

In the Bible, unbelievers are rebuked again and again, while belief is praised in such lofty words as, "Thus saith the Lord, I remember the affection of thy youth, thy love as a bride when thou wentest after Me in the wilderness, in a land that was not sown" (Jeremiah 2:2). The rabbis are inclined to ascribe sin to a defect in, or a lack of, faith in God. "No man speaks slanderously of another . . . no man deals fraudulently with his neighbor, unless he has first denied (or disbelieved in) the Root of all (namely, God)."[28]

Faith is so precious that Israel was redeemed from Egypt as a reward for their faith. The future redemption is contingent upon the degree of faith shown by Israel.[29] The rabbis denied a share in the life to come not to those who were guilty of wrong deeds, but to those who asserted views that contradicted fundamental beliefs.[30]

In justification of their view, exponents of religious behaviorism cite the passage in which the rabbis paraphrased the words of Jeremiah (16:11), *They have forsaken Me and have not kept My Torah* in the following way: "Would that they had forsaken Me and kept My Torah."[31] However, to regard this passage as a declaration of the primary if not exclusive importance of studying Torah over concern for God is to pervert the meaning of the passage. Such perversion is made possible by overlooking the second part of the passage which reads as follows: "since by occupying themselves with the Torah, the light which she contains would have led them back *to Me*." It was not an ideal that the rabbis envisaged but a last resort. Having forsaken all commandments, if the people had at least continued to study Torah, the light of the Torah would have brought them back to God.

It is true, as said above, that the essence of Judaism is a demand rather than a creed, that by faith alone we do not come close to Him. But the first demand of Judaism is to have faith in God, in Torah, and in the people Israel. It is by faith and love of God that find expression in deeds that we live as Jews. Faith is attachment, and to be a Jew is to be attached to God, Torah, and Israel.

Unquestionably, Judaism stands for verities not only for laws, expecting us to cherish certain thoughts and to be loyal to certain beliefs, not only to perform certain actions. It is both a way of thinking and a way of living, a doctrine and a discipline, faith and action.

We deny the exclusive primacy of dogmas not because we think that Judaism has no beliefs or that Judaism is merely a system of laws and observances, but because we realize that what we believe in surpasses the power and range of human expression.

Moreover, underlying the doctrines of dogmas is an intellectualism which claims that right and correctly expressed thinking is the most important thing. To Jewish tradition, however, right living is what counts most. Follow the pattern of the right living, even though you do not know how to formulate adequately its basic theory.

A dogma is something that is carried out totally in the mind by an act of belief. The mind, however, is but a part of man; the capital of the human realm, not the whole realm. A dogma, therefore, can only be a partial representation of the religious situation.

The danger of dogmas lies in their tendency to serve as *vicarious faith*, as if all we had to do were to accept on authority a fixed set of principles without the necessity of searching for a way of faith. But dogmas, if they are to serve any purpose at all, should be a summary or an epitome of faith rather than a substitute for it.

Not the confession of belief, but the active acceptance of the kingship of God and its order is the central demand of Judaism. Asserting "I believe in . . ." will not make a person a Jew, just as asserting "I believe in the United States of America" will not make a person an American A citizen is he who accepts the allegiance to the Constitution, its rights and obligations. Thus our relation to God cannot be expressed in a belief but rather in the accepting of an order that determines all of life.

Another statement which seems to express an anti-agadic spirit is that of the Babylonian Amora Ula. "Since the day the Temple in Jerusalem was destroyed all that is left to the Holy One are the four cubits of halakhah";[32] as if God were not present outside the realm of halakhah. Those who quote this passage as a statement of disparagement of agadah fail to notice that the passage is hardly an expression of jubilation. Its intention rather is to convey profound grief at the fact that man's attentiveness to God became restricted to matters of halakhah; that God is absent in world affairs, in matters that lie outside the limits of halakhah. This, indeed, is why we pray for redemption.

30. HALAKHAH AND AGADAH

Halakhah represents the strength to shape one's life according to a fixed pattern; it is a form-giving force. Agadah is the expression of man's ceaseless striving which often defies all limitations. Halakhah is the rationalization and schematization of living; it defines, specifies, sets measure and limit, placing life into an exact system. Agadah deals with man's ineffable relations to God, to other men, and to the world. Halakhah deals with details, with each commandment separately; agadah with the whole of life, with the totality of religious life. Halakhah deals with the law; agadah with the meaning of the law. Halakhah deals with subjects that can be expressed literally; agadah introduces us to a realm which lies beyond the range of expression. Halakhah teaches us how to perform common acts; agadah tells us how to participate in the eternal drama. Halakhah gives us knowledge; agadah gives us aspiration.

Halakhah gives us the norms for action; agadah, the vision of the ends of living. Halakhah prescribes, agadah suggests; halakhah decrees, agadah inspires; halakhah is definite; agadah is allusive.

When Isaac blessed Jacob he said: "God give thee the dew of heaven, the fat of the earth, and plenty of corn and wine." Remarked the Midrash: "Dew of heaven is Scripture, the fat of the earth is mishnah, corn is halakhah, wine is agadah."[1]

Halakhah, by necessity, treats with the laws in the abstract, regardless of the totality of the person. It is agadah that keeps on reminding that the purpose of performance is to transform the performer, that the purpose of observance is to train us in achieving spiritual ends. "It is well known that the purpose of all mitzvot is to purify the heart, for the heart is the essence."[2] The chief aim and purpose of the mitzvot performed with our body is to arouse our attention to the mitzvot that are fulfilled with the mind and heart, for these are the pillars on which the service of God rests.[3]

To maintain that the essence of Judaism consists exclusively of halakhah is as erroneous as to maintain that the essence of Judaism consists ex-

175

clusively of agadah. The interrelationship of halakhah and agadah is the very heart of Judaism. Halakhah without agadah is dead, agadah without halakhah is wild.

Halakhah thinks in the category of quantity; agadah is the category of quality. Agadah maintains that he who saves one human life is as if he had saved all mankind. In the eyes of him whose first category is the category of quantity, one man is less than two men, but in the eyes of God one life is worth as much as all of life. Halakhah speaks of the estimable and measurable dimensions of our deeds, informing us how *much* we must perform in order to fulfill our duty, about the size, capacity, or content of the doer and the deed. Agadah deals with the immeasurable, inward aspect of living, telling us *how* we must think and feel; *how* rather than *how much* we must do to fulfill our duty; the manner, not only the content, is important.

To reduce Judaism to law, to halakhah, is to dim its light, to pervert its essence and to kill its spirit. We have a legacy of agadah together with a system of halakhah, and although, because of a variety of reasons, that legacy was frequently overlooked and agadah became subservient to halakhah, halakhah is ultimately dependent upon agadah. Halakhah, the rationalization of living, is not only forced to employ elements which are themselves unreasoned; its ultimate authority depends upon agadah. For what is the basis of halakhah? The event at Sinai, the mystery of revelation, belongs to the sphere of agadah. Thus while the content of halakhah is subject to its own reasoning, its authority is derived from agadah.

Halakhah does not deal with the ultimate level of existence. The law does not create in us the motivation to love and to fear God, nor is it capable of endowing us with the power to overcome evil and to resist its temptations, nor with the loyalty to fulfill its precepts. It supplies the weapons, it points the way; the fighting is left to the soul of man.

The code of conduct is like the score to a musician. Rules, principles, forms may be taught; insight, feeling, the sense of rhythm must come from within. Ultimately, then, the goal of religious life is quality rather than quantity, not only *what* is done, but *how* it is done.

Obedience to the letter of the law regulates our daily living, but such obedience must not stultify the spontaneity of our inner life. When the law becomes petrified and our observance mechanical, we in fact violate and distort its very spirit. He who does not know that observance of the law means constant decision is a *foolish pietist.* "What is a foolish pietist? A woman is drowning in the river, and he says: It is improper for me to look upon her and rescue her."[4]

30. Halakhah and Agadah

Halakhah is an *answer* to a question, namely: What does God ask of me? The moment that question dies in the heart, the answer becomes meaningless. That question, however, is agadic, spontaneous, personal. It is an outburst of insight, longing, faith. It is not given; it must come about. The task of religious teaching is to be a midwife and bring about the birth of the question. Many religious teachers are guilty of ignoring the vital role of the question and condoning spiritual sterility. But the soul is never calm. Every human being is pregnant with problems in a preconceptual form. Most of us do not know how to phrase our quest for meaning, our concern for the ultimate. Without guidance, our concern for the ultimate is not thought through and what we express is premature and penultimate, a miscarriage of the spirit.

The question is not immutable in form. Every generation must express the question in its own way. In this sense agadah may be employed as denoting all religious thinking in the tradition of Judaism.

It would be a fatal error to isolate the law, to disconnect it from the perplexities, cravings, and aspirations of the soul, from spontaneity and the totality of the person. In the spiritual crisis of the modern Jew the problem of faith takes precedence over the problem of law. Without faith, inwardness and the power of appreciation, the law is meaningless.

To reduce Judaism to inwardness, to agadah, is to blot out its light, to dissolve its essence and to destroy its reality. Indeed, the surest way to forfeit agadah is to abolish halakhah. They can only survive in symbiosis. Without halakhah agadah loses its substance, its character, its source of inspiration, its security against becoming secularized.

By inwardness alone we do not come close to God. The purest intentions, the finest sense of devotion, the noblest spiritual aspirations are fatuous when not realized in action. Spiritualism is a way for angels, not for man. There is only one function that can take place without the aid of external means: dreaming. When dreaming, man is almost detached from concrete reality. Yet spiritual life is not a dream and is in constant need of action. Action is the verification of the spirit. Does friendship consist of mere emotion? Of indulgence in feeling? Is it not always in need of tangible, material means of expression? The life of the spirit too needs concrete actions for its actualization. The body must not be left alone; the spirit must be fulfilled in the flesh. The spirit is decisive; but it is life, all of life, where the spirit is at stake. To consecrate our tongue and our hands we need extraordinary means of pedagogy.

It is impossible to decide whether in Judaism supremacy belongs to halakhah or to agadah, to the lawgiver or to the Psalmist. The rabbis may have sensed the problem. Rav said: The world was created for the sake of David, so that he might sing hymns and psalms to God. Samuel said:

177

The world was created for the sake of Moses, so that he might receive the Torah.[5]

A view of the supremacy of agadah is reflected in the following tradition: It is said of Rabbi Yohanan ben Zakkai that his studies included all fields of Jewish learning, *great matters or small matters. Great matters* mean *maaseh merkavah* (mystical doctrines), *small matters* the discussions of *Abaye* and *Rava* (legal interpretations).[6] Here the study of the law is called "a small matter" compared with the study of mystical wisdom.

Maimonides, one of the greatest scholars of the law of all times, declares: "It is more precious to me to teach some of the fundamentals of our religion than any of the other things I study."[7]

Jewish thinking and living can only be adequately understood in terms of a dialectic pattern, containing opposite or contrasted properties. As in a magnet, the ends of which have opposite magnetic qualities, these terms are opposite to one another and exemplify a *polarity* which lies at the very heart of Judaism, the polarity of ideas and events, of mitzvah and sin, of kavvanah and deed, of regularity and spontaneity, of uniformity and individuality, of halakhah and agadah, of law and inwardness, of love and fear, of understanding and obedience, of joy and discipline, of the good and the evil drive, of time and eternity, of this world and the world to come, of revelation and response, of insight and information, of empathy and self-expression, of creed and faith, of the word and that which is beyond words, of man's quest for God and God in search of man. Even God's relation to the world is characterized by the polarity of justice and mercy, providence and concealment, the promise of reward and the demand to serve Him for His sake. Taken abstractedly, all these terms seem to be mutually exclusive, yet in actual living they involve each other; the separation of the two is fatal to both. There is no halakhah without agadah, and no agadah without halakhah. We must neither disparage the body nor sacrifice the spirit. The body is the discipline, the pattern, the law; the spirit is inner devotion, spontaneity, freedom. The body without the spirit is a corpse; the spirit without the body is a ghost. Thus a mitzvah is both a discipline and an inspiration, an act of obedience and an experience of joy, a yoke and a prerogative. Our task is to learn how to maintain a harmony between the demands of halakhah and the spirit of agadah.

Since each of the two principles moves in the opposite direction, equilibrium can only be maintained if both are of equal force. But such a condition is rarely attained. Polarity is an essential trait of all things. Tension, contrast, and contradiction characterize all of reality. In the language of the *Zohar*, this world is called *alma deperuda,* "the world of separation." Discrepancy, contention, ambiguity, and ambivalence afflict all of life, including the study of the Torah; even the sages of the Talmud disagree on many details of the law.[8]

The tension between regularity and spontaneity, between the fixed pattern of the law and the inwardness of the person, has often been a source of embarrassment and agony. We are not always ready to rise to a level from which we could respond, for example, to the grandeur of our liturgy. But the law expects us to confront that grandeur thrice daily. The words, the forms, remain the same, yet we are told that a sacred act should be done for the first time, as it were. The voice proclaimed: "These words which I command thee *this day* shall be upon thy heart" (Deuteronomy 6:6). "They are not to be regarded as an old set of ordinances . . . but as new words toward which men eagerly rush to hear them"; new as if they were given *this day, today.*[9]

Trying to remain loyal to both aspects of Jewish living, we discover that the pole of regularity is stronger than the pole of spontaneity, and, as a result, there is a perpetual danger of our observance and worship becoming mere habit, a mechanical performance. The fixed pattern and regularity of our services tend to stifle the spontaneity of devotion. Our great problem, therefore, is how not to let the principle of regularity (keva) impair the power of spontaneity (kavvanah). It is a problem that concerns the very heart of religious living, and is as easy to solve as other central problems of existence. It is a part of human freedom to face that challenge and to create an answer in every situation, every day of our life. Palliatives may be found, but no cure to polarity is available in this "world of separation."

The simplest way to obviate the problem is to abrogate the principle of regularity, to worship only when we are touched by the spirit and to observe only what is relevant to our minds. But in abrogating regularity we deplete spontaneity. Our spiritual resources are not inexhaustible. What may seem to be spontaneous is in truth a response to an occasion. The soul would remain silent if it were not for the summons and reminder of the law. There may be moments in which the soul fails to respond, but abiding at the threshold of the holy we are unconsciously affected by its power.

We cannot rely on the inspirations of the heart if we detach ourselves from the inspiration of the prophets. Our own moments of illumination are brief, sporadic, and rare. In the long interims the mind is often dull, bare, and vapid. There is hardly a soul that can radiate more light than it receives. To perform a mitzvah is to meet the spirit. The spirit, however, is not something we can acquire once and for all but something we must be with. For this reason the Jewish way of life is to reiterate the ritual, to meet the spirit again and again, the spirit in oneself and the spirit that hovers over all beings.

The way to kavvanah is through the deed; the way of faith is a way of living. Halakhah and agadah are correlated: halakhah is the string, agadah is the bow. When the string is tight the bow will evoke the melody. But the string may jar in the fumbler's hand.

Being bound to an order and stability of observance, to a discipline of worship at set hours and fixed forms is a celestial routine. Nature does not cease to be natural because of its being subject to regularity of seasons. Loyalty to external forms, dedication of the will is itself a form of worship. The mitzvot sustain their halo even when our minds forget to light in us the attentiveness to the holy. The path of loyalty to the routine of sacred living runs along the borderline of the spirit; though being outside, one remains very close to the spirit. Routine holds us in readiness for the moments in which the soul enters into accord with the spirit.

While love is hibernating, our loyal deeds speak. It is right that the good actions should become a habit, that the preference of justice should become our second nature; even though it is not native to the self. A good person is not he who does the right thing, but he who is in the habit of doing the right thing.

What lends meaning to the acts of ritual is not only the particular intention which is cotemporal with the acts but primarily the decision of faith to accept the ritual way of living. It is that decision—*the general intention,* the basic kavvanah—and the accumulated insight throughout many moments of religious experience that bestows devotional meaning upon all ritual acts of our life.

The problem of particular kavvanah is *secondary* to the problem of *general piety.* Love and fear at all times decide the value of every particular act.

It is true that a person may know the acts of loving-kindness, without always knowing the spirit of loving-kindness. Yet it also is true that acts are a challenge to the soul. Indeed, one must be deliberately callous to remain forever deaf to the spirit of the acts he is engaged in performing day after day, year after year. How else can one learn the joy of loving-kindness, if not by enacting it?

Deeds not only follow intention; they also engender kavvanah. There is no static polarity of kavvanah and deed, of devotion and action. The deed may bring out what is dormant in the mind, and acts in which an idea is lived, moments which are filled with dedication make us eloquent in a way which is not open to the naked mind. Kavvanah comes into being with the deed. Actions teach.

31. THE MEANING OF OBSERVANCE

A serious difficulty is the problem of the meaning of Jewish observance. The modern Jew cannot accept the way of static obedience as a short cut to the mystery of the divine will. His religious situation is not conducive to an attitude of intellectual or spiritual surrender. He is not ready to sacrific his liberty on the altar of loyalty to the spirit of his ancestors. He will only respond to a demonstration that there is meaning to be found in what is expected of him. His primary difficulty is not in his inability to comprehend *the divine origin* of the law; his essential difficulty is in his inability to sense *the presence of divine meaning* in the fulfillment of the law.

There are many perspectives from which observance may be judged. The sociological: does it contribute to the good of society or to the survival of the people? The esthetic: does it enhance our sense of form and beauty? The moral: does it help us to realize the good? There is also the dogmatic: observance is the will of God and no other justification is called for. Since Jewish observance embraces the totality of existence, a *synoptic approach* would bring forth its relevance in terms of all higher values, and would open a comprehensive view of its meaning.

Judaism is concerned with the happiness of the individual as well as with the survival of the Jewish people, with the redemption of all men and with the will of one God. It claims, however, that happiness is contingent upon faithfulness to God; that the unique importance of the survival of the people is in its being a partner to a covenant with God; that the redemption of all men depends upon their serving His will. The perspective, therefore, from which the individual, the community and all mankind are judged is that of religious insight and conviction. Without minimizing the profound relevance of other perspectives, we will try to answer the question of how observance is related to religious insight.

The problem of how to live as a Jew cannot be solved in terms of common sense and common experience. The order of Jewish living is a spiritual one; it has a spiritual logic of its own which cannot be apprehended unless its basic terms are lived and appreciated. Its meaning can be better comprehended in personal response than in detached definitions. Life must be *earned spiritually*, not only materially. We must keep alive the sense of wonder through deeds of wonder.

181

What kind of meaning do we look for? There is no understanding of meaning as such. Meaning is always related to a system of meanings. The kind of meaning we look for depends on the kind of system we choose. The most common system is that of psychology. A mitzvah is considered to be meaningful when proved to be capable of satisfying a personal need.

However, the essence of religion does not lie in the satisfaction of a human need. As long as man sees religion as a source of satisfaction for his own needs, it is not God whom he serves but his own self. Such satisfaction can be obtained from civilization, which supplies abundant means to gratify our needs.

Indeed, most of our attention is given to the expedient, to that which is conducive to our advantage and which would enhance our ability to exploit the resources of this planet. If our philosophy were a projection of man's actual behavior, we would have to define the value of the earth as a source of supply for our industries, and the ocean as a fish pond. However, as we have seen, there is more than one aspect of nature that commands our attention. We go out to meet the world not only by the way of expediency but also by the way of wonder. In the first we accumulate information in order to dominate; in the second we deepen our appreciation in order to respond. Power is the language of expediency; poetry the language of wonder.

He who goes to pray is not intent upon enhancing his store of knowledge; he who performs a ritual does not expect to advance his interests. Sacred deeds are designed to make living *compatible with our sense of the ineffable*. The mitzvot are forms of expressing in deeds the appreciation of the ineffable. They are terms of the spirit in which we allude to that which is beyond reason. To look for rational explanations, to scrutinize the mitzvot in terms of common sense is to quench their intrinsic meaning. What would be the value of proving that the observance of the dietary laws is helpful in the promotion of health, that keeping the Sabbath is conducive to happiness? It is not *utility* that we seek in religion but *eternity*. The criterion of religion is not in its being in agreement with our *common sense* but in its being compatible with our *sense of the ineffable*. The purpose of religion is not to satisfy the needs we feel but to create in us the need of serving ends, of which we otherwise remain oblivious.

The problem of ethics is, what is the ideal or principle of conduct that is *rationally* justifiable? To religion the problem of living is, what is the ideal or principle of living that is *spiritually* justifiable? The legitimate question concerning the forms of Jewish observance is the question: Are they spiritually meaningful?

We should, therefore, not evaluate the mitzvot by the amount of rational meaning we may discover at their basis. Religion is not within but beyond the limits of mere reason; its task is not to compete with reason, to be a source of speculative ideas, but to aid us where reason is of little aid. Its meaning must be understood in terms compatible with the sense of the ineffable. Frequently, where concepts fail, where rational understanding ends, the meaning of observance begins. Its purpose is not to serve hygiene, happiness, or the vitality of man; its purpose is to add holiness to hygiene, grandeur to happiness, spirit to vitality.

Indeed, any reason we may advance for our loyalty to the Jewish order of living merely points to one of its many facets. To say that the mitzvot have meaning is less accurate than saying that they lead us to wells of emergent meaning, to experiences which are full of hidden brilliance of the holy, suddenly blazing in our thoughts.

Those who, in order to save the Jewish way of life, bring its meaning under the hammer, sell it in the end to the lowest bidder. The highest values are not in demand and are not saleable on the marketplace.

Works of piety are like works of art. They are functional, they serve a purpose, but their essence is intrinsic. A mitzvah is the perpetuation of an insight or an act of bringing together the passing with the everlasting, the momentary with the eternal.

If insights of the individual are to be conveyed to others and to become a part of social life, or even if they are to be stored up effectively for one's own future understanding, they must assume the forms of deeds, of mitzvot.

Religion without mitzvot is an experience without the power of expression, a sense of mystery without the power of sanctification; a question without an answer.

Explanations for the mitzvot are like insights of art criticism; the interpretation can never rival the creative acts of the artist. Reason in the realm of religion is like a whetstone that makes iron sharp, as the saying goes, though unable itself to cut.

Explanations of the mitzvot come and go; theories change with the temper of the age, but the song of the mitzvot continues. Explanations are translations; they are both useful and inadequate. A translator of the Iliad into German once remarked, "Dear reader, study Greek and throw my translation into the fire." The same applies to the holy: explanations are not substitutes.

Significantly, the Hebrew term for the explanation of the mitzvot is *ta'am,* or *ta'ame hamitzvot.* Yet *ta'am* means also taste, or flavor. It is the flavor that a person perceives in doing a mitzvah which communicates its meaning.

The true meaning is not to be found in a stagnant concept, fixed and determined once and for all. The exclusive meaning-flavor is not something formulations can convey. It is born with the act of fulfillment, and our appreciation grows with our experience.

Mitzvot are not only expressions of meanings given once and for all, but ways of evoking new meaning again and again. They are acts of inspiration rather than acts of compliance. They are the songs that express our wonder.

How must man, a being who is in essence the likeness of God, think, feel, and act? How can he live in a way compatible with the presence of God? Unless we are aware of the problem, we are unable to appreciate the answer.

All mitzvot are means of evoking in us the awareness of living in the neighborhood of God, of living in the holy dimension. They call to mind the inconspicuous mystery of things and acts, and are reminders of our being the stewards, rather than the landlords of the universe; reminders of the fact that man does not live in a spiritual wilderness, that *every act* of man is an encounter of the human and the holy.

All mitzvot first of all express reverence. They are indications of our awareness of God's eternal presence, celebrating His presence in action. The benedictions are in the present tense. We say, "Blessed be Thou Who *creates . . . Who brings forth.*" To say a benediction is to be aware of His continuous creation.

What are all prophetic utterances if not an expression of God's anxiety for man and His concern with man's integrity? A reminder of God's stake in human life; a reminder that there is no privacy? No one can conceal himself, no one can be out of His sight. He dwells with Israel "in the midst of their uncleanness" (Leviticus 16:16). Living is not a private affair of the individual. Living is what man does with God's time, what man does with God's world.

To the vulgar mind, a deed consists of the self trying to exploit the non-self. To the pious man, a deed is an encounter of the human and the holy, of man's will and God's world. Both are hewn from the same rock and destined to be parts of one great mosaic.

There is no dichotomy between the happiness of man and the designs of God. To discover the absence of that dichotomy, to live that identity, is the true reward of religious living. God shares man's joy, if man is open to God's concern. The satisfaction of a human need is a dedication to a divine end.

31. The Meaning of Observance

The world is torn by conflicts, by folly, by hatred. Our task is to cleanse, to illumine, to repair. Every deed is either a clash or an aid in the effort of redemption. Man is not one with God, not even with his true self. Our task is to bring eternity into time, to clear in the wilderness a way, to make plain in the desert a highway for God. "Happy is the man in whose heart are the highways" (Psalm 84:6). Before fulfilling a mitzvah we pray: "Blessed be Thou . . . Who hast sanctified us with His mitzvot . . ." The meaning of a mitzvah is in its power of sanctification.

What is a sacred deed? An encounter with the divine; a way of living in fellowship with God; a flash of holiness in the darkness of profanity; the birth of greater love; endowment with deeper sensibility.

The mitzvot are formative. The soul grows by noble deeds. The soul is illumined by sacred acts. Indeed, the purpose of all mitzvot is to refine man.[1] They were given for the benefit of man: to protect and to ennoble him, to discipline and to inspire him. We ennoble the self by disclosing the divine. God is hiding in the world and our task is to let the divine emerge from our deeds.

To do a mitzvah is to outdo oneself, to go beyond one's own needs and to illumine the world. But whence should come fire to illumine the world? Time and again we discover how blank, how dim and abrupt is the light that comes from within. There is not enough strength within our power to transcend ourselves, to ensoul our deeds. Our strenuous effort is too feeble to outsoar the petty movements of the ego.

But there is *an ecstasy of deeds,* luminous moments in which we are raised by overpowering deeds above our own will; moments filled with outgoing joy, with intense delight. Such exaltation is a gift. To him who strives with heart and soul to give himself to God and who succeeds as far as is *within his power,* the gates of greatness break open and he is able to attain that which is *beyond his power.*[2]

The gift of greatness does not come to those who do not toil to shatter their own smallness. The mitzvah does not conjure holiness out of nothing, it only adds to what man contributes. Nothing will light the wonder in us, when our craving is dormant and our heart both dim and content. We must render kindness to acquire goodness; we must do the good to attain the holy.

The following may be used as an illustration of this thought. "A man planted trees, trimmed their roots, cleared the soil of thorns and weeds, watered the trees when necessary, and applied fertilizers to them; then he prays to God that the trees should yield fruit. But if he neglects tending them and looking after them, he does not deserve that the Creator, blessed be He, should give him fruit from them."[3]

The spark of man may be enhanced and inflamed by a flash of God. "If a man sanctifies himself a little, he becomes greatly sanctified. If he sanctify himself below, he becomes sanctified from above."⁴ Holiness is not exclusively the product of the soul but the outcome of moments in which God and soul meet in the light of a good deed.

32. MITZVAH AND SIN

If the frequency and intensity with which a word is used may serve as an index of its importance to the mentality of a people, then the word *"mitzvah"* is one of supreme importance. Indeed, the role of the term mitzvah in both Hebrew and Yiddish is almost without parallel. Just as *salvation* is the central concept in Christian piety, so does *mitzvah* serve as a focus of Jewish religious consciousness. It is, next to Torah, the basic term of Judaism, serving as a general name for both positive and negative rules, for both directives and restrictions.

A definition or paraphrase of the word mitzvah is difficult to frame. In other languages there are separate words for the different meanings which in Hebrew are conveyed by the single word "mitzvah." It denotes not only commandment, but also *the law,* man's *obligation* to fulfill the law, and *the act* of fulfilling the obligation or the deed, particularly an act of benevolence or charity.

Its meanings range from the acts performed by the high priest in the Temple to the most humble gesture of kindness to one's fellow man, from acts of external performance to inner attitudes, in relation to others as well as in relation to oneself. It is often used in the wide sense of *religion* or *religious.* It combines all levels of human and spiritual living. Every act done in agreement with the will of God is a mitzvah.¹

But the scope of meaning of the word mitzvah is even wider. Beyond the meanings it denotes—namely commandment, law, obligation, and deed—it connotes numerous attributes which are implied in addition to its primary meanings. It has the connotation of goodness, value, virtue, meritoriousness, piety, and even holiness. Thus while it is possible to say good, virtuous, valuable, meritorious, pious, or holy deed, it would be a tautology to say a good, meritorious, pious, or holy mitzvah.

The basic term of Jewish living is "mitzvah" rather than "law" (*din*). Even the sin of Adam and Eve was described as a loss of a mitzvah. After

186

the forbidden fruit, we are told, their eyes were unclosed and "they knew that they were naked" (Genesis 3:7). "One mitzvah was entrusted to them, and they had stripped themselves of it."[2]

To the mind of the Jew mitzvah bears more reality and is a term more frequently and more prominently used than *averah*. In the Christian vocabulary the frequency and importance of the two terms is just the reverse. Christianity has not taken over the idea of mitzvah and, as we have seen, there is no precise equivalent for it in Western languages. On the other hand, the term "sin" has assumed the connotation of something substantial, a meaning not implied in *averah*.

Life revolves around the right and the wrong deed, but we have been trained to be more *mitzvah-conscious* than *averah* or sin-conscious.

Both poles, mitzvah and sin, are real. We are taught to be *mitzvah-conscious* in regard to the present moment, to be mindful of the constant opportunity to do the good. We are also taught to be *sin-conscious* in regard to the past, to realize and to remember our failures and transgressions. The power of both mitzvah and sin must be fully apprehended. The exclusive fear of sin may lead to a deprecation of works; the exclusive appreciation of mitzvah may lead to self-righteousness. The first may result in a denial of the relevance of history, in an overly eschatological view; the second in a denial of Messianism, in a secular optimism. Against both deviations Judaism warns repeatedly.

Two things must always be present to our minds: God and our own sins (Psalms 16:8; 51:5). Three times daily we pray, *Forgive us, our Father, for we have sinned; pardon us, our King, for we have transgressed.* According to a Talmudic saying, every soul when about to be born into this world, is admonished: "Be righteous, and be never wicked; and even if all the world tells you, 'you are righteous' consider yourself wicked."[3] Indeed, "who can say: I have made my heart clean, I am pure from my sin?" (Proverbs 20:9).

The burden of sins is light to those who are oblivious. It was not light to him who said, "Out of the depths have I called Thee, O Lord. . . . If Thou shouldst mark iniquities, who could stand?" (Psalms 130:1,3).

Twice daily we are told, "Do not follow after your own heart and your own eyes, which you are inclined to go after wantonly" (Numbers 15:39). The house of Israel says, "Our transgressions and our sins are upon us, and we waste away because of them; how, then, can we live?" (Ezekiel 33:10). Indeed, "we are neither so arrogant nor so hardened as to say before Thee, O Lord our God and God of our fathers, 'we are righteous and have not sinned'; verily, we have sinned" (The liturgy of the Day of Atonement).

We fail and sin not only in our deeds. We also fail and sin in our hearts.

187

Evil in the heart is the source of evil in deeds. The envy of Cain, the greed of the generation of the Flood, the pride of those who built the Tower of Babel brought misery upon mankind. "Envy, greed, and pride destroy the lives of man."[4] Indeed, this is the diagnosis of the human situation: "The Lord saw that the wickedness of man was great in the earth, and that every drive of the thought of his heart was only evil continually" (Genesis 6:5).

"The wickedness of man" may refer to sinful deeds, but the central part of the diagnosis, repeated in Genesis 8:21, refers to "the drive of the heart." The only one of the Ten Commandments which is said twice and with which they are concluded is: Thou shalt not covet.

Daily we pray, *My God, the soul which Thou hast placed within me is pure.* What must we do to keep it pure? How shall we maintain our integrity in a world where power, success, and money are valued above all else? How shall we control "envy, greed, and pride"? "Thou hast given me a holy soul, but through my deeds I have defiled it," exclaimed Ibn Gabirol.[5]

The emphasis upon the consciousness of mitzvah must not in any way weaken our attentiveness to the fact that we are always ready to betray Him, that even while engaged in a righteous act we are exposed to sin. "Be not sure of thyself till the day of thy death," said Hillel.[6] We have been taught that man may be impregnated with the spirit of the holy all the days of his life, yet one moment of carelessness is sufficient to plunge him in the abyss. *There is but one step between me and death* (I Samuel 20:3).

Life is lived on a spiritual battlefield. Man must constantly struggle with "the evil drive," "for man is like unto a rope, one end of which is pulled by God and the other end by Satan." "Woe to me for my *yotzer* [Creator], woe to me for my *yetzer* [the evil drive]," says a Talmudic epigram.[7] If a man yield to his lower impulses, he is accountable to his Creator; if he obey his Creator, then he is plagued by sinful thoughts.

Should we, then, despair because of our being unable to retain perfect purity? We should, if perfection were our goal. However, we are not obliged to be perfect once and for all, but only to rise again and again beyond the level of the self. Perfection is divine, and to make it a goal of man is to call on man to be divine. All we can do is to try to wring our hearts clean in *contrition.* Contrition begins with a feeling of shame at our being incapable of disentanglement from the self. To be contrite at our failures is holier than to be complacent in perfection.

In the world of Jewish piety two voices may be heard. One voice is severe, uncompromising: good deeds done out of impure motives are entirely inadequate.[8] The other voice is one of moderation: good deeds are precious even if their motivation is not pure.[9]

What are the facts? Even the finest intention is not strong enough to fill all corners of the soul which at all sides is open to intrusions of the ego. Judged by the severe, uncompromising standard of total purity of intention, who could stand? It is, indeed, the voice of moderation that has generally prevailed. Thus we are taught to believe that "alien thoughts" or even improper motives do not vitiate the value of a sacred deed.

The soul is frail, but God is full of compassion for the distress of the soul, for the failure of the heart. It is said in the Talmud: "There are some who desire [to help others] but have not the means; whilst others have the means [and help] but have not the desire [to help]." Yet both kinds of people are holy in the eyes of God.[10]

Judaism insists upon the deed and hopes for the intention. Every morning we pray:

Make sweet, we beseech thee, O Lord our God, the words of Thy Torah in our mouth . . . so that we study Thy Torah *for its own sake.*

While constantly keeping the goal in mind, we are taught that one must continue to observe the law even when one is not ready to fulfill it "for the sake of God." For the good, even if it is not done for its own sake, will teach us eventually how to act for the sake of God. We must continue to perform the sacred deeds even though we may be compelled to bribe the self with human incentives. Purity of motivation is the goal; constancy of action is the way. It is useless endeavor to fight the ego in the open; like a wounded hydra, it produces two heads for every one cut off. We must not indulge in self-scrutinization; we must not concentrate upon the problem of egocentricity. The way to purify the self is to avoid dwelling upon the self and to concentrate upon the task.

Any religious or ethical teaching that places the main emphasis upon the virtues of inwardness such as faith and the purity of motivation must come to grief. If faith were the only standard, the effort of man would be doomed to failure. Indeed, the awareness of the weakness of the heart; the unreliability of human inwardness may perhaps have been one of the reasons that compelled Judaism to take recourse to actions instead of relying upon inward devotion. Perhaps this is the deeper meaning of the rabbis' counsel: one should always do the good, even though it is not done for its own sake. It is the act that teaches us the meaning of the act.

The way to pure intention is paved with good deeds. The good is carried out in acts, and there is an intense fascination that comes from a good deed counteracting the pressure and ardor of the ego. The ego is de-deemed by the absorbing power and the inexorable provocativeness of a just task which we face. It is the deed that carries us away, that transports the soul, proving to us that the greatest beauty grows at the greatest distance from the center of the ego.

Deeds set upon ideal goals, deeds performed not with careless ease and routine but in exertion and submission to their ends are stronger than the surprise and attack of caprice. Serving sacred goals may change mean motives. For such deeds are exacting. Whatever our motive may have been prior to the act, the act itself demands undivided attention. Thus the desire for reward is not the driving force of the poet in his creative moments, and the pursuit of pleasure or profit is not the essence of a religious or moral act.

At the moment in which an artist is absorbed in playing a concerto the thought of applause, fame or remuneration is far from his mind. His complete attention, his whole being is involved in the music. Should any extraneous thought enter his mind, it would arrest his concentration and mar the purity of his playing. The reward may have been on his mind when he negotiated with his agent, but during the performance it is the music that claims his complete concentration.

Man's situation in carrying out a religious or moral deed is similar. Left alone, the soul is subject to caprice. Yet there is power in the deed that purifies desires. It is the act, life itself, that educates the will. The good motive comes into being while doing the good.

If the initial motive is strong and pure, obtrusive intentions which emerge during the act may even serve to invigorate it, for the initial motive may absorb the vigor of the intruder into its own strength. Man may be replete with selfish motives but a deed and God are stronger than selfish motives. The redemptive power discharged in carrying out the good purifies the mind. The deed is wiser than the heart.

A disciple of the Rabbi Mendel of Kotzk complained to his master of his inability to worship God without becoming self-conscious and tinged with a sense of pride. Is there a way of worship in which the self does not intrude? he asked.

—Have you ever encountered a wolf while walking alone in the forest?

—I did, he retorted.

—What was on your mind at that moment?

—Fear, nothing but fear and the will to escape.

—You see, in such a moment you were in fear without being conscious or proud of your fear. It is in such a way that we may worship God.

Though deeply aware of how impure and imperfect all our deeds are, the fact of our doing must be cherished as the highest privilege, as a source of joy, as that which endows life with ultimate preciousness. We believe that moments lived in fellowship with God, acts fulfilled in imitation of God's will, never perish; the validity of the good remains regardless of all impurity.

Traditionally, the Jew is taught to feel delight in being able to fulfill the law, albeit imperfectly, rather than to feel anxiety because of his being unable to fulfill it perfectly. "Serve Him with joy; come before His presence with singing" (Psalms 100:2).

Israel feels a certain ease and delight in the fulfillment of the law which to a hired servant is burdensome and perplexing. For "the son who serves his father serves him with joy, saying, Even if I do not entirely succeed [in carrying out His commandments], yet, as a loving father, He will not be angry with me. In contrast, a hired servant is always afraid lest he may commit some fault, and therefore serves God in a condition of anxiety and confusion." Indeed, when Israel feels uneasy because of their having to stand in judgment before God, the angels say unto them, "Fear ye not the judgment. . . . Know ye not Him? He is your next of kin, He is your brother, and what is more, He is your father."[11]

33. THE PROBLEM OF EVIL

There are those who sense the ultimate question in moments of wonder, in moments of joy; there are those who sense the ultimate question in moments of horror, in moments of despair. It is both the grandeur and the misery of living that makes man sensitive to the ultimate question. Indeed, his misery is as great as his grandeur.

How did Abraham arrive at his certainty that there is a God who is concerned with the world? Said Rabbi Isaac: Abraham may be "compared to a man who was traveling from place to place when he saw *a palace in flames*. Is it possible that there is no one who cares for the palace? he wondered. Until the owner of the palace looked at him and said, 'I am the owner of the palace.' Similarly, Abraham our father wondered, 'Is it conceivable that the world is without a guide?' The Holy One, blessed be He, looked out and said, 'I am the Guide, the Sovereign of the world.' "[1]

The world is in flames, consumed by evil. Is it possible that there is no one who cares?

There is one line that expresses the mood of the Jewish man throughout the ages: "The earth is given into the hand of the wicked" (Job 9:24).

How does the world look in the eyes of God? Are we ever told: the Lord saw that the righteousness of man was great in the earth? That He was glad to have made man on the earth? The general tone of the Biblical view of history is set after the first ten generations: "The Lord saw the wickedness of man was great in the earth . . . And the Lord was sorry that He had made man on the earth, and it grieved Him to His heart" (Genesis 6:5–6, cf. 8:21). One great cry resounds throughout the Bible: The wickedness of man is great on the earth.

The experience of the easy and endless opportunities for evil, and the awareness of the dreadful danger, threatens to outweigh all delight of living. The answer to that danger is either despair or the question: God, where art Thou? "Where is the God of justice?" (Malachi 2:17).

This essential predicament of man has assumed a peculiar urgency in our time, living as we do in a civilization where factories were established in order to exterminate millions of men, women, and children; where soap was made of human flesh. What have we done to make such crimes possible? What are we doing to make such crimes impossible?

Modern man may be characterized as a being who is callous to catastrophes. A victim of enforced brutalization, his sensibility is being increasingly reduced; his sense of horror is on the wane. The distinction between right and wrong is becoming blurred. All that is left to us is our being horrified at the loss of our sense of horror.

Even more frustrating than the fact that evil is real, mighty and tempting is the fact that it thrives so well in the disguise of the good, that it can draw its nutriment from the life of the holy. In this world, it seems, the holy and the unholy do not exist apart, but are mixed, interrelated and confounded. It is a world where idols may be rich in beauty, and where the worship of God may be tinged with wickedness.

It was not the lack of religion but the perversion of it that the prophets of Israel denounced. "Many an altar has Ephraim raised, altars that only serve for sin" (Hosea 8:11). "The priests said not: Where is the Lord? And they that handle the law knew Me not" (Jeremiah 2:8). The greater the man, the more he is exposed to sin.[2] Piety is at times evil in disguise, an instrument in the pursuit of power. "The tragedies in human history, the cruelties and fanaticisms, have not been caused by the criminals . . . but by the good people . . . by idealists who did not understand the strange mixture of self-interest and ideals which is compounded in all human motives." The great contest is not "between God-fearing believers

192

and unrighteous unbelievers." Biblical religion has emphasized "the *inequality of guilt* just as much as the equality of sin." "Especially severe judgments fall upon the rich and the powerful, the mighty and the noble, the wise and the righteous."[3] Indeed the most horrible manifestation of evil is when it acts in the guise of good. "Such monstrous evil deeds could religion urge man to commit" (Lucretius).

The dreadful confusion, the fact that there is nothing in this world that is not a mixture of good and evil, of holy and unholy, of silver and dross, is, according to Jewish mysticism, the central problem of history and the ultimate issue of redemption. The confusion goes back to the very process of creation.

"When God came to create the world and reveal what was hidden in the depths and disclose the light out of darkness, they were all wrapped in one another, and therefore light emerged from darkness, and from the impenetrable came forth the profound. So, too, from good issues evil and from mercy issues judgment, and all are intertwined, the good impulse and the evil impulse. . . ."[4]

There are no easy solutions for problems that are at the same time intensely personal and universal, urgent and eternal. Technological progress creates more problems than it solves. Efficiency experts or social engineering will not redeem humanity. Important as their contributions may be, they do not reach the heart of the problem. Religion, therefore, with its demands and visions, is not a luxury but a matter of life and death. True, its message is often diluted and distorted by pedantry, externalization, ceremonialism, and superstition. But this precisely is our task: to recall the urgencies, the perpetual emergencies of human existence, the rare cravings of the spirit, the eternal voice of God, to which the demands of religion are an answer.

The power to make distinctions is a primary operation of intelligence. We distinguish between white and black, beautiful and ugly, pleasant and unpleasant, gain and loss, good and evil, right and wrong. The fate of mankind depends upon the realization that the distinction between good and evil, right and wrong, is superior to all other distinctions. As long as such realization is lacking, pleasantness in alliance with evil will be preferred to unpleasantness in alliance with good. To teach humanity the primacy of that distinction is of the essence to the Biblical message.

The ego is a powerful rival of the good. When coupled with gain, when virtue pays, the good has a chance to prevail. When the good is to be realized at a loss, with no reward, it is easily defeated. Now, since it is of the essence of virtue that the good is not to be done for the sake of a reward, what is the chance of the good ever to prevail over the interests of the ego? Who is our help in the struggle with evil?

Does not goodness tend to turn impotent in the face of temptations? Crime, vice, sin offer us rewards; while virtue demands self-restraint, self-denial. Sin is thrilling and full of excitement. Is virtue thrilling? Are there many mystery stories that describe virtue? Are there many best-selling novels that portray adventures in goodness?

If the nature of man were all we had, then surely the outlook would be dim. But we also have the aid of God, the commandment, the mitzvah. The central Biblical fact is *Sinai*, the covenant, the word of God. Sinai was superimposed on the failure of Adam. The fact that we were given the knowledge of His will is a sign of some ability to cope with evil. The voice is more than a challenge. It is powerful enough to shake the wilderness of the soul, to strip the ego bare, to flash forth His will like fire.

To the Jew, Sinai is at stake in every act of man, and the supreme issue is not good and evil but God, and His commandment to love good and to hate evil; not the sinfulness of man but the commandment of God.

"The Lord created the evil inclination in man and He created the Torah to temper it."[5] The life of man was compared with "a lonely settlement which was kept in disorder by invading bands. What did the king do? He appointed a commander to protect it." The Torah is a safeguard, the Torah is an antidote.[6]

We are never alone in our struggle with evil. A mitzvah, unlike the concept of duty, is not anonymous and impersonal. To do a mitzvah is to give an answer to His will, to respond to what He expects of us. This is why an act of mitzvah is preceded by a prayer: "Blessed be Thou . . ."

What is a mitzvah? A prayer in the form of a deed. And to pray is to sense His presence. "In all thy ways thou shalt know Him." Prayer should be part of all our ways. It does not have to be always on our lips; it must always be on our minds, in our hearts.

In the light of the Bible, the good is more than a value; it is a *divine concern,* a way of God. This is the profound implication of the oneness of God: all deeds are relevant to Him. He is present in all our deeds. "The Lord is good to all and His compassion is over all that He has made" (Psalms 145:10). There is no reverence for God without reverence for man. Love of man is the way to the love of God. The fear lest we hurt a poor man must be as deep as the fear of God, for *He that oppresses the poor blasphemes his maker, but he who is gracious unto the needy honors Him* (Proverbs 14:31).

What we are discussing as a moral issue is but an aspect of the larger metaphysical problem about the relation of good and evil. Which of the two is self-subsistent? Is good ultimately a parasite on the body of evil? Or is it just the opposite: is it evil that lives as a parasite on the body of the good?

In our intellectual climate there seems to be only one answer to that problem. Ideals have a high mortality rate in our generation. Contemporary thinking looks like a graveyard of discredited ideals. With his moral efforts man, it is felt, can build castles in the air. All our norms are nothing but desires in disguise.

He who accepts this world as the ultimate reality will, if his mind is realistic and his heart sensitive to suffering, tend to doubt that the good is either the origin or the ultimate goal of history. To the Jewish mind, evil is an instrument rather than an iron wall; a temptation, an occasion, rather than an ultimate power.

The words of the Psalmist, *Depart from evil, and do good* (34:15), contain the epitome of right living. Yet, it seems that Jewish tradition believes that the right way of departing from evil is to do good; it puts the accent on the second half of the sentence.

Evil is not man's ultimate problem. Man's ultimate problem is his relation to God. Evil entered history as a result of man's disobedience to God, as a result of his having forfeited the only mitzvah he had (not to eat the fruit of the tree of knowledge). The Biblical answer to evil is not the good but the *holy*. It is an attempt to raise man to a higher level of existence, where man is not alone when confronted with evil. Living in "the light of the face of God" bestows upon man a power of love that enables him to overcome the powers of evil. The seductiveness of vice is excelled by the joys of the mitzvah. "Ye shall be men of holiness unto Me" (Exodus 22:30). How do we receive that quality, that power? "With every new mitzvah which God issues to Israel, He adds holiness to them."[7]

We do not wage war with evil in the name of an abstract concept of duty. We do the good not because it is a value or because of expediency, but because we owe it to God. God created man, and what is good "in His eyes" is good for man. Life is human as well as divine. Man is a child of God, not only a value to society. We may explore things without God; we cannot decide about values without Him.

We do not conceive of values as absolute essences which are laid up in heaven, to use the language of Plato. Values are not eternal ideas, existing independently of God and man. If not for the will of God, there would be no goodness; if not for the freedom of man, goodness would be out of place in history. Greek philosophy is concerned with *values;* Jewish thought dwells on *mitzvot*.

Evil is not only a threat, it is also a challenge. Neither the recognition of the peril nor faith in the redemptive power of God is sufficient to solve the tragic predicament of the world. We cannot stem the tide of evil by taking refuge in temples, by fervently imploring the restrained omnipotence of God.

The mitzvah, the humble single act of serving God, of helping man, of cleansing the self, is our way of dealing with the problem. We do not know how to solve the problem of *evil,* but we are not exempt from dealing with *evils.* The power of evil does not vitiate the reality of good. Significantly, Jewish tradition, while conscious of the possibilities of evil in the good, stresses the possiblities of further good in the good. Ben Azzai said, "Be eager to do a minor mitzvah, and flee from transgression; for one mitzvah leads to (brings on) another mitzvah, and one transgression leads to another transgression; for the reward of a mitzvah is a mitzvah, and the reward of a transgression is a transgression."[8]

At the end of days, evil will be conquered by the One; in historic times, evils must be conquered one by one.[9]

Jewish tradition, though conscious of the perils and pitfalls of existence, is a constant reminder of the grand and everlasting opportunities to do the good. We are taught to love life in this world because of the possibilities of charity and sanctity, because of the many ways open to us in which to serve the Lord. "More precious, therefore, than all of life in the world to come is a single hour of life on earth—an hour of repentance and good deeds."[10]

In stressing the fundamental importance of the mitzvah, Judaism assumes that man is endowed with the ability to fulfill what God demands, at least to some degree. This may, indeed, be an article of prophetic faith: the belief in our ability to do His will. "For this commandment (mitzvah) which I command thee this day, it is not too hard for thee, neither is it far off. . . . But the word is very nigh unto thee, in thy mouth and in thy heart, that thou mayest do it" (Deuteronomy 30:11–14). Man's actual failures rather than his essential inability to do the good are constantly stressed by Jewish tradition. In spite of all imperfection, the worth of good deeds remains in all eternity.

The idea with which Judaism starts is not the realness of evil or the sinfulness of man but rather the wonder of creation and the ability of man to do the will of God. There is always an opportunity to do a mitzvah, and precious is life because at all times and in all places we are able to do His will. This is why despair is alien to Jewish faith.

It is true that the commandment to be holy is exorbitant, and that our constant failures and transgressions fill us with contrition and grief.

196

Yet we are never lost. We are the sons of Abraham. Despite all faults, failures, and sins, we remain parts of the Covenant. His compassion is greater than His justice. He will accept us in all our frailty and weakness. "For He knows our drive [yetzer], He remembers that we are dust" (Psalms 103:14).

Judaism would reject the Kantian axiom, "I ought, therefore I can"; it would claim, instead, "Thou art commanded, therefore thou canst." Judaism, as we have said, claims that man has the resources to fulfill what God commands, at least to some degree. On the other hand, we are continually warned lest we rely on man's own power and the belief that man, by his power alone, is capable of redeeming the world. Good deeds alone will not redeem history; it is the obedience to God that will make us worthy of being redeemed by God.[11]

If Judaism had relied exclusively on the human resources for the good, on man's ability to fulfill what God demands, on man's power to achieve redemption, why did it insist upon the promise of messianic redemption? Indeed, messianism implies that any course of living, even the supreme human efforts, must fail in redeeming the world. It implies that history for all its relevance is not sufficient to itself.

There are two problems: the particular sins, the examples of breaking the law, and the general and radical problem of "the evil drive" in man. The law deals with the first problem; obedience to the law prevents evil deeds. Yet, the problem of the evil drive is not solved by observance. The prophets' answer was eschatological. "Behold, the days come, saith the Lord, when I will make a new covenant with the house of Israel . . . not like the covenant which I made with their fathers . . . I will put my law within them, and I will write it upon their hearts" (Jeremiah 31:31–34). "A new heart I will give you, and a new spirit I will put within you; and I will take out of your flesh the heart of stone and give you a heart of flesh. And I will put My spirit within you, and cause you to walk in My statutes and be careful to keep My ordinances" (Ezekiel 36:26–27).

The world is in need of redemption, but the redemption must not be expected to happen as an act of sheer grace. Man's task is to make the world worthy of redemption. His faith and his works are preparations for *ultimate redemption*.

34. PRAYER: AN ACT OF SPIRITUAL ECSTASY

As a tree torn from the soil, as a river separated from its source, the human soul wanes when detached from what is greater than itself. Without the holy, the good turns chaotic; without the good, beauty becomes accidental. It is the pattern of the impeccable which makes the average possible. It is the attachment to what is spiritually superior: loyalty to a sacred person or idea, devotion to a noble friend or teacher, love for a people or for mankind, which holds our inner life together. But any ideal, human, social, or artistic, if it forms a roof over all of life, shuts us off from the light. Even the palm of one hand may bar the light of the entire sun. Indeed, we must be open to the remote in order to perceive the near. Unless we aspire to the utmost, we shrink to inferiority.

Prayer is our attachment to the utmost. Without God in sight, we are like the scattered rungs of a broken ladder. To pray is to become a ladder on which thoughts mount to God to join the movement toward Him which surges unnoticed throughout the entire universe. We do not step out of the world when we pray; we merely see the world in a different setting. The self is not the hub, but the spoke of the revolving wheel. In prayer we shift the center of living from self-consciousness to self-surrender. God is the center toward which all forces tend. He is the source, and we are the flowing of His force, the ebb and flow of His tides.

Prayer takes the mind out of the narrowness of self-interest, and enables us to see the world in the mirror of the holy. For when we betake ourselves to the extreme opposite of the ego, we can behold a situation from the aspect of God. Prayer is a way to master what is inferior in us, to discern between the signal and the trivial, between the vital and the futile, by taking counsel with what we know about the will of God, by seeing our fate in proportion to God. Prayer clarifies our hope and intentions. It helps us discover our true aspirations, the pangs we ignore, the longings we forget. It is an act of self-purification, a quarantine for the soul. It gives us the opportunity to be honest, to say what we believe, and to stand for what we say. For the accord of assertion and conviction, of thought and conscience, is the basis of all prayer.

Prayer teaches us what to aspire to. So often we do not know what to cling to. Prayer implants in us the ideals we ought to cherish. Redemption, purity of mind and tongue, or willingness to help, may hover as ideas before our mind, but the idea becomes a concern, something to long for, a goal to be reached, when we pray: "Guard my tongue from evil and my lips from speaking guile; and in the face of those who curse me, let my soul be silent."[1]

Prayer is the essence of spiritual living. Its spell is present in every spiritual experience. Its drive enables us to delve into what is beneath our beliefs and desires, and to emerge with a renewed taste for the infinite simplicity of the good. On the globe of the microcosm the flow of prayer is like the Gulf Stream, imparting warmth to all that is cold, melting all that is hard in our life. For even loyalties may freeze to indifference if detached from the stream which carries the strength to be loyal. How often does justice lapse into cruelty, and righteousness into hypocrisy. Prayer revives and keeps alive the rare greatness of some past experience in which things glowed with meaning and blessing. It remains important, even when we ignore it for a while, like a candlestick set aside for the day. Night will come, and we shall again gather round its tiny flame. Our affection for the trifles of living will be mixed with longing for the comfort of all men.

However, prayer is no panacea, no substitute for action. It is, rather, like a beam thrown from a flashlight before us into the darkness. It is in this light that we who grope, stumble, and climb, discover where we stand, what surrounds us, and the course which we should choose. Prayer makes visible the right, and reveals what is hampering and false. In its radiance, we behold the worth of our efforts, the range of our hopes, and the meaning of our deeds. Envy and fear, despair and resentment, anguish and grief, which lie heavily upon the heart, are dispelled like shadows by its light.

Sometimes prayer is more than a light before us; it is a light within us. Those who have once been resplendent with this light find little meaning in speculations about the efficacy of prayer.

The idea of prayer is based upon the assumption of man's ability to accost God, to lay our hopes, sorrows, and wishes before Him. But this assumption is not an awareness of a particular ability with which we are endowed. We do not feel that we possess a magic power of speaking to the Infinite; we merely witness the wonder of prayer, the wonder of man addressing himself to the Eternal. Contact with Him is not our achievement. It is a gift, coming down to us from on high like a meteor, rather than rising up like a rocket. Before the words of prayer come to the lips, the mind must believe in God's willingness to draw near to us, and in our ability to clear the path for His approach. Such belief is the idea that leads us toward prayer.

Prayer is not a soliloquy. But is it a dialogue with God?[2] Does man address Him as person to person? It is incorrect to describe prayer by analogy with human conversation; we do not communicate with God. We only make ourselves communicable to Him. Prayer is an emanation of what is most precious in us toward Him, the outpouring of the heart before Him. It is not a relationship between person and person, between subject and subject, but an endeavor to become the object of His thought.

Prayer is like the light from a burning glass in which all the rays that emanate from the soul are gathered to a focus. There are hours when we are resplendent with the glowing awareness of our share in His secret interests on earth. We pray. We are carried forward to Him who is coming close to us. We endeavor to divine His will, not merely His command. Prayer is an answer to God: "Here am I. And this is the record of my days. Look into my heart, into my hopes and my regrets." We depart in shame and joy. Yet prayer never ends, for faith endows us with a bold craving that He draw near to us and approach us as a father —not only as a ruler; not only through our walking in His ways, but through His entering into our ways. The purpose of prayer is to be brought to His attention, to be listened to, to be understood by Him; not to know Him, but to *be known* to Him. To pray is to behold life not only as a result of His power, but as a concern of His will, or to strive to make our life a divine concern. For the ultimate aspiration of man is not to be a master, but an object of His knowledge. To live "in the light of His countenance," to become a thought of God—this is the true career of man.

But are we worthy of being known, of entering into His mercy, of being a matter of concern to Him? It seems as if the meaning of prayer lies in man's aspiration to be thought of by God as one who is thinking of Him. Man waxes in God when serving the sacred, and wanes when he betrays his task. Man lives in His mind when He abides in man's life.

There is no human misery more strongly felt than the state of being forsaken by God. Nothing is so terrible as rejection by Him. It is a horror to live deserted by God, and effaced from His mind. The fear of being forgotten even for an instant is a powerful spur to a pious man to bring himself to the attention of God, to keep his life *worth* being known to Him. He prefers to be smitten by His punishment rather than to be left alone. In all his prayers he begs, explicitly or implicitly, "Do not forsake me, O Lord."

To many psychologists, prayer is but a function, a shadow cast by the circumstances of our lives, growing and diminishing in accordance with our various needs and wants. Consequently, to understand the nature of prayer, it is enough to become familiar with the various occasions on which it is offered. But is it possible to determine the value of a work of art by discovering the occasion of its creation? Assuming that we can ascertain whether Cervantes wrote his *Don Quixote* in order to pay his debts, or to attain fame and impress his friends, would that have any bearing upon either the intrinsic value or our appreciation of his art? Nor is the factor which induces a person to pray the essence of prayer. The essence is inherent in the act of prayer itself. It can be detected only inside the consciousiness of man during the act of worship.

The drive toward practical consequences is not the force that inspires a person at the moment of his chanting praise to God. Even in supplication, the thought of aid or protection does not constitute the inner act of prayer. The hope of results may be the motive that leads the mind into prayer, but not the content which fills the worshiper's consciousness in the essential moment of prayer. The artist may give a concert for the sake of the promised remuneration, but, in the moment when he is passionately seeking with his fingertips the vast swarm of swift and secret sounds, the consideration of subsequent reward is far from his mind. His whole being is immersed in the music. The slightest shift of attention, the emergence of any ulterior motive, would break his intense concentration, and his single-minded devotion would collapse, his control of the instrument would fail. Even an artisan can never be true to his task unless he is motivated by love of the work for its own sake. Only by wholehearted devotion to his trade can he produce a consummate piece of craftsmanship. Prayer, too, is primarily kavvanah, the yielding of the entire being to one goal, the gathering of the soul into focus.

The focus of prayer is not the self. A man may spend hours meditating about himself, or be stirred by the deepest sympathy for his fellow man, and no prayer will come to pass. Prayer comes to pass in a complete turning of the heart toward God, toward His goodness and power. It is the momentary disregard of our personal concerns, the absence of self-centered thoughts, which constitute the art of prayer. Feeling becomes prayer in the moment in which we forget ourselves and become aware of God. When we analyze the consciousness of a supplicant, we discover that it is not concentrated upon his own interests, but on something beyond the self. The thought of personal need is absent, and the thought of divine grace alone is present in his mind. Thus, in beseeching Him for bread, there is *one* instant, at least, in which our mind is directed neither to our hunger nor to food, but to His mercy. This instant is prayer.

We start with a personal concern and live to feel the utmost. For the fate of the individual is a counterpoint in a larger theme. In prayer we come close to hearing the eternal theme and discerning our place in it. It is as if our life were a seamless garment, continuous with the Infinite. Our poverty is His. His property is ours. Overwhelmed with awe of His share in our lives, we extend ourselves to Him, expose our goals to His goodness, exchange our will for His wisdom. For this reason, the analogy between prayer and petitioning another human being is like the analogy between the ocean and a cup of water. For the essence of prayer lies in man's self-transcending, in his surpassing the limits of what is human, in his relating the purely natural to the Divine.

Prayer is an invitation to God to intervene in our lives, to let His will prevail in our affairs; it is the opening of a window to Him in our will, an effort to make Him the Lord of our soul. We submit our interests to His concern, and seek to be allied with what is ultimately right. Our approach to the holy is not an intrusion, but an answer. Between the dawn of childhood and the door of death, man encounters things and events out of which comes a whisper of truth, not much louder than stillness, but exhorting and persistent. Yet man listens to his fears and his whims, rather than to the gentle petitions of God. The Lord of the universe is suing for the favor of man, but man fails to realize his correlation. It is the disentanglement of our heart from cant, bias, and ambition, the staving in of the bulk of stupid conceit, the cracking of hollow self-reliance, that enables us to respond to this request for our service.

The purpose of prayer is not the same as the purpose of speech. The purpose of speech is to inform; the purpose of prayer is to partake.

Ultimately the goal of prayer is not to translate a word but to translate the self; not to render an ancient vocabulary in modern terminology, but to transform our thoughts into thoughts of prayer. Prayer is the soul's *imitation of the spirit,* of the spirit that is contained in the liturgical word.

The privilege of praying is man's greatest distinction. For what is there in man to induce reverence, to make his life sacred and his rights inalienable? The possession of knowledge, wealth, or skill does not compose the dignity of man. A person possessing none of these gifts may still lay claim to dignity. Our reverence for man is aroused by something in him beyond his own and our reach, something that no one can deprive him of. It is his right to pray, his ability to worship, to utter the cry that can reach God: "If . . . they cry out to Me, I will surely hear their cry" (Exodus 22:22).

The main ends of prayer are to move God, to let Him participate in our lives, and to interest ourselves in Him. What is the meaning of praise if not to make His concern our own? Worship is an act of inner agree-

202

ment with God. We can only petition Him for things we need when we are sure of His sympathy for us. To praise is to feel God's concern; to petition is to let Him feel our concern. In prayer we establish a living contact with God, between our concern and His will, between despair and promise, want and abundance. We affirm our adherence by invoking His love.

Prayer is *spiritual ecstasy*. It is as if all our vital thoughts in fierce ardor would burst the mind to stream toward God. A keen single force draws our yearning for the utmost out of the seclusion of the soul. We try to see our visions in His light, to feel our life as His affair. We begin by letting the thought of Him engage our minds, by realizing His name and entering into a reverie which leads through beauty and stillness, from feeling to thought, and from understanding to devotion. For the coins of prayer bear the image of God's dreams and wishes for fear-haunted man.

At the beginning of all action is an inner vision in which things to be are experienced as real. Prayer, too, is frequently an inner vision, an intense dreaming for God—the reflection of the Divine intentions in the soul of man. We dream of a time "when the world will be perfected under the Kingship of God, and all the children of flesh will call upon Thy name, when Thou wilt turn unto Thyself all the wicked of the earth."[3] We anticipate the fulfillment of the hope shared by both God and man. To pray is to dream in league with God, to envision His holy visions.

35. PRAYER: EXPRESSION AND EMPATHY

Prayer is an event that comes to pass between the soul of man and the word. It is from this point of view, that we have to distinguish between two main types of prayer: prayer as *an act of expression* and prayer as *an act of empathy*.

The first type comes to pass when we feel the urge to set forth before God a personal concern. Here the concern, and even the mood and the desire to pray, come first; the word follows. It is the urge to pray that leads to the act of praying.

While it is true that the prayer of expression is a common and universal phenomenon, it is inaccurate to assume, as most people do, that prayer occurs primarily as an act of expression. The fact is that the more common type of prayer is *an act of empathy*. There need be no prayerful mood in us when we begin to pray. It is through our reading and feeling the words of the prayers, through the imaginative projection of our consciousness into the meaning of the words, and through empathy for the ideas with which the words are pregnant, that this type of prayer comes to pass. Here the word comes first, the feeling follows.

In the Book of Psalms some chapters begin with the words, *To David, a Psalm,* while others begin, *A Psalm to David.* The Talmud explains: when David began to sing and then the inspiration came to him it was *To David a Psalm;* when first the inspiration came to him and then he sang, it was *A Psalm to David.*[1]

In the prayer of empathy, we begin by turning to the words of the liturgy. At first, the words and their meaning seem to lie beyond the horizon of the mind. How remote is the meaning of *Blessed be Thou* to the thoughts in which we are usually immersed. We must, therefore, remember that the experience of prayer does not come all at once. It grows in the face of the word that comes ever more to light in its richness, buoyancy, and mystery. Gradually, going out to meet its meaning, we rise to the greatness of prayer. On the way to the word, on its slopes and ridges, prayer matures—we purify ourselves into beings who pray.

The concepts which indicate the divine surpass the bounds of human consciousness. The words which tell of it exceed the power of the soul, and, over and above that, they demand an intensity of dedication which is rarely present. To name Him is a risk, a forcing of the consciousness beyond itself. To refer to Him means almost to get outside oneself. Every praying person knows how serious an act the utterance of His name is, for the word is not a tool but a reflection of the object which is designates. We often discover that the word is greater than the mind. What we feel is so much less than what we say.

In the prayer of expression we often arrive at thoughts that lie beyond our power of expression. In the prayer of empathy we often arrive at words that lie beyond our power of empathy. It is in such tensions that our worship gains in strength and our knowledge in intuitive depth.

Genuine prayer is an event in which man surpasses himself. Man hardly comprehends what is coming to pass. Its beginning lies on this side of the word, but the end lies beyond all words. What is happening is not always brought about by the power of man. At times all we do is to utter a word with all our heart, yet it is as if we lifted up a whole world. It is as if someone unsuspectingly pressed a button and a gigantic wheel-work were stormily and surprisingly set in motion.

We do not turn the light of prayer on and off at will, as we control sober speculation; we are seized by the overwhelming spell of its grandeur. It is amazement, not understanding; awe, not reasoning; a challenge, a sweep of emotion, the tide of the spirit, a claim on our wills by the living will of God.

The service of prayer, the worship of the heart, fulfills itself not in the employment of words as a human expression but in the celebration of words as a holy reality. One is ashamed to open his experiences, to disclose his feelings before the face of God; only rarely does he fully overcome his inhibition. What he can do most easily is this: to capture the substance of the word with aroused attention and devotion and offer it with trembling. The power which streams from words unites itself with the elemental power that rises from the memory. Thoughts are being transcended, experiences of the past illumined, desires transformed. A thought becomes a wish, a wish a desire, a desire a demand, a demand an expectation, an expectation a vision. These steps represent at once stages of personal attitude as well as objective events.

Praying means to take hold of a word, the end, so to speak, of a line that leads to God. The greater the power, the higher the ascent in the word. But praying also means that the echo of the word falls like a plummet into the depth of the soul. The purer the readiness, so much the deeper penetrates the word.

Those who plead for the primacy of the prayer of expression over the prayer of empathy ought to remember that the ability to express what is hidden in the heart is a rare gift, and cannot be counted upon by all men. What, as a rule, makes it possible for us to pray is our ability to affiliate our own minds with the pattern of fixed texts, to unlock our hearts to the words, and to surrender to their meanings. The words stand before us as living entities full of spiritual power, of a power which often surpasses the grasp of our minds. The words are often the givers, and we the recipients. They inspire our minds and awaken our hearts.

Most of do not know the answer to one of the most important questions, namely, What is our ultimate concern? We do not know what to pray for. It is the liturgy that teaches us what to pray for.

It is good that there are words sanctified by ages of worship, by the honesty and love of generations. If it were left to ourselves, who would know what word is right to be offered as praise in the sight of God or which of our perishable thoughts is worthy of entering eternity?

On the other hand, one may ask: Why should we follow the order of the liturgy? Should we not say, one ought to pray when he is ready to pray? The time to pray is all the time. There is always an opportunity to disclose the holy, but when we fail to seize it, there are definite moments in the liturgical order of the day, there are words in the liturgical order of our speech to remind us. These words are like mountain peaks pointing to the unfathomable. Ascending their trails we arrive at prayer.

There is danger in the prayer of empathy, the danger of relying on the word, of depending upon the text, of forgetting that the word is a challenge to the soul rather than a substitute for the outburst of the heart. Even in prayer of empathy the word is, at best, the inspirer, not the source. The source is the soul. Prayer as a way of speaking is a way that leads nowhere. The text must never be more important than *kavvanah*, than inner devotion. The life of prayer depends not so much upon loyalty to custom as upon inner participation; not so much upon the length as upon the depth of the service.

Those who run precipitately through the liturgy, rushing in and out of the prayer texts, as if the task were to cover a maximum of space in a minimum of time, will derive little from worship. To be able to pray is to know how to stand still and to dwell upon a word. This is how some worshipers of the past would act: "They would repeat the same word many times, because they loved and cherished it so much that they could not part from it."[2]

There is a classical principle in regard to prayer: *"Better is a little with kavvanah than much without it."*[3] Quality is more decisive than than quantity. Jewish piety throughout the ages expressed itself by adding more prayers to the liturgy. The prayer book of the last centuries contains many more texts than the prayer book in the time of the Talmud or in the time of Saadia. A pilgrimage through the entire order of the daily morning prayer in its present form is like a journey through a vast collection of precious works of art. To absorb all their beauty, even to a small degree, would take many hours of concentration as well as the ability to experience an immense variety of insights, one after the other. But the time allotted to daily prayer is too brief, and all we are able to accomplish is a hasty glance.

To abridge the service without deepening the concentration would be meaningless. It is just as possible to read a brief service without kavvanah as to go through a long service without kavvanah. On the other hand, those of us who are anxious to omit no word out of reverence for the treasures of the liturgy are paying a high price for their loyalty. Judaism is faced with a dilemma, with a conflict between two requirements: the loyalty to the order and the requirement of *kavvanah*.

Two brief stories may be told relative to the two main types of prayer, the expressive and the empathic.

There was a young shepherd who was unable to recite the Hebrew prayers. The only way in which he worshiped was "Lord of the world!

It is apparent and known unto you, that if you had cattle and gave them to me to tend, though I take wages for tending from all others, from you I would take nothing, because I love you."

One day a learned man passing by heard the shepherd pronounce his offer and shouted at him: "Fool, do not pray thus."

The shepherd asked him: "How should I pray?"

Thereupon the learned man taught him the benedictions in order, the recitation of the *Shema*[4] and the "silent prayer," so that henceforth he would not say what he was accustomed to say.

After the learned man had gone away, the shepherd forgot all that had been taught him, and did not pray. And he was even afraid to say what he had been accustomed to say, since the righteous man had told him not to.

One night the learned man had a dream, and in it he heard a voice: "If you do not tell him to say what he was accustomed to say before you came to him, know that misfortune will overtake you, for you have robbed me of one who belongs to the world to come."

At once the learned man went to the shepherd and said to him: "What prayer are you making?"

The shepherd answered: "None, for I have forgotten what you taught me, and you forbade me to say 'If you had cattle.' "

Then the learned man told him what he had dreamed and added: "Say what you used to say."

"Behold, here is one who had neither Torah nor words; he only had it in his heart to do good, and this was esteemed in heaven, as if this were a great thing. *'The Merciful One desires the Heart.'*[5] Therefore, let men think good thoughts, and let these thoughts be turned to the Holy One, blessed be He."[6]

Now, many of us are so much on the side of the shepherd boy as to be opposed to the institution of regular prayer, claiming that one should pray when and as we feel inspired to do so. For such there is a story, told by Rabbi Israel Friedmann, the Rizhiner, about a small Jewish town, far off from the main roads of the land. But it had all the necessary municipal institutions: a bathhouse, a cemetery, a hospital, and law court; as well as all sorts of craftsmen—tailors, shoemakers, carpenters, and masons. One trade, however, was lacking: there was no watchmaker. In the course of years many of the clocks became so annoyingly inaccurate that their owners just decided to let them run down, and ignore them altogether. There were others, however, who maintained that as long as the clocks ran, they should not be abandoned. So they wound their clocks day after day though they knew that they were not accurate. One day the news spread through the town that a watchmaker had arrived, and everyone rushed to him with their clocks. But the only ones he could repair were those that had been kept running—the abandoned clocks had grown too rusty!

In a sense, prayer begins where expression ends. The words that reach our lips are often but waves of an overflowing stream touching the shore. We often seek and miss, struggle and fail to adjust our unique feelings to the patterns of texts. The soul can only intimate its persistent striving, the riddle of its unhappiness, the strain of living twixt hope and fear. Where is the tree that can utter fully the silent passion of the soil? Words can only open the door, and we can only weep on the threshold of our incommunicable thirst after the incomprehensible.

In no other act does man experience so often the disparity between the desire for expression and the means of expression as in prayer. The inadequacy of the means at our disposal appears so tangible, so tragic, that one feels it a grace to be able to give oneself up to music, to a tone, to a song, to a chant. The wave of a song carries the soul to heights which utterable meanings can never reach. Such abandonment is no escape nor an act of being unfaithful to the mind. For the world of unutterable meanings is the nursery of the soul, the cradle of all our ideas. It is not an escape but a return to one's origins.

The sense for the power of words and the sense for the impotence of human expression are equally characteristic of the religious consciousness. "Who can utter the mighty doings of the Lord or utter all his praise?" (Psalms 106:2). He is "exalted above all blessing and praise" (Nehemiah 9:5), "above all the blessings and hymns, extollings and comfortings that are ever uttered in the world" (the *kaddish*). This is the most important guidance:

> Commune with your hearts . . .
> and be still.
>
> (Psalms 4:5)

"The highest form of worship is that of silence and hope."[7] "The language of the heart is the main thing; the spoken word serves merely as an interpreter between the heart and the listener."[8] "The preparations of the heart are man's, but the expression (or answer) of the tongue is from the Lord" (Proverbs 16:1). *"For there is a form of knowledge that precedes the process of expression* (compare Psalms 139:4), and it is God who understands it."[9]

"A certain reader once prayed in the presence of Rabbi Ḥanina and said: 'O God, the great, the mighty, the revered, the majestic, the powerful, the strong, the fearless, the all-wise, the certain, the honorable,' etc., etc. Rabbi Ḥanina waited until he finished and then said to him:

35. Prayer: Expression and Empathy

'Have you exhausted the praises of your Master? Why do you say so much? Even the three attributes which we recite (in the "silent prayer": great, mighty, revered), we do so only because our master Moses put them in his law and because the men of the Great Assembly fixed them in the liturgy. It is as if an earthly king had a million denarii of gold, and we praised him for possessing much silver. Is not such praise insult?"[10]

In a sense, our liturgy is a higher form of silence. It is pervaded by an awed sense of the grandeur of God which resists description and surpasses all expression. The individual is silent. He does not bring forth his own words. His saying the consecrated words is in essence an act of listening to what they convey. *The spirit of Israel speaks, the self is silent.*

Twofold is the meaning of silence. One, the abstinence from speech, the absence of sound. Two, inner silence, the absence of self-concern, stillness. One may articulate words in his voice and yet be inwardly silent. One may abstain from uttering any sound and yet be overbearing.

Both are inadequate: our speech as well as our silence. Yet there is a level that goes beyond both: the level of song. "There are three ways in which a man expresses his deep sorrow: the man on the lowest level cries; the man on the second level is silent; the man on the highest level knows how to turn his sorrow into song."[11] True prayer is a song.

We have stressed the fact that prayer is an event that begins in the individual soul. We have not dwelled upon how much our ability to pray depends upon our being a part of a community of prayer.

It is not safe to pray alone. Tradition insists that we pray with, and as a part of, the community; that public worship is preferable to private worship. Here we are faced with an aspect of the *polarity of prayer.* There is a permanent union between individual worship and community worship, each of which depends for its existence upon the other. To ignore their *spiritual symbiosis* will prove fatal to both.

How can we forget that our ability to pray we owe to the community and to tradition? We have learned how to pray by listening to the voice of prayer, by having been a part of a community of men standing before God. We are often carried toward prayer by the reader: when we hear how he asks questions, how he implores, cries, humbles himself, sings.

Those who cherish genuine prayer, yet feel driven away from the houses of worship because of the sterility of public worship today, seem to believe that private prayer is the only way. Yet, the truth is that private prayer will not survive unless it is inspired by public prayer. The way of the recluse, the exclusive concern with personal salvation, piety in isolation from the community is an act of impiety.

Judaism is not only the adherence to particular doctrines and observ-

209

ances, but primarily living in the spiritual order of the Jewish people, the living *in* the Jews of the past and *with* the Jews of the present. Judaism is not only a certain quality in the souls of the individuals, but primarily the existence of the community of Israel. It is not a doctrine, an idea, a faith, but the covenant between God and the people. Our share in holiness we acquire by living in the Jewish community. What we do as individuals is a trivial episode; what we attain as Israel causes us to become a part of eternity.

The Jew does not stand alone before God; it is as a member of the community that he stands before God. Our relationship to Him is not as an I to a Thou, but as a We to a Thou.

We never pray as individuals, set apart from the rest of the world. The liturgy is an order which we can enter only as a part of the Community of Israel. Every act of worship is an act of participating in an eternal service, in the service of all souls of all ages. Every act of adoration is done in union with all of history, and with all beings above and below:

> We sanctify Thy Name in the world, as they sanctify
> it in the highest heavens . . .
> A crown will be bestowed
> Upon the Lord our God
> By the angels, the multitudes above,
> In union with Israel Thy people
> Assembled below. . . .[12]

And yet—this we must never forget—prayer is primarily an event in the individual souls, an act of emanation, not only an act of participation. Even the worth of public worship depends upon the depth of private worship, of the private worship of those who worship together.

36. PRAYER: KNOW BEFORE WHOM YOU STAND!

There is a classical statement in rabbinic literature that expresses the spiritual minimum of prayer as an act of the consciousness of man: *"Know before Whom you stand."*[1] Three ideas are contained in this definition.*

* The sentence consists of three parts: The main verb in the imperative "know."

36. Prayer: Know before Whom You Stand!

Know (or Understand)

A certain understanding or awareness, a definite attitude of the mind is the condition *sine qua non* of all prayer. Prayer cannot live in a theological vacuum. *It comes out of insight.*

Prayer must not be treated as if it were the result of an intellectual oversight, as if it thrived best in the climate of thoughtlessness. One needs understanding, wisdom of the spirit to know what it means to worship God. Or at least one must endeavor to become free of the folly of worshiping the specious glory of mind-made deities, free of unconditional attachment to the false dogmas that populate our minds.

To live without prayer is to live without God, to live without a soul. No one is able to think of Him unless he has learned how to pray to Him. For this is the way man learns to think of the true God—of the God of Israel. He first is aware of His presence long before he thinks of His essence. And to pray is to sense His presence.

There are people who maintain that prayer is a matter of *emotion.* In their desire to "revitalize" prayer, they would proclaim: Let there be emotion! This is, of course, based on a fallacy. Emotion is an important *component;* it is not the *source* of prayer. The power to pray does not depend on whether a person is of a choleric or phlegmatic temperament. One may be extremely emotional and be unable to generate that power. This is decisive: worship comes out of insight. It is not the result of an intellectual oversight.

What is more, prayer has the power to generate insight; it often endows us with an understanding not attainable by speculation. Some of our deepest insights, decisions and attitudes are born in moments of prayer. Often where reflection fails, prayer succeeds. What thinking is to philosophy, prayer is to religion. And prayer can go beyond speculation. The truth of holiness is not a truth of speculation—it is the truth of worship.

"Rabbi said: I am amazed that the prayer for understanding was not included in the Sabbath liturgy! For if there is no understanding, how is it possible to pray?"[2]

Know before Whom you stand. Such knowledge, such understanding is not easily won. It "is neither a gift we receive undeservedly nor a treasure to be found inadvertently." The art of awareness of God, the art of sensing His Presence in our daily lives, cannot be learned off-hand. "God's grace resounds in our lives like a staccato. Only by retaining the seemingly disconnected notes comes the ability to grasp the theme."

Dependent on this main verb is the clause "before whom you stand," which can be broken up into two segments: the adverbial phrase "before whom," which contains the interrogative pronoun, and "you stand," which is the subject and verb of the subordinate clause.

Before Whom

To have said before *what* would have contradicted the spirit of Jewish prayer. *What* is the most indefinite pronoun. In asking *what,* one is totally uncommitted, uninitiated, bare of any anticipation of an answer; any answer may be acceptable. But he who is totally uncommitted, who does not even have an inkling of the answer, has not learned the meaning of the ultimate question, and is not ready to engage in prayer. If God is a *what,* a power, the sum total of values, how can we pray to it? An "I" does not pray to an "it." Unless, therefore, God is at least as real as my own self; unless I am sure that God has at least as much life as I do, how can I pray?

You Stand

The act of prayer is more than a process of the mind and a movement of the lips. It is an act that happens between man and God—in the presence of God.

Reading or studying the text of a prayer is not the same as praying. What marks the act of prayer is the decision to enter and face the presence of God. To pray means to expose oneself to Him, to His judgment.

If "prayer is the expression of the sense of being at home in the universe,"[3] then the Psalmist who exclaimed, "I am a stranger on earth, hide not Thy commandments from me" (119:19), was a person who grievously misunderstood the nature of prayer. Throughout many centuries of Jewish history the true motivation for prayer was not "the sense of being at home in the universe" but the sense of *not* being at home in the universe. We could not but experience anxiety and spiritual homelessness in the sight of so much suffering and evil, in the countless examples of failure to live up to the will of God. That experience gained in intensity by the soul-stirring awareness that God Himself was not at home in a universe, where His will is defied, where His kingship is denied. *The Shekhinah is in exile,* the world is corrupt, *the universe itself is not at home. . . .*

To pray, then, means to bring God back into the world, to establish His kingship, to let His glory prevail. This is why in the greatest moments of our lives, on the Days of Awe, we cry out of the depth of our disconcerted souls, a prayer of redemption:

And so, Lord our God, grant Thy awe to all Thy works, and your dread to all Thou hast created, that all Thy works may fear Thee, and all who have been created prostrate themselves before Thee, and all form one union to do Thy will with a whole heart.

Great is the power of prayer. For to worship is *to expand the presence*

212

of God in the world. God is transcendent, but our worship makes Him immanent. This is implied in the idea that God is in need of man: His being immanent depends upon us. When we say *Blessed be He,* we extend His glory, we bestow His spirit upon this world. *Yitgadal ve-yitkadash: Magnified and sanctified be God's great name throughout the world. . . .* May there be more of God in this world.

What is decisive is not the mystic experience of our being close to Him; decisive is not our *feeling* but our *certainty* of His being close to us— although even His presence is veiled and beyond the scope of our emotion. Decisive is not our emotion but our *conviction.* If such conviction is lacking, if the presence of God is a myth, then prayer to God is a delusion. If God is unable to listen to us, then we are insane in talking to Him.

The true source of prayer, we said above, is not an emotion but an insight. It is the insight into the mystery of reality, *the sense of the ineffable,* that enables us to pray. As long as we refuse to take notice of what is beyond our sight, beyond our reason; as long as we are blind to the mystery of being, the way to prayer is closed to us. If the rise of the sun is but a daily routine of nature, there is no reason to say, *In mercy Thou givest light to the earth and to those who dwell on it . . . every day constantly.* If bread is nothing but flour moistened, kneaded, baked and then brought forth from the oven, it is meaningless to say, *Blessed art Thou . . . who bringest forth bread from the earth.*

The way to prayer leads through *acts of wonder* and *radical amazement.* The illusion of total intelligibility, the indifference to the mystery that is everywhere, the foolishness of ultimate self-reliance are serious obstacles on the way. It is in moments of our being faced with the mystery of living and dying, of knowing and not-knowing, of love and the inability of love—that we pray, that *we address ourselves to Him who is beyond the mystery.*

Praise is our first response. Aflame with inability to say what His presence means, we can only sing, we can only utter words of adoration.

This is why in Jewish liturgy *praise* rather than *petition* ranks foremost. It is the more profound form, for it involves not so much the sense of one's own dependence and privation as the sense of God's majesty and glory. In praising Him all that is specious, all that is false, is dispelled. We rise to a higher level of living.

213

37.   THE SABBATH: HOLINESS IN TIME

I

Technical civilization is man's conquest of space. It is a triumph frequently achieved by sacrificing an essential ingredient of existence, namely, time. In technical civilization, we expend time to gain space. To enhance our power in the world of space is our main objective. Yet to have more does not mean to be more. The power we attain in the world of space terminates abruptly at the borderline of time. But time is the heart of existence.[1]

To gain control of the world of space is certainly one of our tasks. The danger begins when in gaining power in the realm of space we forfeit all aspirations in the realm of time. There is a realm of time where the goal is not to have but to be, not to own but to give, not to control but to share, not to subdue but to be in accord. Life goes wrong when the control of space, the acquisition of things of space, becomes our sole concern.

Nothing is more useful than power, nothing more frightful. We have often suffered from degradation by poverty, now we are threatened with degradation through power. Many hearts and pitchers are broken at the fountain of profit. Selling himself into slavery to things, man becomes a utensil that is broken at the fountain.

Technical civilization stems primarily from the desire of man to subdue and manage the forces of nature. The manufacture of tools, the art of spinning and farming, the building of houses, the craft of sailing—all this goes on in man's spatial surroundings. The mind's preoccupation with things of space affects, to this day, all activities of man. Even religions are frequently dominated by the notion that the deity resides in space, within particular localities like mountains, forests, trees, or stones, which are, therefore, singled out as holy places; the deity is bound to a particular land, holiness a quality associated with things of space, and the primary question is: Where is the god? There is much enthusiasm for the idea that God is present in the universe, but that idea is taken to mean His presence in space rather than in time, in nature rather than in history; as if He were a thing, not a spirit.

Even pantheistic philosophy is a religion of space: the Supreme Being is thought to be the infinite space. *Deus sive natura* has extension, or space, as its attribute, not time; time to Spinoza is merely an accident of motion, a mode of thinking. And his desire to develop a philosophy *more*

214

37. The Sabbath: Holiness in Time

geometrico, in the manner of geometry, which is the science of space, is significant of his space-mindedness.

The primitive mind finds it hard to realize an idea without the aid of imagination, and it is the realm of space where imagination wields its sway. Of the gods it must have a visible image; where there is no image there is no god. The reverence for the sacred image, for the sacred monument or place, is not only indigenous to most religions, it has been retained by men of all ages, all nations, pious, superstitious, or even anti-religious; they all continue to pay homage to banners and flags, to national shrines, to monuments erected to kings or heroes. Everywhere the desecration of holy shrines is considered a sacrilege, and the shrine may become so important that the idea it stands for is consigned to oblivion. The memorial becomes an aid to amnesia; the means stultify the end. For things of space are at the mercy of man. Though too sacred to be polluted, they are not too sacred to be exploited. To retain the holy, to perpetuate the presence of god, his image is fashioned. Yet a god who can be fashioned, a god who can be confined, is but a shadow of man.

In our daily lives we attend primarily to that which the senses are spelling out for us: to what the eyes perceive, to what the fingers touch. Reality to us is thinghood, consisting of substances that occupy space; even God is considered by most of us a thing.

The result of our thinginess is our blindness to all reality that fails to identify itself as a thing, as a matter of fact. This is obvious in our understanding of time, which, being thingless and insubstantial, appears to us as if it had no reality.[2]

Indeed, we know what to do with space but do not know what to do about time, except to make it subservient to space. Most of us seem to labor for the sake of things of space. As a result we suffer from a deeply rooted dread of time and stand aghast when compelled to look into its face.[3] But things of space are not fireproof; they only add fuel to the flames. Is the joy of possession an antidote to the terror of time which grows to be a dread of inevitable death?

It is impossible for man to shirk the problem of time. The more we think, the more we realize: we cannot conquer time through space. We can only master time in time.

Monuments of bronze live by the grace of the memory of those who gaze at their form, while moments of the soul endure even when banished to the back of the mind. Feelings, thoughts, are our own, while possessions are alien and often treacherous to the self. Though we deal with things, we live in deeds.

The higher goal of spiritual living is not to amass a wealth of information, but to face sacred moments. In a religious experience, for example,

215

it is not a thing that imposes itself on man but a spiritual presence. What is retained in the soul is the moment of insight rather than the place where the act came to pass. A moment of insight is a fortune, transporting us beyond the confines of measured time. Spiritual life begins to decay when we fail to sense the grandeur of what is eternal in time.

Our intention here is not to deprecate the world of space. To disparage space and the blessing of things of space, is to disparage the works of creation, the works which God beheld and saw "it was good." The world cannot be seen exclusively *sub specie temporis*. Time and space are interrelated. To overlook either of them is to be partially blind. What we plead against is man's unconditional surrender to space, his enslavement to things. We must not forget that it is not a thing that lends significance to a moment; it is the moment that lends significance to things.

The Bible is more concerned with time than with space. It sees the world in the dimension of time. It pays more attention to generations, to events, than to countries, to things; it is more concerned with history than with geography. To understand the teaching of the Bible one must accept its premise that time has a meaning for life which is at least equal to that of space; that time has a significance and sovereignty of its own.

One of the most important facts in the history of religion was the transformation of agricultural festivals into commemorations of historical events. The festivals of ancient peoples were intimately linked with nature's seasons. Thus the value of the festive day was determined by the things nature did or did not bring forth. In Judaism, Passover, originally a spring festival, became a celebration of the exodus from Egypt; the Feast of Weeks, an old harvest festival at the end of the wheat harvest (ḥag hakatzir, Exodus 23:16; 34:22), became the celebration of the day on which the Torah was given at Sinai; the Feast of the Booths, an old festival of vintage (ḥag haasif, Exodus 23:16), commemorates the dwelling of the Israelites in booths during their sojourn in the wilderness (Leviticus 23:42 f.). To Israel the unique events of historic time were spiritually more significant than the repetitive processes in the cycle of nature, even though physical sustenance depended on the latter. While the deities of other peoples were associated with places or things, the God of Israel was the God of events: the Redeemer from slavery, the Revealer of the Torah, manifesting Himself in events of history rather than in things or places. Thus, the faith in the unembodied, in the unimaginable was born.

Judaism is a *religion of time* aiming at *the sanctification of time*. Unlike the space-minded man to whom time is unvaried, iterative, homogeneous, to whom all hours are alike, qualitiless, empty shells, the Bible senses the diversified character of time. There are no two hours

216

alike. Every hour is unique and the only one given at the moment, exclusive and endlessly precious.

Judaism teaches us to be attached to *holiness in time,* to be attached to sacred events, to learn how to consecrate sanctuaries that emerge from the magnificent stream of a year. The Sabbaths are our great cathedrals; and our Holy of Holies is a shrine that neither the Romans nor the Germans were able to burn; a shrine that even apostasy cannot easily obliterate: the Day of Atonement. According to the ancient rabbis, it is not the observance of the Day of Atonement, but the Day itself, the "essence of the Day," which, with man's repentance, atones for the sins of man.[4]

Jewish ritual may be characterized as the art of significant forms in time, as *architecture of time.* Most of its observances—the Sabbath, the New Moon, the festivals, the Sabbatical and the Jubilee year—depend on a certain hour of the day or season of the year. It is, for example, the evening, morning, or afternoon that brings with it the call to prayer. The main themes of faith lie in the realm of time. We remember the day of the exodus from Egypt, the day when Israel stood at Sinai; and our Messianic hope is the expectation of a day, of the end of days.

In a well-composed work of art an idea of outstanding importance is not introduced haphazardly, but, like a king at an official ceremony, it is presented at a moment and in a way that will bring to light its authority and leadership. In the Bible, words are employed with exquisite care, particularly those which, like pillars of fire, lead the way in the far-flung system of the Biblical world of meaning.

One of the most distinguished words in the Bible is the word *kadosh,* holy; a word which more than any other is representative of the mystery and majesty of the divine. Now what was the first holy object in the history of the world? Was it a mountain? Was it an altar?

It is, indeed, a unique occasion at which the distinguished word *kadosh* is used for the first time: in the Book of Genesis at the end of the story of creation. How extremely significant is the fact that it is applied to time: "And God blessed the seventh *day* and made it *holy.*"[5] There is no reference in the record of creation to any object in space that would be endowed with the quality of holiness.

This is a radical departure from accustomed religious thinking. The mythical mind would expect that, after heaven and earth have been established, God would create a holy place—a holy mountain or a holy spring—whereupon a sanctuary is to be established. Yet it seems as if to the Bible it is *holiness in time,* the Sabbath, which comes first.

When history began, there was only one holiness in the world, holiness in time. When at Sinai the word of God was about to be voiced, a call for holiness in *man* was proclaimed: "You shall be unto me a holy people." It was only after the people had succumbed to the temptation of worshiping a thing, a golden calf, that the erection of a Tabernacle, of holiness in *space,* was commanded.[6] The sanctity of time came first, the sanctity of man came second, and the sanctity of space last. Time was hallowed by God; space, the Tabernacle, was consecrated by Moses.[7]

While the festivals celebrated events that happened in time, the date of the month assigned for each festival in the calendar is determined by the life in nature. Passover and the Feast of Booths, for example, coincide with the full moon, and the date of all festivals is a day in the month, and the month is a reflection of what goes on periodically in the realm of nature, since the Jewish month begins with the new moon, with the reappearance of the lunar crescent in the evening sky. In contrast, the Sabbath is entirely independent of the month and unrelated to the moon. Its date is not determined by any event in nature, such as the new moon, but by the act of creation. Thus the essence of the Sabbath is completely detached from the world of space. It is a day on which we are called upon to share in what is eternal in time, to turn from the results of creation to the mystery of creation; from the world of creation to the creation of the world.

II

The Sabbath is not for the sake of the weekdays; the weekdays are for the sake of Sabbath.[8] It is not an interlude but the climax of living.

Three acts of God denoted the seventh day: He *rested,* He *blessed,* and He *hallowed* the seventh day (Genesis 2:2–3). To the prohibition of labor is, therefore, added the blessing of delight and the accent of sanctity. Not only the hands of man celebrate the day, the tongue and the soul keep the Sabbath. One does not talk on it in the same manner in which one talks on weekdays. Even thinking of business or labor should be avoided.

Labor is a craft, but perfect rest is an art. It is the result of an accord of body, mind and imagination. To attain a degree of excellence in art, one must accept its discipline, one must adjure slothfulness. The seventh day is a *palace in time* which we build. It is made of soul, of joy and reticence. In its atmosphere, a discipline is a reminder of adjacency to eternity. Indeed, the splendor of the day is expressed in terms of *abstentions,* just as the mystery of God is more adequately conveyed *via negationis,* in the categories of *negative theology* which claims that we can never say what He is, we can only say what He is not. We often feel how poor the edifice would be were it built exclusively of our rituals and deeds which are so awkward and often so obtrusive. How else express glory

218

in the presence of eternity, if not by the silence of abstaining from noisy acts?

For all the idealization, there is no danger of the idea of the Sabbath becoming a fairy tale. With all the romantic idealization, the Sabbath remains a concrete fact, a legal institution and a social order. There is no danger of its becoming a disembodied spirit, for the spirit of the Sabbath must always be in accord with actual deeds, with definite actions and abstentions. The real and the spiritual are one, like body and soul in a living man. It is for the law to clear the path; it is for the soul to sense the spirit.

This is what the ancient rabbis felt: the Sabbath demands all of man's attention, the service and singleminded devotion of total love. The logic of such a conception compelled them to enlarge constantly the system of laws and rules of observance. They sought to ennoble human nature and make it worthy of being in the presence of the royal day.

Yet law and love, discipline and delight, were not always fused. In their illustrious fear of desecrating the spirit of the day, the ancient rabbis established a level of observance which is within the reach of exalted souls but not infrequently beyond the grasp of ordinary men.

The glorification of the day, the insistence upon strict observance, did not, however, lead the rabbis to a deification of the law. "The Sabbath is given unto you, not you unto the Sabbath."[9] The ancient rabbis knew that excessive piety may endanger the fulfilment of the essence of the law.[10] "There is nothing more important, according to the Torah, than to preserve human life . . . Even when there is the slightest possibility that a life may be at stake one may disregard every prohibition of the law."[11] One must sacrifice mitzvot *for the sake of man* rather than sacrifice man *"for the sake of mitzvot."* The purpose of the Torah is "to bring life to Israel, in this world and in the world to come."[12]

Continuous austerity may severely dampen, yet levity would certainly obliterate the spirit of the day. One cannot modify a precious filigree with a spear or operate on a brain with a plowshare.

Labor without dignity is the cause of misery; rest without spirit the source of depravity. Indeed the prohibitions have succeeded in preventing the vulgarization of the grandeur of the day.

Two things the people of Rome anxiously desired—bread and circus games.[13] But man does not live by bread and circus games alone. Who will teach him how to desire anxiously the spirit of a sacred day?

Yet what the spirit offers is often too august for our trivial minds. We accept the ease and relief and miss the inspirations of the day, where it comes from and what it stands for. This is why we pray for understanding:

May Thy children realize and understand that their rest comes from Thee, and that to rest means to sanctify Thy name.

(The Afternoon Prayer for the Sabbath)

Call the Sabbath a delight: [14] a delight to the soul and a delight to the body. Since there are so many acts which one must abstain from doing on the seventh day, "you might think I have given you the Sabbath for your displeasure; I have surely given you the Sabbath for your pleasure." To sanctify the seventh day does not mean: Thou shalt mortify thyself, but, on the contrary: Thou shalt sanctify it with all thy heart, with all thy soul and with all thy senses. "Sanctify the Sabbath by choice meals, by beautiful garments; delight your soul with pleasure and I will reward you for this very pleasure." [15]

Unlike the Day of Atonement, the Sabbath is not dedicated exclusively to spiritual goals. It is a day of the soul as well as of the body; comfort and pleasure are an integral part of the Sabbath observance. Man in his entirety, all his faculties must share its blessing.

The words: "On the *seventh* day God *finished* His work" (Genesis 2:2), seem to be a puzzle. Is it not said: "He *rested* on the *seventh* day"? "In *six* days the Lord made heaven and earth" (Exodus 20:11)? We would surely expect the Bible to tell us that on the sixth day God finished His work. Obviously, the ancient rabbis concluded, there was an act of creation on the seventh day. Just as heaven and earth were created in six days, *menuhah* was created on the Sabbath.

"After the six days of creation—what did the universe still lack? *Menuhah*. Came the Sabbath, came *menuhah,* and the universe was complete." [16]

"Menuhah" which we usually render with "rest" means here much more than withdrawal from labor and exertion, more than freedom from toil, strain or activity of any kind. *Menuhah* is not a negative concept but something real and intrinsically positive. This must have been the view of the ancient rabbis if they believed that it took a special act of creation to bring it into being, that the universe would be incomplete without it.

"What was created on the seventh day? *Tranquility, serenity, peace,* and *repose.*" [17]

To the Biblical mind *menuhah* is the same as happiness [18] and stillness, as peace and harmony. The word with which Job described the state after life he was longing for is derived from the same root as *menuhah*. It is the state wherein man lies still, wherein the wicked cease from troubling and the weary are at rest. [19] It is the state in which there is no strife and no fighting, no fear and no distrust. The essence of good life is *menuhah*. "The Lord is my shepherd, I shall not want, He maketh me to lie down in green pastures; He leadeth me beside the still waters" (the waters of *menuhot*).[20] In later times *menuhah* became a synonym for the life in the world to come, for eternal life.[21]

III

Technical civilization is the product of labor, of man's exertion of power for the sake of gain, for the sake of producing goods. It begins when man, dissatisfied with what is available in nature, becomes engaged in a struggle with the forces of nature in order to enhance his safety and to increase his comfort. To use the language of the Bible, the task of civilization is to subdue the earth, to have dominion over the beast.

How proud we often are of our victories in the war with nature, proud of the multitude of instruments we have succeeded in inventing, of the abundance of commodities we have been able to produce. Yet our victories have come to resemble defeats. In spite of our triumphs, we have fallen victims to the work of our hands; it is as if the forces we had conquered have conquered us.

Is our civilization a way to disaster, as many of us are prone to believe? Is civilization essentially evil, to be rejected and condemned? The faith of the Jew is not a way out of this world, but a way of being within and above this world; not to reject but to surpass civilization. The Sabbath is the day on which we learn the art of *surpassing* civilization.

Adam was placed in the Garden of Eden "to dress it and to keep it" (Genesis 2:15). Labor is not only the destiny of man; it is endowed with divine dignity. However, after he ate of the tree of knowledge he was condemned to toil, not only to labor "In toil shall thou eat . . . all the days of thy life" (Genesis 3:17). Labor is a blessing, toil is the misery of man.

The Sabbath as a day of abstaining from work is not a depreciation but an affirmation of labor, a divine exaltation of its dignity. Thou shalt abstain from labor on the seventh day is a sequel to the command: *Six days shalt thou labor, and do all thy work.*[22]

"Six days shalt thou labor and do all thy work; but the seventh day is Sabbath unto the Lord thy God." Just as we are commanded to keep the Sabbath, we are commanded to labor.[23] "Love work . . . "[24] The duty to work for six days is just as much a part of God's covenant with man as the duty to abstain from work on the seventh day.[25]

To set apart one day a week for freedom, a day on which we would not use the instruments which have been so easily turned into weapons of destruction, a day for being with ourselves, a day of detachment from the vulgar, of independence of external obligations, a day on which we stop worshipping the idols of technical civilization, a day on which we use no money, a day of armistice in the economic struggle with our fellow men and the forces of nature—is there any institution that holds out a greater hope for man's progress than the Sabbath?

The solution of mankind's most vexing problem will not be found in renouncing technical civilization, but in attaining some degree of independence of it.

In regard to external gifts, to outward possessions, there is only one proper attitude—to have them and to be able to do without them. On the Sabbath we live, as it were, *independent of technical civilization:* we abstain primarily from any activity that aims at remaking or reshaping the things of space. Man's royal privilege to conquer nature is suspended on the seventh day.

What are the kinds of labor not to be done on the Sabbath? They are, according to the ancient rabbis, all those acts which were necessary for the construction and furnishing of the Sanctuary in the desert. The Sabbath itself is a sanctuary which we build, *a sanctuary in time.*

It is one thing to race or be driven by the vicissitudes that menace life, and another thing to stand still and to embrace the presence of an eternal moment.

The seventh day is the armistice in man's cruel struggle for existence, a truce in all conflicts, personal and social, peace between man and man, man and nature, peace within man; a day on which handling money is considered a desecration, on which man avows his independence of that which is the world's chief idol. The seventh day is the exodus from tension, the liberation of man from his own muddiness, the installation of man as a sovereign in the world of time.

In the tempestuous ocean of time and toil there are islands of stillness where man may enter a harbor and reclaim his dignity. The island is the seventh day, the Sabbath, a day of detachment from things, instruments and practical affairs as well as of attachment to the spirit.

The Sabbath must all be spent "in charm, grace, peace, and great love . . . for on it even the wicked in hell find peace." It is, therefore, a double sin to show anger on the Sabbath. "Ye shall kindle no fire throughout your habitations on the Sabbath day" (Exodus 35:3), is interpreted to mean: "Ye shall kindle no fire of controversy nor the heat of anger."[26] Ye shall kindle no fire—not even the fire of righteous indignation.

All week we may ponder and worry whether we are rich or poor, whether we succeed or fail in our occupations; whether we accomplish or fall short of reaching our goals. But who could feel distressed when gazing at spectral glimpses of eternity, except to feel startled at the vanity of being so distressed?

The Sabbath is no time for personal anxiety or care, for any activity

222

that might dampen the spirit of joy. The Sabbath is no time to remember sins, to confess, to repent, or even to pray for relief or anything we might need. It is a day for praise, not a day for petitions. Fasting, mourning, demonstrations of grief are forbidden. The period of mourning is interrupted by the Sabbath. And if one visits the sick on the Sabbath, one should say: "It is the Sabbath, one must not complain; you will soon be cured."²⁷ One must abstain from toil and strain on the seventh day, even from strain in the service of God.

For the Sabbath is a day of harmony and peace, peace between man and man, peace within man, and peace with all things. On the seventh day man has no right to tamper with God's world, to change the state of physical things. It is a day of rest for *man and animal* alike:

> In it thou shalt not do any manner of work, thou nor thy son, nor thy daughter, nor thy man-servant, nor thy maid-servant, nor thine *ox*, nor thine *ass*, nor any of thy *cattle*, nor thy stranger that is within thy gates; that thy man-servant and thy maid-servant may rest as well as thou.
>
> (Deuteronomy 5:14)

IV

About the middle of the third century, distinguished scholars speak of the seventh day not as if referring to abstract time, elusive and constantly passing us by. The day was a living presence, and when it arrived they felt as if a guest had come to see them. And, surely, a guest who comes to pay a call in friendship or respect must be given a welcome. It is, indeed, told of Rabbi Yannai that his custom was to don his robes on the eve of the Sabbath, and then address himself to the ethereal guest: *"Come O Bride, Come O Bride."*²⁸ Of another contemporary, Rabbi Ḥanina the Great, we know that at the sunset of Sabbath eve, he would clothe himselc in beautiful robes, burst forth in a dance,²⁹ and exclaim, presumably in the presence of his friends: "Come, let us go out to welcome the *Queen Sabbath.*" ³⁰

There are two aspects to the Sabbath, as there are two aspects to the world. The Sabbath is meaningful to man and is meaningful to God. It stands in a relation to both, and is a sign of the covenant entered into by both. What is the sign? God has sanctified the day, and man must again and again sanctify the day, illumine the day with the light of his soul. The Sabbath is holy by the grace of God, and is still in need of all the holiness which man may lend to it.

The name of the Friday evening service is *kabbalat Shabbat*. What does the phrase mean? The term *"kabbalah"* denotes the act of taking an obligation upon oneself. The term in this sense has the connotation of strictness and restraint. Yet *"kabbalah"* in its verbal form means also: to receive, to welcome, to greet.[31] In the first meaning, it is applied to a law; in the second, to a person. The question arises, in what meaning is the word *"kabbalah"* used when applied to the word *"Shabbat"?*

It has been said that in medieval literature the term *"kabbalat Shabbat"* is used exclusively in the first sense, denoting the act of taking upon oneself the obligation to rest, the moment of cessation from work. Yet it may be proved that in an even earlier period the term has been used in the sense of greeting or welcoming the Sabbath.[32] What, then, does the phrase *"kabbalat Shabbat"* mean?

The answer is, it means both; it has both a legal and a spiritual meaning; they are inseparable from one another. The distinction of the Sabbath is reflected in the twin meanings of the phrase *kabbalat Shabbat* which means to accept the sovereignty as well as to welcome the presence of the day. The Sabbath is a queen as well as a bride.

According to the Talmud, the Sabbath is *me'en 'olam ha-ba,* which means: *somewhat like* eternity or the world to come. This idea that a seventh part of our lives may be experienced as paradise is a scandal to the pagans and a revelation to the Jews. And yet to Rabbi Ḥayim of Krasne the Sabbath contains more than a morsel of eternity. To him the Sabbath is the fountainhead (*ma'yan*) of eternity, the well from which heaven or the life in the world to come takes its source.

Unless one learns how to relish the taste of Sabbath while still in this world, unless one is initiated in the appreciation of eternal life, one will be unable to enjoy the taste of eternity in the world to come. Sad is the lot of him who arrives inexperienced and when led to heaven has no power to perceive the beauty of the Sabbath. . . .

While Jewish tradition offers us no definition of the concept of eternity, it tells us how to experience the taste of eternity or eternal life within time. Eternal life does not grow away from us; it is "planted within us," growing beyond us. The world to come is therefore not only a posthumous condition, dawning upon the soul on the morrow after its departure from the body. The essence of the world to come is Sabbath eternal, and the seventh day in time is an example of eternity.[33] The seventh day has the flavor of the seventh heaven and was given as a foretaste of the world to come; *ot hi le-'olam,* a token of eternity.[34]

A story is told about the rabbi who once entered heaven in his dream. He was permitted to approach the temple in Paradise where the great sages of the Talmud, the Tannaim, were spending their eternal lives. He saw that they were just sitting around tables studying the Talmud. The disappointed rabbi wondered, "Is this all there is to Paradise?" But suddenly he heard a voice: "You are mistaken. The Tannaim are not in Paradise. Paradise is in the Tannaim."

37. The Sabbath: Holiness in Time

We usually think that the earth is our mother, that time is money and profit our mate. The seventh day is a reminder that God is our father, that time is life and the spirit our mate.

There is a world of things and a world of spirit. Sabbath is a microcosm of spirit, as if combining in itself all the elements of the macrocosm of spirit.

Just as the physical world does not owe its existence to the power of man—it is simply there—so does the spirit not owe its existence to the mind of man. The Sabbath is not holy by the grace of man. It was God who sanctified the seventh day.

In the language of the Bible the world was brought into being in the six days of creation, yet its survival depends upon the holiness of the seventh day.

V

Holiness in space, in nature, was known in other religions. New in the teaching of Judaism was that the idea of holiness was gradually shifted from space to time, from the realm of nature to the realm of history, from things to events. The physical world became divested of any inherent sanctity. There were no naturally sacred plants or animals any more. To be sacred, a thing had to be consecrated by a conscious act of man. The quality of holiness is not in the grain of matter. It is a preciousness bestowed upon things by an act of consecration and persisting in relation to God.

The emphasis on time is a predominant feature of prophetic thinking. "The day of the Lord" is more important to the prophets than "the house of the Lord."

Mankind is split into nations and divided in states. It is a moment in time—the messianic end of days—that will give back to man what a thing in space, the Tower of Babel, had taken away. It was the vision of the messianic day in which the hope of restoring the unity of all men was won.[35]

There is no mention of a sacred place in the Ten Commandments. On the contrary, following the event at Sinai, Moses is told: "In every place where I cause My name to be mentioned I will come unto thee and bless thee" (Exodus 20:24). The awareness that sanctity is not bound to a particular place made possible the rise of the synagogue. The temple was only in Jerusalem, while the synagogue was in every village. There are fixed times, but no fixed place of prayer.

In the Bible, no thing, no place on earth, is holy by itself. Even the site on which the only sanctuary was to be built in the Promised Land is never called holy in the Pentateuch, nor was it determined or specified

225

in the time of Moses. More than twenty times it is referred to as "the place which the Lord your God *shall choose.*"

The temple became a sacred place, yet its sacredness was not self-begotten. Its sanctity was established, yet the paradox of a sanctity in space was sensed by the prophets.

The pious people of Israel would sing:

> Let us go into His dwelling-place;
> Let us worship at His footstool.
> (Psalms 132:7)

but the prophet proclaimed:

> Thus saith the Lord:
> The heaven is my throne,
> And the earth is my footstool;
> Where is the house that ye may build unto Me?
> And where is the place that may be My resting-place?
> (Isaiah 66:1)

If God is everywhere, He cannot be just somewhere. If God has made all things, how can man make a thing for Him?[36] In the Sabbath liturgy we recite till this day:

> His glory fills the universe.
> His angels ask one another:
> Where is the place of His glory?

The sense of holiness in time is expressed in the manner in which the Sabbath is celebrated. No ritual object is required for keeping the seventh day, unlike most festivals on which such objects are essential to their observance, as, for example, unleavened bread, Shofar, Lulab and Etrog, or the Tabernacle. On that day the symbol of the Covenant, the phylacteries, displayed on all days of the week, is dispensed with. Symbols are superfluous: the Sabbath is itself the symbol.

VI

The Sabbath as experienced by man cannot survive in exile, a lonely stranger among days of profanity. It needs the companionship of all other days. All days of the week must be spiritually consistent with the Day of Days. All our life should be a pilgrimage to the seventh day; the thought and appreciation of what this day may bring to us should be ever present in our minds. For the Sabbath is the counterpoint of living; the melody sustained throughout all agitations and vicissitudes which menace our conscience; our awareness of God's presence in the world.

Inner liberty depends upon being exempt from domination of things as well as from domination of people. There are many who have acquired a high degree of political and social liberty, but only very few are not enslaved to things. This is our constant problem—how to live with people and remain free, how to live with things and remain independent.

In a moment of eternity, while the taste of redemption was still fresh to the former slaves, the people of Israel were given the Ten Words, the Ten Commandments. In its beginning and end, the Decalogue deals with the liberty of man. The first Word—*I am the Lord thy God, who brought thee out of the Land of Egypt, out of the house of bondage*—reminds him that his outer liberty was given to him by God, and the tenth Word— *Thou shalt not covet!*—reminds him that he himself must achieve his inner liberty.

When today we wish to bring a word into special prominence we either underline it or print it in italics. In ancient literature, emphasis is expressed through direct repetition (epizeuxis), by repeating a word without any intervening words. The Bible, for example, says: "Justice, Justice shalt thou follow" (Deuteronomy 16:20); "Comfort ye, comfort ye My people" (Isaiah 40:1). Of all the Ten Commandments, only one is proclaimed twice, the last one: "Thou shalt not covet . . . Thou shalt not covet." Clearly it was reiterated in order to stress its extraordinary importance. Man is told not to covet "thy neighbor's house," "thy neighbor's wife, nor his man-servant nor his maid-servant, nor his ox, nor his ass, nor any thing belonging to thy neighbor."

We know that passion cannot be vanquished by decree. The tenth injunction would, therefore, be practically futile, were it not for the "commandment" regarding the Sabbath day to which about a third of the text of the Decalogue is devoted, and which is an epitome of all other commandments. We must seek to find a relation between the two "commandments." Do not covet anything belonging to thy neighbor; I have given thee something that belongs to Me. What is that something? A day.

Judaism tries to foster the vision of life as a pilgrimage to the seventh day; the longing for the Sabbath all days of the week which is a form of longing for the eternal Sabbath all the days of our lives. It seeks to displace the coveting of things in space for *coveting the things in time,* teaching man to covet the seventh day all days of the week. God himself coveted that day, He called it *Ḥemdat Yamim,* a day to be coveted. It is as if the command: *Do not covet things of space,* were correlated with the unspoken word: *Do covet things of time.*

VII

Pagans project their consciousness of God into a visible image or associate Him with a phenomenon in nature, with a thing of space. In the

Ten Commandments, the Creator of the universe identifies Himself by an event in history, by an event in time, the liberation of the people from Egypt, and proclaims: "Thou shalt not make unto thee any graven image or any likeness of any thing that is in heaven above, or that is in the earth, or that is in the water under the earth."

Monuments of stone are destined to disappear; days of spirit never pass away. About the arrival of the people at Sinai we read in the Book of Exodus: "In the third month after the children of Israel were gone forth out of the land of Egypt, on *this day* they came into the wilderness of Sinai" (19:1). Here was an expression that puzzled the ancient rabbis: on *this day?* It should have been said: on *that day*. This can only mean that the day of giving the Torah can never become past; that day is this day, every day. The Torah, whenever we study it, must be to us "as if it were given us today."[37] The same applies to the day of the exodus from Egypt: "In every age man must see himself as if he himself went out of Egypt."[38]

The worth of a great day is not measured by the space it occupies in the calendar.

In the realm of spirit, there is no difference between a second and a century, between an hour and an age. Rabbi Judah the Patriarch cried: "There are those who gain eternity in a lifetime, others who gain it in one brief hour."[39] One good hour may be worth a lifetime; an instant of returning to God may restore what has been lost in years of escaping from Him. "Better is one hour of repentence and good deeds in this world than the whole life in the world to come."[40]

Technical civilization, we have said, is man's triumph over space. Yet time remains impervious. We can overcome distance but can neither recapture the past nor dig out the future. Man transcends space, and time transcends man.

Every one of us occupies a portion of space. He takes it up exclusively. The portion of space which my body occupies is taken up by myself in exclusion of anyone else. Yet, no one possesses time. There is no moment which I possess exclusively. This very moment belongs to all living men as it belongs to me. We share time, we own space. Through my ownership of space, I am a rival of all other beings; through my living in time, I am a contemporary of all other beings. We pass through time, we occupy space. We easily succumb to the illusion that the world of space is for our sake, for man's sake. In regard to time, we are immune to such an illusion.

According to the Book of Exodus, Moses beheld his first vision "in a flame of fire, out of the midst of a bush: and he looked, and, behold, the bush burned with fire, and the bush was not consumed" (3:2). Time is

228

like an eternal burning bush. Though each instant must vanish to open the way to the next one, time itself is not consumed.

Time is the process of creation, and things of space are results of creation. When looking at space we see the products of creation; when intuiting time we hear the process of creation. Things of space exhibit a deceptive independence. They show off a veneer of limited permanence. Things created conceal the Creator. It is the dimension of time wherein man meets God, wherein man becomes aware that every instant is an act of creation, a Beginning, opening up new roads for ultimate realizations. Time is the presence of God in the world of space, and it is within time that we are able to sense the unity of all beings.

Creation, we are taught, is not an act that happened once upon a time, once and for ever. The act of bringing the world into existence is a continuous process. God called the world into being, and that call goes on. There is this present moment because God is present. Every instant is an act of creation. A moment is not a terminal but a flash, a signal of Beginning. Time is perpetual innovation, a synonym for continuous creation. Time is God's gift to the world of space.

A world without time would be a world without God, a world existing in and by itself, without renewal, without a Creator. A world without time would be a world detached from God, a thing in itself, reality without realization. A world in time is a world going on through God; realization of an infinite design; not a thing in itself but a thing for God.

To witness the perpetual marvel of the world's coming into being is to sense the presence of the Giver in the given, to realize that the source of time is eternity, that the secret of being is the eternal within time.

We cannot solve the problem of time through the conquest of space, through either pyramids or fame. We can only solve the problem of time through sanctification of time. To men alone time is elusive; to men with God time is eternity in disguise.

This is the task of men: to conquer space and sanctify time.

We must conquer space in order to sanctify time. All week long we are called upon to sanctify life through employing things of space. On the Sabbath it is given us to share in the holiness that is in the heart of time.

Part V

The Meaning of This Hour

38. WHAT IS MAN?

What is human about a human being? What do I see when I see man? We know that man is more similar to an ape than an ape is to a toad. We are told that "man has not only developed from the realm of animals; he *was, is,* and *shall always* remain an animal." But is this the whole truth about man? Is this an answer to the question, "What do I see when I see a man?"

A textbook used in our American colleges contains the following definition. A human being is "an ingenious assembly of portable plumbing." What glory to be a man!

We must not take lightly man's pronouncements about himself. They surely reveal as well as affect his basic attitudes. Is it not right to say that we often treat man as if he were made in the likeness of a machine rather than in the likeness of God?

A definition in the Eleventh Edition of the *Encyclopaedia Britannica* is surely bound to inspire reverence for the greatness of man. It says: "Man is a seeker after the greatest degree of comfort for the least necessary expenditure of energy."

In pre-Nazi Germany the following statement of man was frequently quoted: "The human body contains a sufficient amount of fat to make seven cakes of soap, enough iron to make a medium-sized nail, a sufficient amount of phosphorus to equip two thousand match-heads, enough sulphur to rid one's self of one's fleas." Perhaps there was a connection between this statement and what the Nazis actually did in the extermination camps: to make soap of human flesh.

As descriptions of one of many aspects of the nature of man, these definitions may indeed be correct. But when pretending to express his totality or meaning, they contribute to the gradual liquidation of man's self-understanding. And the liquidation of the self-understanding of man may lead to the self-extinction of man.

It seems that the depth and mystery of a human being is something that no science can grasp. The knowledge of man we get from science for all its usefulness strikes us as an oversimplification; its definitions become meaningless when applied to actual human beings. Am I addressing myself at this moment to an ingenious assemblage of portable plumbing?

Perhaps this is the central issue in religious education: to become aware

233

of the sacred image of man. Man is our chief problem. His physical and mental reality is beyond dispute; his meaning, his spiritual relevance, is a question that cries for an answer.

There are three aspects of human existence which seem to be basic to the Bible.

1. Man is created in the image of God.
2. Man is dust.
3. Man is an object of Divine concern.

Nothing is more alien to the spirit of Judaism than the veneration of images and symbols. The Third Commandment, "You shall not make yourself a graven image," implies the rejection not only of images fashioned by man but also of "any likeness, of anything that is in Heaven above, or that is in the Earth beneath, or that is in the water under the earth." It would even be alien to the spirit of the Bible to assert that the world is a symbol of God.

And yet there is something in the world that the Bible does regard as a symbol of God. It is not a temple nor a tree, it is not a statue nor a star. The one symbol of God is *man, every man*. God Himself created man in His image, or to use the Biblical terms, in his *tzelem* and *demut*. How significant is the fact that the term, *"tzelem"*, which is frequently used in a damnatory sense for a man-made image of God, as well as the term, *"demut"*—of which Isaiah claims (40:18) no *demut* can be applied to God—are employed in denoting man as an image and likeness of God!

Not that the Bible was unaware of man's frailty and wickedness. With supreme frankness the failures and shortcomings of kings and prophets, of men such as Moses and David, are recorded. And yet, Jewish tradition insisted that not only man's soul but also his body is symbolic of God. This is why even the body of a criminal condemned to death must be treated with reverence, according to the book of Deuteronomy (21:23). He who sheds the blood of a human being, "it is accounted to him as though he diminished (or destroyed) the Divine image." Hillel characterized the body as an "icon" of God, as it were, and considered keeping clean one's own body as an act of reverence for its Creator.

As not one man or one particular nation but all men and all nations are endowed with the likeness of God, there is no danger of ever worshipping man, because only that which is extraordinary and different may become an object of worship. But the Divine likeness is something all men share.

This is a conception of far reaching importance to Biblical piety. What it implies can hardly be summarized. Reverence for God is shown in our reverence for man. The fear you must feel of offending or hurting a human being must be as ultimate as your fear of God. An act of violence is an act of desecration. To be arrogant toward man is to be blasphemous toward God.

> He who oppresses the poor blasphemes his
>   Maker,
> He who is gracious to the needy honors Him.
>   (Proverbs 14:31)

And what is more, Biblical piety may be expressed in the form of a supreme imperative: Treat yourself as a symbol of God. In the light of this imperative we can understand the meaning of that astounding commandment: "You shall be holy, for I the Lord your God am holy" (Leviticus 19:2).

Now there are two ways in which the Bible speaks of the creation of man. In the first chapter of the book of Genesis (which is devoted to the creation of the physical universe) man is described as having been created in the image and likeness of God. In the second chapter (which tells us of the commandment not to eat of the fruit of the tree of knowledge) man is described as having been formed *out of the dust* of the earth. Together image and dust express the polarity of the nature of man. He is formed of the most inferior stuff in the most superior image.

Dust thou art, and unto dust thou shalt return (Genesis 3:19). These words with which the Lord addressed Adam after he sinned convey a basic part of the Biblical understanding of man. The fact of man having been created "in the image and likeness of God" is mentioned as a Divine secret and uttered in a Divine monologue, while the fact of man being dust is conveyed to man in a dialogue with man. Nowhere in the Bible does man, standing before God, say, "I am Thy image and likeness." Abraham, pleading with God to save the city of Sodom, knows: "Behold now, I have taken upon me to speak unto the Lord, who am but *dust and ashes*" (Genesis 18:27). Job prays: "Remember, I beseech Thee, that Thou hast fashioned me as clay" (10:9). And his last words are: "I abhor my words, and repent, seeing I am dust and ashes" (42:6; see 30:19). In this spirit, the Psalmist describes men as beings "that go down to the dust" (Psalms 22:30). This miserable fact, however, is also a comfort to him who discovers his failures, his spiritual feebleness. The Psalmist is consoled in the knowledge that God understands our nature; He remembers that we are dust (Psalms 103:14).

Man, then, is involved in a polarity of a divine image and worthless dust. He is a duality of mysterious grandeur and pompous aridity, a vision of God and a mountain of dust. It is because of his being dust that his iniquities may be forgiven, and it is because of his being an image that his righteousness is expected.

That the end of man is dust is an indisputable fact. But so is the end of the beast. And yet, the Bible emphasizes the absolute difference between man and all other creatures. Plants and animals were brought forth by the earth, by the waters (Genesis 1:11, 20:24); they emerged from "nature" and became an "organic" part of nature. Man, on the other hand, is an artifact. The Lord both created and formed him (1:26; 2:7). He came into being by a special act of creation. He did not come forth out of dust; he did not grow out of the earth. The Lord both created and formed him (1:26; 2:7). He owes his existence not to the forces of nature but to the Creator of all. He is set apart from both the plants and the beasts by the fact of God being directly involved in man's coming into being. It is the knowledge of this fact that inspired the Psalmist's prayer: "Thy hands have made me and fashioned me; give me understanding that I may learn Thy commandments" (Psalms 119:73).

The idea of God as the father of man expresses not merely man's creaturely dependence on God or his personal affinity to God. It expresses the idea that man's ultimate confrontation is not with the world but with God; not only with a Divine law but with *a Divine concern;* not only with His wisdom and power, but also with His love and care.

Man is man because something Divine is at stake in his existence. He is not an innocent bystander in the cosmic drama. There is in us more kinship with the Divine than we are able to believe. The souls of men are candles of the Lord, lit on the cosmic way, rather than fireworks produced by the combustion of nature's explosive compositions, and every soul is indispensable to Him. Man is needed, he is *a need of God.*

Life is a *partnership* of God and man; God is not detached from or indifferent to our joys and griefs. Authentic vital needs of man's body and soul are a divine concern. This is why human life is holy. God is a partner and a partisan in man's struggle for justice, peace and holiness, and it is because of His being in need of man that He entered a *covenant* with him for all time, a mutual bond embracing God and man, a relationship to which God, not only man, is committed.

God does not judge the deeds of man impassively, in a spirit of cool detachment. His judgment is imbued with a feeling of intimate concern. He is the father of all men, not only a judge; He is a lover engaged to his people, not only a king. God stands in a passionate relationship to man. His love or anger, His mercy or disappointment is an expression of His profound participation in the history of Israel and all men.

This is the central message of the Biblical prophets. God is involved in the life of man. A personal relationship, an intimate concern binds Him to mankind. Behind the various manifestations of His pathos is one motive, one need: The Divine need for human righteousness.

And precious are the deeds of righteousness in the eyes of the Lord. The idea of man having been created in the image of God was interpreted, it sems, not as *an analogy of being* but as *an analogy of doing.* Man is called upon to act in the likeness of God. "As He is merciful be thou merciful."

The future of the human species depends upon our degree of reverence for the individual man. And the strength and validity of that reverence depend upon our faith in God's concern for man.

In terms of the cosmic process all of human history counts as much as a match struck in the darkness, and the claim that there is unique and eternal value to the life of the individual must be dismissed as an absurdity. From the perspective of astronomy the exterminations of millions of human beings would not be different from the extermination of insects or roaches.

Only if there is a God who cares, a God to whom the life of every individual is an event—and not only a part of an infinite process—can our sense for the sanctity and preciousness of the individual man be maintained.

There are many questions about man which have often been raised. What is his nature? Why is he mortal? None of these issues are central in Biblical thinking.

The problem that challenged the Biblical mind was not the obscurity of his nature but the paradox of his existence. The starting-point was not a question about man but the distinction of man; not the state of ignorance about the nature of man but rather a state of amazement at what we know about man, namely: Why is man so significant in spite of his insignificance? Not the question, Why is man mortal? But the question, Why is he so distinguished?

The problem that challenged the Biblical mind was not man in and by himself. Man is never seen in isolation but always in relation to God who is the Creator, the King, and the Judge of all beings. The problem of man revolved around God's relation to man.

> Lord,
> What is man,
> That thou takest knowledge of him?
> Or the son of man,
> That thou makest account of him?
> Man is like unto a breath;
> His days are as a shadow
> That passeth away.
>
> (Psalms 144:3–4)

When I behold Thy heavens,
The work of Thy fingers,
The moon and the stars
Which Thou hast established—
What is man
That Thou shouldst be mindful of him?
And the son of man
That Thou shouldst think of him?
And make him
But a little lower than the Divine,
And crown him with glory and honour,
And make him rule over the works of Thy hands?
Thou hast put all things under his feet:
Sheep and oxen, all of them,
Yea, and the beasts of the field;
The fowl of the air, and the fish of the sea,
That pass through the paths of the seas.

(Psalms 8:2–9)

The insignificance of man compared with the grandeur of God under-scores the paradox of God's concern for him. Neither Job nor the Psalmist offers an answer to the overwhelming enigma which thus remains the central mystery of human existence. Yet the acceptance of that fact of Divine concern established the Biblical approach to the existence of man. It is from the perspective of that concern that the quest for an understanding of man begins.

Today the realization of the dangerous greatness of man, of his immense power and ability to destroy all life on earth, may help us to intuit man's relevance in the divine scheme. If this great world of ours is not a trifle in the eyes of God, if the creator is at all concerned with His creation, then man—who has the power to devise both culture and crime, but who is also able to be a proxy for divine justice—is important enough to be the object of divine concern.

Nowhere in Plato's Socratic dialogues do we find a direct solution to the problem, "What is man?" There is only an indirect answer, "Man is declared to be that creature who is constantly in search of himself—a creature who in every moment of his existence must examine and scrutinize the conditions of his existence" (Cassirer). He is a being in search of meaning.

The Greek approach must be contrasted with the Biblical contention that "unless the Lord builds the house, those who build it labor in vain" (Psalms 127:1). The pursuit of meaning is meaningless, unless there is a meaning in pursuit of man.

To the Biblical mind man is not only a creature who is constantly in

238

search of himself but also *a creature God is constantly in search of*. Man is a creature in search of meaning because there is a meaning in search of him, because there is God's beseeching question, "Where art thou?"

Man is prone to ignore this chief question of his existence as long as he finds tranquillity in the ivory tower of petty presumption. But when the tower begin to totter, when death wipes away that which seemed mighty and independent, when in evil days the delights of success are replaced by the nightmare of futility, he becomes conscious of the peril of evasiveness, of the emptiness of small objectives. His apprehension lest in winning small prizes he would gamble his life away, throws his soul open to questions he was trying to avoid.

But what is man's answer to God's beseeching cry?

> Thus says the Lord:
> Why, when I came was there no man?
> When I called, was there no one to answer?
> (Isaiah 50:2a)

Man not only refuses to answer; he often sets out to defy and to blaspheme. Abundant are the references in the Bible not only to man's callousness, but also to his rebellion. The human species is capable of producing not only saints and prophets, but also scoundrels and "enemies of God." The idea of the divine image of man offers no explanation to the dreadful mystery of the evil urge in the heart of man.

> The heart is deceitful above all things and desperately corrupt;
> Who can understand it?
> (Jeremiah 17:9)

Because of the tension of "The good urge" and "the evil urge," human life is full of perils. The only safeguard against constant danger is constant vigilance, constant guidance. If human nature were all we had, there would be little reason to be hopeful. Yet we also have the word of God, the commandment, the *mitzvah*. The central Biblical fact is Sinai. Sinai was superimposed on the failure of Adam. It initiated an order of living, an answer to the question, How should man, a being created in the image of God, think, act, and feel?

Ugly and somber is the world to the prophetic eye; drunk with lust for power, infatuated with war, driven by envy and greed. Man has become a nightmare. History is being made by "guilty men, whose own might is their god" (Habakkuk 1:11).

The meaning of having been created in the image of God is veiled in an enigma. But perhaps we may surmise the intention was for man to be *a witness for God*, a symbol of God. Looking at man one should sense the presence of God. But instead of living as a witness, he became an impostor; instead of being a symbol, he became an idol. In his bristling presumption he developed *a false sense of sovereignty* which fills the world with terror.

We are proud of the achievements of our technological civilization. But our pride may result in our supreme humiliation. The pride in maintaining, "My power and the might of my hand have gotten me this wealth" (Deuteronomy 8:17), will cause us to say "Our god" to the work of our hands (Hosea 14:4).

One shudders to think that involved in our civilization is a demonic force trying to exact vengeance on God.

After having eaten the forbidden fruit, the Lord sent forth man from Paradise, to till the ground from which he was taken. But man who is more subtle than any other creature that God has made, what did he do? He undertook to build a Paradise by his own might and is driving out God from his Paradise. For generations all looked well. But now we have discovered that our Paradise is built upon the top of a volcano. The Paradise we have built may turn out to be a vast camp for the extermination of man.

This is a time to cry out. One is ashamed to be human. One is embarrassed to be called religious in the face of religion's failure to keep alive the image of God in the face of man. We see the writing on the wall but are too illiterate to understand what it says. There are no easy solutions to grave problems. All we can honestly preach is a *theology of dismay*. We have imprisoned God in our temples and slogans, and now the word of God is dying on our lips. We have ceased to be symbols. There is darkness in the East, and smugness in the West. What of the night? What of the night? What is history? Wars, victories, and wars. So many dead. So many tears. So little regret. So many fears. And who could sit in judgment over the victims of cruelty whose horror turns to hatred? Is it easy to keep the horror of wickedness from turning into a hatred of the wicked? The world is drenched in blood, and the guilt is endless. Should not all hope be abandoned?

What saved the prophets from despair was their messianic vision and the idea of man's capacity for repentance. That vision and that idea affected their understanding of history.

History is not a blind alley, and guilt is not an abyss. There is always a way that leads out of guilt: repentance or turning to God. The prophet is a person who living in dismay has the power to transcend his dismay. Over all the darkness of experience hovers the vision of a different day.

In that day there shall be a highway from Egypt to Assyria; the Assyrian will come to Egypt, and the Egyptian into Assyria, and the Egyptians will worship with the Assyrians.

In that day Israel shall be a third with Egypt and Assyria, a blessing in the midst of the earth which the Lord of Hosts has blessed, saying,

Blessed be My People Egypt,
and Assyria, the work of My hands,
and Israel, My inheritance.

(Isaiah 19:23–25.)

Egypt and Assyria are locked up in deadly wars. Hating each other, they are both the enemies of Israel. Abominable are their idolatries, and frightful are their crimes. How does Isaiah, the son of a people which cherishes the privilege of being called by the Lord "My people," "the work of My hands" (Isaiah 60:21), feel about Egypt and Assyria?

Our God is also the God of our enemies, without their knowing Him and despite their defying Him. The enmity between the nations will turn to friendship. They will live together when they will worship together. All three will be equally God's chosen people.

39. UNDERSTANDING THE BIBLE

I

There are two approaches to the Bible that prevail in philosophical thinking. The first approach claims that the Bible is a naïve book, it is poetry or mythology. Beautiful as it is, it must not be taken seriously, for in its thinking it is primitive and immature. How could you compare it with Hegel or Hobbes, John Locke or Schopenhauer? The father of the depreciation of the intellectual relevance of the Bible is Spinoza, who may be blamed for many distorted views of the Bible in subsequent philosophy and exegesis.

The second approach claims that Moses taught the same ideas as Plato or Aristotle, that there is no serious disagreement between the teachings of the philosophers and the teachings of the prophets. The difference, it is claimed, is merely one of expression and style. Aristotle, for example, used unambiguous terms, while the prophets employed metaphors. The father of this approach is Philo. Theology was dominated by the theory of Philo, while general philosophy took the attitude of Spinoza.

There is a story of a cub reporter who was sent to cover a wedding.

When he came back he said dejectedly that he had no story because the bridegroom did not show up. . . .

It is true that one looks in vain for a philosophical vocabulary in the Bible. But the serious student must not look for what he already has. The categories within which philosophical reflection about religion has been operating are derived from Athens rather than from Jerusalem. Judaism is a confrontation with the Bible, and a philosophy of Judaism must be a confrontation with the thought of the Bible.

The Bible is not the only work in which a concern for ultimate religious problems is found. In many lands and at many ages man has searched for God. Yet the Biblical period is the grand chapter in the history of man's wrestling with God (and of God's wrestling with man). And just as in a study of moral values we cannot ignore the great tradition of moral philosophy, we must not in our wrestling with religious issues ignore the insights accumulated in the Bible. It is, therefore, the age of the Bible, a thousand years of illumination, to which we will turn for guidance.

What do we and the people to the Bible have in common? The anxieties and joys of living; the sense of wonder and the resistance to it; the awareness of the hiding God and moments of longing to find a way to Him.

The central thought of Judaism is *the living God*. It is the perspective from which all other issues are seen. And the supreme problem in any philosophy of Judaism is: what are the grounds for man's believing in the realness of the living God? Is man at all capable of discovering such grounds?

Two sources of religious thinking are given us: *memory* (tradition) and *personal* insight. We must rely on our memory and we must strive for fresh insight. We *hear* from tradition, we also *understand* through our own seeking. The prophets appeal to the spiritual power in man: "Know, therefore, this day, and lay it to your heart, that the Lord is God in heaven above and on the earth beneath; there is no other" (Deuteronomy 4:39). The psalmist calls on us "O taste and see that the Lord is good" (34:9). How does one know? How does one taste?

An allusion to the need for every man's own quest for God was seen homiletically in the Song of the Red Sea:

> This is my God, and I will glorify Him;
> The God of my father, and I will exalt Him.
> (Exodus 15:2)

Out of his own insight a person must first arrive at the understanding: *This is my God, and I will glorify Him,* and subsequently he will attain the realization that He is *the God of my father, and I will exalt Him.*[1]

It is not given to all men to identify the divine. His light may shine upon us, and we may fail to sense it. Devoid of wonder, we remain deaf to the sublime. We cannot sense His presence in the Bible except by being responsive to it. Only living with its words, only sympathy with its pathos, will open our ear to its voice. Biblical words are like musical signs of a divine harmony which only the finest chords of the soul can utter. It is the sense of the holy that perceives the presence of God in the Bible.

We can never approach the Bible alone. It is to *man with God* that the Bible opens itself.

To sense the presence of God in the Bible, one must learn *to be present* to God in the Bible. Presence is not a concept, but a situation. To understand love it is not enough to read tales about it. One must be involved in the prophets to understand the prophets. One must be inspired to understand inspiration. Just as we cannot test thinking without thinking, we cannot sense holiness without being holy. Presence is not disclosed to those who are unattached and try to judge, to those who have no power to go beyond the values they cherish; to those who sense the story, not the pathos; the idea, not the realness of God.

The Bible is the frontier of the spirit where we must move and live in order to discover and to explore. It is open to him who gives himself to it, who lives with it intimately.

We can only sense the presence by being responsive to it. We must learn to respond before we may hear; we must learn to fulfill before we may know. *It is the Bible that enables us to know the Bible.* It is through the Bible that we discover what is in the Bible. Unless we are confronted with the word, unless we continue our dialogue with the prophets, unless we respond, the Bible ceases to be Scripture.

II

In our encounter with the Bible we may take either a fundamentalist attitude which regards every word as literally valid, making no distinction between the eternal and the temporal, and allowing no place for personal or historic understanding, or for the voice of the conscience. Or we may take a rationalist attitude which, taking science as the touchstone of religion, regards Scripture as a poetic product or myth, useful to men of an inferior civilization and therefore outdated at any later period of history.

Philosophy of religion has to carry on a battle on two fronts, trying to winnow false notions of the fundamentalist, and to dampen the over-confidence of the rationalists. The ultimate task is to lead us to a higher plane of knowledge and experience, to attachment through understanding.

We must beware of the obscurantism of a mechanical deference to the

Bible. The prophetic words were given to us to be understood, not merely to be mechanically repeated. The Bible is to be understood by the spirit that grows with it, wrestles with it, and prays with it.

By insisting upon the objective revelational character of the Bible, dogmatic theology has often lost sight of the profound and decisive share of man.

The prophet is not a passive recipient, a recording instrument, affected from without without participation of heart and will, nor is he a person who acquires his vision by his own strength and labor. The prophet's personality is rather a unity of inspiration and experience, invasion and response. God does not reveal Himself; he only reveals His way. Judaism does not speak of God's self-revelation, but of the revelation of His teaching for man. The Bible reflects God's revelation of His relation to history, rather than of a revelation of His very Self. Even His will or His wisdom is not completely expressed through the prophets. Prophecy is superior to human wisdom, and God's love is superior to prophecy. This spiritual hierarchy is explicitly stated by the rabbis.

"They asked *Wisdom:* What should be the punishment of a sinner? And Wisdom said: *Misfortune pursues sinners* (Proverbs 13:21). They asked *Prophecy:* What should be the punishment of a sinner? And Prophecy said: *The soul that sins shall die* (Ezekiel 18:4, 20). They asked *the Holy One,* blessed be He: What should be the punishment of a sinner? And He said: *Let him repent, and he will be atoned for.*"[2]

God is infinitely more sublime than what the prophets were able to comprehend, and the heavenly wisdom is more profound than what the Torah contains in its present form.

"There are five incomplete phenomena (or unripe fruits). The incomplete experience of death is sleep; an incomplete form of prophecy is dream; the incomplete form of the world to come is the Sabbath; the incomplete form of the heavenly light is the orb of the sun; the incomplete form of heavenly wisdom is the Torah."[3]

The word Torah is used in two senses: the supernal Torah, the existence of which preceded the creation of the world,[4] and the revealed Torah. Concerning the supernal Torah the rabbis maintained: "The Torah is hidden from the eyes of all living. . . . Man knows not the price thereof."[5] "Moses received Torah"—but not all of the Torah—"at Sinai."[6] And not all that was revealed to Moses was conveyed to Israel; the meaning of the commandments is given as an example.[7] Together with the gratitude for the word that was disclosed, there is a yearning for the meaning yet to be disclosed. "The Lord gave Israel the Torah and spoke to them face to face, and the memory of that love is more delightful to them than any other joy. They have been promised that He will return to them once more in order to reveal the secret meaning of the Torah and its concealed content. Israel implores Him to fulfill this promise. This is the meaning of the verse: *Let Him kiss me with the kisses of His mouth—for Thy love is better than wine.*"[8]

There is a theory in Jewish literature containing a profound parabolical truth which maintains that the Torah, which is eternal in spirit, assumes different forms in various eons. The Torah was known to Adam when he was in the Garden of Eden, although not in its present form. Commandments such as those concerning charity to the poor, the stranger, the orphan, and the widow, would have been meaningless in the Garden of Eden. In that eon the Torah was known in its spiritual form.[9] Just as man assumed a material form when he was driven out of the Garden of Eden, so has the Torah assumed a material form. If man had retained "the garments of light," his spiritual form of existence, the Torah, too, would have retained its spiritual form.[10]

God is not only in heaven but in this world as well. But in order to dwell in this world, the divine must assume a form which this world could bear, "shells" in which the light is concealed. The Torah, too, in order to enter the world of history, is encased in "shells," since it could not exist or be fulfilled in its perfect form in a world which is stained with imperfections.[11]

The words of Scripture are the only lasting record of what was conveyed to the prophets. At the same time they are neither identical with, nor the eternally adequate rendering of, the divine wisdom. As a reflection of His infinite light, the text in its present form is, to speak figuratively, one of an endless number of possible reflections. In the end of the days, it was believed, countless unknown rearrangements of the words and letters and unknown secrets of the Torah would be made known. Yet in its present form the text contains that which God wishes us to know.[12]

There is another aspect to the part played by the prophet. According to the rabbis, *"The same idea is revealed to many prophets, but no two prophets use the same expression."* The fact that the four hundred prophets of King Ahab employed *the same* phrases was regarded as proof that they were not divinely inspired.[13] When in the court of justice two people testifying to the same event use identical language, they are suspected of having conspired to bear false witness. The prophets bear witness to an event. The event is divine, but the formulation is done by the individual prophet. According to this conception, the idea is revealed; the expression is coined by the prophet. The expression "the word of God" would not refer to the word as a sound or a combination of sounds. Indeed, it has often been maintained that what reached the ear of man was not identical with what has come out of the spirit of the eternal God. For

"Israel could not possibly have received the Torah as it came forth from the mouth of the Lord, for the word of the Lord is fire and the Lord is 'a fire that consumes fire.' Surely man would flash into blaze, if he were exposed to the word in itself. Therefore, the word became clothed before it entered the world of creation. And so the Psalmist speaks of revelation as 'coals that flamed forth from Him' (Psalms 18:9). The word of God in itself is like a burning flame, and the Torah that we received is merely a part of the coal to which the flame is attached. And yet, even in this form it would have remained beyond our comprehension as long as we are mortals. The word had to descend further and to assume the form of darkness (*'arafel*) in order to become perceptible to man."[14]

Out of the experience of the prophets came the words, words that try to interpret what they perceived. To this very day, these words make present what happened in the past. As the meaning and wonder of the event inspired the spiritual comprehension of the prophet, the meaning and wonder of the Biblical words continue to inspire the understanding of man.

The Bible reflects its divine as well as its human authorship. Expressed in the language of a particular age, it addresses itself to all ages; disclosed in particular acts, its spirit is everlasting. The will of God is in time and in eternity. God borrowed the language of man and created a work such as no men had ever made. It is the task of faith to hold fast to that work, to treasure its mixture of timeliness and eternity and to continually understand the polarity of its contents.

An outstanding mark of Biblical writing is its *ruthless honesty*. None of the prophets is pictured as faultless, none of the heroes is impeccable. The Glory is enveloped in a cloud, and redemption is attained at the price of exile. There is neither perfection nor sweetness nor sentimentality in the Bible's approach. Abraham has the courage to exclaim, "The judge of all the earth shall not act justly?" And Job dares to question the fairness of the Almighty. Accusing his friends who offer apologies for God as being "plasterers of lies," Job pleads:

> Will you speak falsely for God,
> And talk deceitfully for Him?
> Will you show partiality toward Him,
> Will you plead the case of God?
> Will it be well with you when He searches you out?
> Or can you deceive Him, as one deceives a man?
> He will surely rebuke you,
> If in secret you show partiality.
>
> (Job 13:7–10)

Resignation and acceptance of the inscrutable will of God are expressions of normal piety. In contrast, though *not* in contradiction, stands the prophet who, instead of being unquestioning and submissive in the face of God, dares to challenge His judgment, to remind Him of His covenant and to plead for His mercy. In the spirit of piety, Jew and Christian will accept evil as well as good, and pray, "Thy will be done,"[15] while the prophet will plead, "Turn from Thy fierce wrath and repent of this evil against Thy people" (Exodus 32:12).

Abraham challenged the intention of the Lord to destroy Sodom. In the name of God's mercy, we too have the right to challenge the harsh statements of the prophets.

III

The Bible is not an intellectual sinecure, and its acceptance should not be like setting up a talismanic lock that seals both the mind and the conscience against the intrusion of new thoughts. Revelation is not *vicarious thinking*. Its purpose is not to substitute for but to extend our understanding. The prophets tried to extend the horizon of our conscience and to impart to us a sense of the divine partnership in our dealings with good and evil and in our wrestling with life's enigmas. They tried to teach us how to think in the categories of God: His holiness, justice and compassion. The appropriation of these categories, far from exempting us from the obligation to gain new insights in our own time, is a challenge to look for ways of translating Biblical commandments into programs required by our own conditions. The full meaning of the Biblical words was not disclosed once and for all. Every hour another aspect is unveiled. The word was given once; the effort to understand it must go on for ever. It is not enough to accept or even to carry out the commandments. To study, to examine, to explore the Torah is a form of worship, a supreme duty. For the Torah is an invitation to perceptivity, a call for *continuous understanding*.

Taken as vicarious thinking, the Bible becomes a stumbling block. He who says, I have *only* the Torah, does not even have the Torah. The Karaites claimed to adhere to a purely Biblical religion. However, Judaism is not a purely Biblical religion. Moses was not the founder of Judaism. Long before he was born the children of Israel cherished traditions that dated back to the days of Abraham. The oral Torah is, in parts, older than the written Torah. The Sabbath, we are told, was known to Israel before the event at Sinai took place. Not all of the Mosaic teachings were incorporated in the Pentateuch. Numerous principles and rules remained "oral teaching" handed down from generation to generation.

And it was concerning both the written and the "oral teaching" that the covenant at Sinai was concluded.

We approach the laws of the Bible through the interpretation and the wisdom of the rabbis. Without their interpretation the text of the laws is often unintelligible. Thus Judaism is based upon a minimum of revelation and a maximum of interpretation, upon the will of God and upon the understanding of Israel. For that understanding we are dependent upon Israel's unwritten tradition. The prophets' inspirations and the sages' interpretations are equally important. There is a partnership of God and Israel in regard to both the world and the Torah: He created the earth and we till the soil; He gave us the text and we refine and complete it. "The Holy One, blessed be He, gave the Torah unto Israel like wheat from which to derive fine flour, or like flax from which to make a garment."[16]

The Bible is a seed, God is the sun, but we are the soil. Every generation is expected to bring forth new understanding and new realization.

The word is the word of God, and its understanding He gave unto man. The source of authority is not the word as given in the text but Israel's understanding of the text. At Sinai we received both the word and the spirit to understand the word. The savants are heirs to the prophets; they determine and interpret the meaning of the word. There is much liberty and much power in the insights of the sages: they have the power to set aside a precept of the Torah when conditions require it. Here on earth, their opinion may overrule an opinion held in heaven.

Some of that original understanding and response of Israel was poured into words, conveyed from mouth to mouth, entrusted to writing, but much, of which words were only a reflection, remained unsaid, unwritten, a tradition transmitted from soul to soul, inherited like the power to love, and kept alive by constant communion with the Word, by studying it, by guarding it, by living it and by being ready to die for it. In the hands of many peoples it becomes a *book;* in the life of Israel it remained a *voice,* a Torah within the heart (Isaiah 51:7).

For Israel's understanding of the word was not cheaply or idyllically won. It was acquired at the price of millennia of wrestling, of endurance and bitter ordeals of a stubborn people, of unparalleled martyrdom and self-sacrifice of men, women and children, of loyalty, love and constant study. What modern scholar could vie with the intuition of such a people? The Torah is not only our mother, it is "our life and the length of our days; we will meditate (on her words) day and night" (Evening liturgy).

Without our continuous striving for understanding, the Bible is like paper money without security. Yet such understanding requires austere discipline and can only be achieved in attachment and dedication, in retaining and reliving the original understanding as expressed by the prophets and the ancient sages.

There is always the danger of trying to interpret the Bible in terms of paganism. As there is *false prophecy,* there is *false understanding.* It is possible to commit murder in the name of the Torah; one may be a scoundrel and act within the letter of the law (Naḥmanides). There has, indeed, been so much pious abuse that the Bible is often in need of being saved from the hands of its admirers.

For centuries the prohibition of writing down "the oral teaching" was regarded as a basic tenet. "Those who write down the halakhah are like those who burn the Torah."[17] He "who writes down the agadah loses his share in the world to come."[18] Then the rabbis decided to submit "the oral teaching" to the written form. In justification of the bold reform, they interpreted the verse in Psalms 119:126 to mean: "There comes a time when you may abrogate the Torah in order to do the work of the Lord." Hence, the rabbis maintained, it is better that one part of the Torah shall be abrogated than the whole Torah be forgotten.[19] The accumulation of the vast amount of learning, the scattering of Jewish communities, and the weakening of memory militated against the oral system.

Rabbi Mendel of Kotzk asked: How could the ancient rabbis abolish the fundamental principle of Judaism, not to write down what is to be kept as an oral tradition, on the basis of a single verse in the book of Psalms? The truth is that the oral Torah was never written down. The meaning of the Torah has never been contained by books.

IV

The Bible is an answer to the question: how to sanctify life. And if we say we feel no need for sanctification, we only prove that the Bible is indispensable. Because it is the Bible that teaches us how to feel the need for sanctification.

What have the prophets done for the human situation? Let us try to recall but a few out of many things.

The Bible showed man his independence of nature, his superiority to conditions, and called on him to realize the tremendous implications of simple acts. Not only the stars but also the deeds of man travel a course that either reflects or perverts a thought of God. The degree of our appreciation of the Bible is, therefore, determined by the degree of our sensitivity to the divine dignity of human deeds. The insight into the divine implications of human life is the distinct message of the Bible.

The Bible has shattered man's illusion of being alone. God does not stand aloof from our cries; He is not only a pattern, but a power, and life is a response, not a soliloquy.

The Bible shows the way of God with man and the way of man with God. It contains both the complaint of God against the wicked and the shriek of the smitten man, demanding justice of God.

And there dwell also in its pages reminders of man's incredible callousness and obstinacy, of his immense capacity to bring about his doom as well as the assurance that beyond all evil is the compassion of God.

He who seeks an answer to the most pressing question, what is living? will find an answer in the Bible: man's destiny is to be a partner rather than a master. There is a task, a law, and a way: the task is redemption, the law, to do justice, to love mercy, and the way is the secret of being *human and holy*. When we are gasping with despair, when the wisdom of science and the splendor of the arts fail to save us from fear and the sense of futility, the Bible offers us the only hope: history is a circuitous way for the steps of the Messiah.

40. RELIGION IN MODERN SOCIETY

Little does religion ask of contemporary man. It is ready to offer comfort; it has no courage to challenge. It is ready to offer edification; it has no courage to break the idols, to shatter the callousness. The trouble is that religion has become "religion"—institution, dogma, securities. It is not an event any more. Its acceptance involves neither risk nor strain. Religion has achieved respectability by the grace of society, and its representatives publish as a frontispiece the *nihil obstat* signed by social scientists.

To be free one must attain a degree of independence. Yet, the complexities of society have enmeshed contemporary man in a web of relationships which make his independence most precarious.

Inherent in man is the desire to be in agreement with others. Yet today, with a mass of miscellaneous associations and unprecedented excitements, it is a grim task, indeed, to agree with all and to retain the balance of integrity.

Loaded with more vulnerable interests than he is able to protect, bursting with fears of being squeezed by a multiplicity of tasks and responsibilities, modern man feels too insecure to remain upright.

Good and evil have always had a tendency to live in promiscuity, but in more integrated societies man, it seems, found it easier to discriminate between the two, while in our turbulent times circumstances often stupefy our power of discernment; it is as if many of us have become value-blind in the epidemics of needs.

The glory of a free society lies not only in the consciousness of my right to be free, and my capacity to be free, but also in the realization of my fellow man's right to be free, and his capacity to be free. The issue we face is how to save man's belief in his capacity to be free. Our age may be characterized as the *age of suspicion*. It has become an axiom that the shortest way to the understanding of man is to suspect his motives. This seems to be the contemporary version of the Golden Rule: *Suspect thy neighbor as thyself*. Suspicion breeds suspicion. It creates a chain reaction. Honesty is not necessarily an anachronism.

The insecurity of freedom is a bitter fact of historic experience. In times of unemployment, vociferous demagogues are capable of leading the people into a state of mind in which they are ready to barter their freedom for any bargain. In times of prosperity, hidden persuaders are capable of leading the same people into selling their conscience for success. Unless a person learns how to rise daily to a higher plane of living, to care for that which surpasses his immediate needs, will he in a moment of crisis insist upon loyalty to freedom?

The threat to freedom lies in the process of reducing human relations to a matter of fact. Human life is not a drama any more, it is a routine. Uniqueness is suppressed, repetitiveness prevails. We teach our students how to recognize the labels, not how to develop a taste. Standardization corrodes the sense of ultimate significance. Man to his own self becomes increasingly vapid, cheap, insignificant. Yet without the sense of ultimate significance and ultimate preciousness of my own existence, freedom becomes a hollow phrase.

The central problem of this generation is emptiness in the heart, the decreased sensitivity to the imponderable quality of the spirit, the collapse of communication between the realm of tradition and the inner world of the individual. The central problem is that we do not know how to think, how to pray, or how to cry, or how to resist the deceptions of the silent persuaders. There is no community of those who worry about integrity.

One of the chief problems of contemporary man is the problem: What to do with time? Most of our life we spend time in order to gain space, namely things of space. Yet when the situation arrives in which no things of space may be gained, the average man is at a loss as to what to do with time.

With the development of automation the number of hours to be spent professionally will be considerably reduced. The four-day week may become a reality within this generation. The problem will arise: What to do with so much leisure time? The problem will be *too much* time rather than too little time. But too much time is a breeding ground for crime. Idleness is unbearable, and the most popular method to solve the problem of time is to kill time. Yet time is life, and to kill time is murder.

The average man has not only forgotten how to be alone; he finds it even difficult to be with his fellow man. He not only runs away from himself; he runs away from his family. To children "Honor your father and your mother" is an irrational commandment. The normal relationship is dull; deviation is where pleasure is found.

The average man does not know how to stand still, how to appreciate a moment, an event, for its own sake. When witnessing an important event or confronted with a beautiful sight, all he does is take a picture. Perhaps this is what our religious traditions must teach the contemporary man: to stand still and to behold, to stand still and to hear.

Judaism claims that the way to nobility of the soul is the art of sanctifying time. Moral dedications, acts of worship, intellectual pursuits are means in the art of sanctification of time. Personal concern for justice in the marketplace, for integrity in public affairs and in public relations, is a prerequisite for our right to pray.

Acts of worship counteract the trivialization of existence. Both involve the person, and give him a sense of living in ultimate relationships. Both of them are ways of teaching man how to stand alone and not be alone, of teaching man that God is a refuge, not a security.

But worship comes out of wisdom, out of insight, it is not an act of insight. Learning, too, is a religious commandment. Learning is an indispensable form of purification as well as ennoblement. I do not mean memorization, erudition; I mean the very act of study, of being involved in wisdom, and of being overwhelmed by the marvel and mystery of God's creation.

Religion's major effort must be to counteract the deflation of man, the trivialization of human existence. Our religious traditions claim that man is capable of sacrifice, discipline, of moral and spiritual exaltation, that every man is capable of an ultimate commitment.

Ultimate commitment includes the consciousness of being accountable for the acts we perform under freedom; the awareness that what we own we owe; the capacity for repentance; that a life without the service of God is a secret scandal.

Faith in God cannot be forced upon man. The issue is not only lack of faith but the vulgarization of faith, the misunderstanding and abuse of freedom. Our effort must involve a total reorientation about the nature of man and the world. And our hope lies in the certainty that all men are capable of sensing the wonder and mystery of existence, that all men have a capacity for reverence. Awe, reverence, precedes faith; it is at the root of faith. We must grow in awe in order to reach faith. We must be guided by awe to be worthy of faith. Awe is "the beginning and gateway of faith, the first precept of all, and upon it the whole world is established."

The grandeur and mystery of the world that surrounds us is not something which is perceptible only to the elect. All men are endowed with a sense of wonder, with a sense of mystery. But our system of education fails to develop it and the anti-intellectual climate of our civilization does much to suppress it. Mankind will not perish for lack of information; it may collapse for want of appreciation.

Education for reverence, the development of a sense of awe and mystery, is a prerequisite for the preservation of freedom.

We must learn how to bridle the outrageous presumption of modern man, to cultivate a sense of wonder and reverence, to develop an awareness that something is asked of man. Freedom is a burden that God has thrust upon man. Freedom is something we are responsible for. If we succeed, we will help in the redemption of the world; if we fail, we may be crushed by its abuse. Freedom as man's unlimited lordship is the climax of absurdity, and the central issue we face is man's false sense of sovereignty.

Tragic is the role of religion in contemporary society. The world is waiting to hear the Voice, and those who are called upon to utter the word are confused and weak in faith. "The voice of the Lord is powerful, the voice of the Lord is full of majesty" (Psalms 29:4). Where is its power? Where is its majesty?

A story is told about a community where a man was accused of having transgressed the seventh commandment. The leaders of the community went to the Rabbi and voicing their strong moral indignation demanded stern punishment of the sinner. Thereupon the Rabbi turned his face to the wall and said: O, Lord. Thy glory is in heaven, Thy presence on earth is invisible, imperceptible. In contrast to Thy invisibility, the object of that man's passion stood before his eyes, full of beauty and enravishing his body and soul. How could I punish him?

R. Simon said: "When the Holy One, blessed be He, came to create Adam, the ministering angels formed themselves into groups and parties, some of them saying, 'Let him be created,' whilst others urged, 'Let him not be created.' Thus it is written, Love and Truth fought together, Righteousness and Peace combated each other (Psalms 85: 11); Love said, 'Let him be created, because he will dispense acts of love'; Truth said, 'Let him not be created, because he is compounded of falsehood';

Righteousness said, 'Let him be created, because he will perform righteous deeds'; Peace said, 'Let him not be created because he is full of strife.' What did the Lord do? He took Truth and cast it to the ground. Said the ministering angels before the Holy One, blessed be He, 'Sovereign of the Universe! Why dost Thou despise Thy seal? Let Truth arise from the earth!' Hence it is written, Let truth spring up from the earth" (Psalms 85:12).

God had to bury truth in order to create man.

How does one ever encounter the truth? The truth is underground, hidden from the eye. Its nature and man's condition are such that he can neither produce nor invent it. However, there is a way. If you bury the lies, truth will spring up. Upon the grave of the specious we encounter the valid. Much gravedigging has to be done. The most fatal trap into which religious thinking may fall is *the equation of faith with expediency*. The genuine task of our traditions is to educate a sense for the inexpedient, a sensitivity to God's demand.

Perhaps we must begin by disclosing *the fallacy of absolute expediency*. God's voice may sound feeble to our conscience. Yet there is a divine cunning in history which seems to prove that the wages of absolute expediency is disaster. We must not tire of reminding the world that something is asked of man, of every man; that the value of charity is not to be measured in terms of public relations. Foreign aid when offered to underdeveloped countries, for the purpose of winning friends and influencing people, turns out to be a boomerang. Should we not learn how to detach expediency from charity? The great failure of American policy is not in public relations. The great failure is in private relations.

The spirit is a still small voice, and the masters of vulgarity use loudspeakers. The voice has been stifled, and many of us have lost faith in the possibility of a new perceptiveness.

Discredited is man's faith in his own integrity. We question man's power to sense any ultimate significance. We question the belief in the compatibility of existence with spirit.

Yet, man is bound to break the chains of despair, to stand up against those who deny him the right and the strength to believe wholeheartedly. Ultimate truth may be hidden from man, yet the power to discern between the valid and the specious has not been taken from us.

Surely God will always receive a surprise of a handful of fools—who do not fail. There will always remain a spiritual underground where a few brave minds continue to fight. Yet our concern is not how to worship in the catacombs but rather how to remain human in the skyscrapers.

41. THE MEANING OF THIS HOUR

Emblazoned over the gates of the world in which we live is the escutcheon of the demons. The mark of Cain[1] in the face of man has come to overshadow the likeness of God. There has never been so much guilt and distress, agony, and terror. At no time has the earth been so soaked with blood. Fellow men turned out to be evil ghosts, monstrous and weird. Ashamed and dismayed, we ask: Who is responsible?

History is a pyramid of efforts and errors; yet at times it is the Holy Mountain on which God holds judgment over the nations. Few are privileged to discern God's judgment in history. But all may be guided by the words of the Baal Shem: If a man has beheld evil, he may know that it was shown to him in order that he learn his own guilt and repent; for what is shown to him is also within him.

We have trifled with the name of God. We have taken the ideals in vain. We have called for the Lord. He came. And was ignored. We have preached but eluded Him. We have praised but defied Him. Now we reap the fruits of our failure. Through centuries His voice cried in the wilderness. How skillfully it was trapped and imprisoned in the temples! How often it was drowned or distorted! Now we behold how it gradually withdraws, abandoning one people after another, departing from their souls, despising their wisdom. The taste for the good has all but gone from the earth. Men heap spite upon cruelty, malice upon atrocity.

The horrors of our time fill our souls with reproach and everlasting shame. We have profaned the word of God, and we have given the wealth of our land, the ingenuity of our minds and the dear lives of our youth to tragedy and perdition. There has never been more reason for man to be ashamed than now. Silence hovers mercilessly over many dreadful lands. The day of the Lord is a day without the Lord. Where is God? Why didst Thou not halt the trains loaded with Jews being led to slaughter? It is so hard to rear a child, to nourish and to educate. Why dost Thou make it so easy to kill? Like Moses, we hide our face; for we are afraid to look upon *Elohim,* upon His power of judgment. Indeed, where were we when men learned to hate in the days of starvation? When raving madmen were sowing wrath in the hearts of the unemployed?

255

Let modern dictatorship not serve as an alibi for our conscience. We have failed to fight *for* right, *for* justice, *for* goodness; as a result we must fight *against* wrong, *against* injustice, *against* evil. We have failed to offer sacrifices on the altar of peace; thus we offered sacrifices on the altar of war. A tale is told of a band of inexperienced mountain climbers. Without guides, they struck recklessly into the wilderness. Suddenly a rocky ledge gave way beneath their feet and they tumbled headlong into a dismal pit. In the darkness of the pit they recovered from their shock only to find themselves set upon by a swarm of angry snakes. For each snake the desperate men slew, ten more seemed to lash out in its place. Strangely enough, one man seemed to stand aside from the fight. When indignant voices of his struggling companions reproached him for not fighting, he called back: "If we remain here, we shall be dead before the snakes. I am searching for a way of escape from the pit for all of us."

Our world seems not unlike a pit of snakes. We did not sink into the pit in 1939, or even in 1933. We had descended into it generations ago, and the snakes have sent their venom into the bloodstream of humanity, gradually paralyzing us, numbing nerve after nerve, dulling our minds, darkening our vision. Good and evil, that were once as real as day and night, have become a blurred mist. In our everyday life we worshiped force, despised compassion, and obeyed no law but our unappeasable appetite. The vision of the sacred has all but died in the soul of man. And when greed, envy and the reckless will to power came to maturity, the serpents cherished in the bosom of our civilization broke out of their dens to fall upon the helpless nations.

The outbreak of war was no surprise. It came as a long expected sequel to a spiritual disaster. Instilled with the gospel that truth is mere advantage and reverence weakness, people succumbed to the bigger advantage of a lie—"the Jew is our misfortune"—and to the power of arrogance—"tomorrow the whole world shall be ours," "the peoples' democracies must depend upon force." The roar of bombers over Rotterdam, Warsaw, London, was but the echo of thoughts bred for years by individual brains, and later applauded by entire nations. It was through our failure that people started to suspect that science is a device for exploitation; parliaments pulpits for hypocrisy, and religion a pretext for a bad conscience. In the tantalized souls of those who had faith in ideals, suspicion became a dogma and contempt the only solace. Mistaking the abortions of their conscience for intellectual heroism, many thinkers employ clever pens to scold and to scorn the reverence for life, the awe for truth, the loyalty to justice. Man, about to hang himself, discovers it is easier to hang others.

The conscience of the world was destroyed by those who were wont to blame others rather than themselves. Let us remember. We revered the instincts but distrusted the prophets. We labored to perfect engines and let our inner life go to wreck. We ridiculed supersitition until we lost our ability to believe. We have helped to extinguish the light our fathers had kindled. We have bartered holiness for convenience, loyalty for success, love for power, wisdom for information, tradition for fashion.

We cannot dwell at ease under the sun of our civilization as our ancestors thought we could. What was in the minds of our martyred brothers in their last hours? They died with disdain and scorn for a civilization in which the killing of civilians could become a carnival of fun, for a civilization which gave us mastery over the forces of nature but lost control over the forces of our self.

Tanks and planes cannot redeem humanity, nor the discovery of guilt by association nor suspicion. A man with a gun is like a beast without a gun. The killing of snakes will save us for the moment but not forever. The war has outlasted the victory of arms as we failed to conquer the infamy of the soul: the indifference to crime, when committed against others. For evil is indivisible. It is the same in thought and in speech, in private and in social life. The greatest task of our time is to take the souls of men out of the pit. The world has experienced that God is involved. Let us forever remember that the sense for the sacred is as vital to us as the light of the sun. There can be no nature without spirit, no world without the Torah, no brotherhood without a father, no humanity without attachment to God.

God will return to us when we shall be willing to let Him in—into our banks and factories, into our Congress and clubs, into our courts and investigating committees, into our homes and theaters. For God is everywhere or nowhere, the Father of all men or no man, concerned about everything or nothing. Only in His presence shall we learn that the glory of man is not in his will to power, but in his power of compassion. Man reflects either the image of His presence or that of a beast.

Soldiers in the horror of battle offer solemn testimony that life is not a hunt for pleasure, but an engagement for service; that there are things more valuable than life; that the world is not a vacuum. Either we make it an altar for God or it is invaded by demons. There can be no neutrality. Either we are ministers of the sacred or slaves of evil. Let the blasphemy of our time not become an eternal scandal. Let future generations not loathe us for having failed to preserve what prophets and saints, martyrs and scholars have created in thousands of years. The apostles of force have shown that they are great in evil. Let us reveal that we can be as great in goodness. We will survive if we shall be as fine and sacrificial in our homes and offices, in our Congress and clubs, as our soldiers are on the fields of battle.

There is a divine dream which the prophets and rabbis have cherished and which fills our prayers, and permeates the acts of true piety. It is the dream of a world, rid of evil by the grace of God as well as by the efforts of man, by his dedication to the task of establishing the kingship of God in the world. God is waiting for us to redeem the world. We should not spend our life hunting for trivial satisfactions while God is waiting constantly and keenly for our effort and devotion.

The Almighty has not created the universe that we may have opportunities to satisfy our greed, envy and ambition. We have not survived that we may waste our years in vulgar vanities. The martyrdom of millions demands that we consecrate ourselves to the fulfillment of God's dream of salvation. Israel did not accept the Torah of their own free will. When Israel approached Sinai, God lifted up the mountain and held it over their heads, saying: "Either you accept the Torah or be crushed beneath the mountain."

The mountain of history is over our heads again. Shall we renew the covenant with God?

SOURCES

The following abbreviations are used in referring to the two volumes of Heschel's Philosophy of Religion:

I. *Man is Not Alone: A Philosophy of Religion,* New York: Farrar, Straus and Young, Inc., 1951.
II. *God in Search of Man: A Philosophy of Judaism,* New York: Farrar, Straus and Cudahy, Inc., 1955.

PART I: WAYS TO HIS PRESENCE

1. Three Starting Points
   From an address given before the Seminar on Religion in a Free Society of The Fund for the Republic in New York City, May 9, 1958 (see also II, p. 3), and from II, pp. 31–32.
2. The Sublime
   From II, pp. 33–34, 36–37, 39–41.
3. Wonder
   From II, pp. 43–51.
4. The Mystery
   From II, pp. 56–58; I, pp. 30–32, 5, 19–21, 8, 21; II, pp. 62–63, 61, 66–69.
5. Awe and Reverence
   From II, pp. 74–78; I, pp. 26–27.
6. The Glory
   From II, pp. 80–85.
7. A Question Addressed to Us
   From II, pp. 108, 110–113.
8. I Am What Is Not Mine
   From I, pp. 45–49.
9. An Ontological Presupposition
   From II, pp. 114–122.
10. Faith
    From II, pp. 136–138, 140–143, 147.
11. Revelation
    From II, pp. 174–175, 168–173, 178–180, 184, 185, 187, 198–199.
12. Response Through Deeds
    From II, pp. 311–313, 281–292.

Sources

PART II: THE GOD OF THE PROPHETS

13. The Worship of Nature
   From II, pp. 88–98; from a revised English version of *Die Prophetie* soon to be published; II, pp. 98–99.
14. How to Identify the Divine
   From I, pp. 100–109.
15. One God
   From I, pp. 111–123.
16. The Divine Concern
   From I, pp. 135–139, 142–146, 148–150, 129, 126–129.
17. Process and Event
   From II, pp. 209–212.
18. The Divine Pathos
   This chapter contains "The Divine Pathos: The Basic Category of Prophetic Theology," an excerpt from Part III, ch. 1 ("Die pathetische Theologie") of *Die Prophetie,* Cracow, 1936, and is the work of William Wolf. It appeared originally in the quarterly journal *Judaism,* Vol. 2, No. 1 (January, 1953). In addition, material from the manuscript of the forthcoming English version of *Die Prophetie* has been incorporated in this chapter.
19. Prophetic Sympathy
   The material for this chapter is taken from the manuscript of the forthcoming English version of *Die Prophetie.*

PART III: MAN AND HIS NEEDS

20. The Problem of Needs
   From an address given before the Seminar on Religion in a Free Society of the Fund for the Republic in New York City, May 9, 1958; I, p. 190.
21. The Illusion of Human Self-Sufficiency
   From I, pp. 193–199, 210–215.
22. Needs and Ends
   From I, pp. 219–227.
23. God Is in Need of Man
   From I, pp. 241–244, 246–251.
24. Needs as Spiritual Opportunities
   From I, pp. 262–269.
25. Freedom
   From II, pp. 409–411; I, pp. 142, 146, 142; II, pp. 411–413.

PART IV: RELIGIOUS OBSERVANCE

26. Religion and Law
   From II, pp. 293–303.
27. Law and Life
   From II, pp. 306–311.

28. Kavvanah
    From II, pp. 314–317.
29. Religious Behaviorism
    From II, pp. 320–331.
30. Halakhah and Agadah
    From II, pp. 336–345.
31. The Meaning of Observance
    From II, pp. 348–352, 354, 356–359.
32. Mitzvah and Sin
    From II, pp. 361–366, 402–406.
33. The Problem of Evil
    From II, pp. 357–372, 374–380.
34. Prayer: An Act of Spiritual Ecstasy
    From an article, "Prayer," published originally in the *Review of Religion* (Columbia University Press), Vol. IX, No. 2 (January, 1945) and now forming ch. 1 of *Man's Quest for God: Studies in Prayer and Symbolism,* New York: Charles Scribner's Sons, 1954. The material selected in this chapter is taken from the following pages of *Man's Quest for God:* 6–11, 14–17.
35. Prayer: Expression and Empathy
    From *Man's Quest for God,* pp. 27–30, 32–37, 39, 41, 43–46.
36. Prayer: Know Before Whom You Stand!
    From an address delivered before the Rabbinical Assembly of America at Atlantic City, New Jersey, in 1953 and originally published as "The Spirit of Prayer" in *The Proceedings of the Rabbinical Assembly of America,* 1953. Expanded in form, it is now ch. 3 of *Man's Quest for God.* The selection is from pp. 59–64 of that work.
37. The Sabbath: Holiness in Time
    From *The Sabbath: Its Meaning for Modern Man,* New York: Farrar, Straus & Young, Inc., 1951, pp. 3–6; *The Earth Is the Lord's,* pp. 13 f; *The Sabbath,* pp. 6–10, 14–19, 22–23, 27–30, 53–54, 61–62, 74–76, 79–82, 89–90, 98–101.

PART V: THE MEANING OF THIS HOUR

38. What Is Man?
    From an address delivered before the convention of the Religious Education Association in Chicago, November, 1957, and published in *Religious Education,* March-April, 1958, pp. 97–102, and *The Christian Century,* December 11, 1957, pp. 1473–1475.
39. Understanding the Bible
    From II, pp. 24–27, 252–253, 272–273, 259, 261–266, 268–269, 273–276, 237–238.
40. Religion in Modern Society
    From an address given before the Seminar on Religion in a Free Society of The Fund for the Republic at the World Affairs Center, New York City, May 9, 1958.

41. The Meaning of This Hour
    The essential part of this essay was originally delivered in March, 1938, at a conference of Quaker leaders in Frankfurt on the Main. It was expanded and published in a 1943 issue of *The Hebrew Union College Bulletin* and is printed here in the final version found in *Man's Quest for God*, pp. 147–151.

BIBLIOGRAPHY

The Writings of Abraham J. Heschel

BOOKS

Poems [Yiddish], Warsaw: Insel Verlag, 1933.

Maimonides: Eine Biographie [German], Berlin: Erich Reiss Verlag, 1935. [French edition: *Maïmonide,* transl. by Germaine Bernard, Paris: Payot, 1936.]

Die Prophetie [German], Cracow: The Polish Academy of Sciences (Mémoires de la Commission Orientaliste No. 22), 1936. [An exposition in English of the ideas presented in *Die Prophetie* can be found in Harold Knight, *The Hebrew Prophetic Consciousness,* London and Redhill: Lutterworth Press, 1947.]

Don Jizchak Abravanel [German], Berlin: Erich Reiss Verlag, 1937. [Polish translation by Ozjasz Tilleman, Lwow, 1938.]

A Concise Dictionary of Hebrew Philosophical Terms, Cincinnati: Hebrew Union College, 1941 [*Mimeographed*].

The Quest for Certainty in Saadia's Philosophy, New York: Philip Feldheim, 1944. [First published as two separate articles in *The Jewish Quarterly Review, N.S.,* Vol. 33 (1943), Nos. 2-3, pp. 265-313, and Vol. 34 (1944), No. 4, pp. 391-408.]

Pikkuah Neshamah [Hebrew], New York: Baronial Press, 1949.

The Earth Is the Lord's: The Inner Life of the Jew in East Europe, New York: Henry Schuman, 1950. [Spanish edition: *La Tierra es del Señor,* transl. by Segisfredo Krebs, Buenos Aires: Editorial Candelabro, 1952; Yiddish edition: New York: Schocken Books, 1946.]

Man Is Not Alone: A Philosophy of Religion, New York: Farrar, Straus, and Young, Inc., and Philadelphia: The Jewish Publication Society of America, 1951.

The Sabbath: Its Meaning for Modern Man, New York: Farrar, Straus, and Young, 1951.

Man's Quest for God: Studies in Prayer and Symbolism, New York: Charles Scribner's Sons, 1954.

God in Search of Man: A Philosophy of Judaism, New York: Farrar, Straus, and Cudahy, 1933, and Philadelphia: The Jewish Publication Society of America, 1956. Paperback Edition, New York: Meridian Books and Philadelphia: Jewish Publication Society of America, 1959.

Bibliography

Les Bâtisseurs du Temps, transl. by Georges Levitte, Paris: Les Editions de Minuit (Collection Aleph), 1957. [Contains French translations of *The Earth Is the Lord's,* chapters 2-7, 9, 12, 15, and *The Sabbath,* Prologue, chapters 1, 3, 7, and Epilogue.]

Theology of Ancient Judaism (Torah min ha-shamayim be-ispaklaryah shel ha-dorot) [Hebrew], London and New York: Soncino Press, Vol. I, 1962; Vol. II, 1965.

The Prophets, New York and Evanston: Harper and Row, and Philadelphia: Jewish Publication Society of America, 1962.

The Sabbath, Expanded Edition, New York: Farrar, Straus and Co., 1963 [Contains an additional chapter "Space, Time and Reality". [Spanish translation: *El Shabat y el Hombre Moderno,* Buenos Aires: Editorial Paidós, 1964.]

The Earth Is the Lord's and The Sabbath [Paperback Edition], Cleveland and New York: Meridian Books (World Publ. Co.) and Philadelphia: Jewish Publication Society of America, 1963.

The Insecurity of Freedom: Essays in Applied Religion, New York: Farrar, Straus and Giroux, 1965.

Bibliography

ESSAYS AND ARTICLES

"Persönlichkeiten der jüdischen Geschichte" [Eight essays on Tannaim], in *Jüdisches Gemeindeblatt*, Berlin, February 23, March 8, March 29, April 12, April 26, May 17, May 31, August 16, 1936.

"Der Begriff des Seins in der Philosophie Gabirols," in *Festschrift Jakob Freimann* zum 70. Geburtstag, Berlin, 1937, pp. 67-77.

"Der Begriff der Einheit in der Philosophie Gabirols," in *Monatsschrift für die Geschichte und Wissenschaft des Judentums*, Vol. 82 (1938), pp. 89-111.

"Das Gebet als Ausserung und Einfühlung," in *Monatsschrift für die Geschichte und Wissenschaft des Judentums*, Vol. 83 (1939), pp. 562-567.

"Das Wesen der Dinge nach der Lehre Gabirols," in *Hebrew Union College Annual*, Vol. 14 (1939), pp. 359-385.

"Antwort an Einstein," in *Aufbau* (New York), Vol. 6, No. 38 (September 20, 1940), p. 3.

"On the Essence of Prayer" [Hebrew], in *Bitzaron Hebrew Monthly*, Vol. 3, No. 5 (February, 1941), pp. 346-353.

"Zevi Diesendruck," in *The American Jewish Year Book*, Vol. 43, Philadelphia: The Jewish Publication Society of America, 1941-1942, pp. 391-398.

"An Analysis of Piety," in *The Review of Religion*, Vol. 6, No. 3 (March, 1942), pp. 293-307. [Hebrew translation in *"Sefer Hashanah,"* Vol. 6, New York, 1942, pp. 61-72.]

"The Holy Dimension," in *The Journal of Religion*, Vol. 23, No. 2 (April, 1943), pp. 117-124.

"Faith," in *The Reconstructionist*, Vol. 10, No. 13 (November 3, 1944), pp. 10-14, No. 14 (November 17, 1944), pp. 12-16.

"The Meaning of This War," in *Liberal Judaism*, Vol. 11, No. 10 (February, 1944), pp. 18-21.

"A Cabbalistic Commentary on the Prayerbook" [Hebrew], in *Studies in Memory of Moses Schorr*, ed. by L. Ginzberg and A. Weiss, New York: The Professor Moses Schorr Memorial Committee, 1944, pp. 113-126.

"Prayer," in *The Review of Religion*, Vol. 9, No. 2, (January, 1945), pp. 153-168.

"Did Maimonides Strive for Prophetic Inspiration?" [Hebrew], in *Louis Ginzberg Jubilee Volume* (Hebrew Section), New York: The American Academy for Jewish Research, 1945, pp. 159-188.

"The Eastern European Era in Jewish History," in *Yivo Annual of Jewish Social Science*, Vol. 1, New York: Yiddish Scientific Institute-Yivo, 1946, pp. 86-106; reprinted as introductory essay in Roman Vishniac, *Polish Jews: A Pictorial Record*, New York: Schocken Books, 1947, pp. 7-17; [Yiddish: in *Yivo Bleter*, Vol. 25, No. 2 (March-April, 1945), pp. 163-183; Hebrew: transl. by Yehudah

Bibliography

Yaari, in *Luah Ha-aretz* for the Year 1947-48, Tel Aviv: Haim Publishing Co., Ltd., 1947, pp. 98-124.]

"The Two Great Traditions," in *Commentary*, Vol. 5, No. 5 (May, 1948), pp. 416-422.

"Rabbi Phineas of Koretz" [Hebrew], in *Alei Ayin: The Salman Schocken Jubilee Volume*, Jerusalem, 1948-1952, pp. 213-244, [Yiddish: "Reb Pinkhes Koritser," in *Yivo Bleter*, Vol. 33 (1949), pp. 9-48.]

"The Mystical Element in Judaism," in *The Jews: Their History, Culture, and Religion*, ed. by Louis Finkelstein, New York: Harper & Brothers, and Philadelphia: The Jewish Publication Society of America, 1949, pp. 602-623 [in Vol. 1 of the 2-volume edition, and in Vol. 2 of the 4-volume edition].

"After Majdanek: On the Poetry of Aaron Zeitlin" [Yiddish], in *Yiddisher Kemfer*, Vol. 29, No. 771 (October 1, 1948), pp. 28-30.

"Inspiration [*ruah ha-kodesh*] in the Middle Ages" [Hebrew], in *Alexander Marx Jubilee Volume* (Hebrew Section), New York: The Jewish Theological Seminary of America, 1950, pp. 175-208.

"Rabbi Gershon of Kuty" [Hebrew], in *Hebrew Union College Annual*, Vol. 23, 1950-1951, part II, pp. 17-71.

"Between Civilization and Eternity," in *Commentary*, Vol. 12, No. 4 (October, 1951), pp. 375-378.

"To Be a Jew: What Is It?", in *Zionist Quarterly*, Vol. 1, No. 1 (Summer, 1951), pp. 78-84. [A Yiddish version of this article appeared in *Yiddisher Kemfer*, Vol. 28, No. 718 (September 12, 1947), pp. 25-28.]

"Unknown Documents on the History of Hasidism" [Yiddish], in *Yivo Bleter*, Vol. 36 (1952), pp. 113-135.

"Architecture of Time," in *Judaism*, Vol. 1, No. 1 (January, 1952), pp. 44-51.

"Space, Time, and Reality: The Centrality of Time in the Biblical World View," in *Judaism*, Vol. 1, No. 3 (July, 1952), pp. 262-269.

"The Divine Pathos: The Basic Category of Prophetic Theology," in *Judaism*, Vol. 2, No. 1 (January, 1953), pp. 61-67. [An excerpt of Part 3, chapter 1 of *Die Prophetie*, translated into English by William Wolf.]

"The Moment at Sinai," in *The American Zionist*, Vol. 43, No. 7 (February 5, 1953), pp. 18-20.

"The Spirit of Prayer," in *Proceedings of the Rabbinical Assembly of America*, Vol. 17 (1953), pp. 151-215 [Hebrew transl. by "A. L.," in *Megillot* (New York), Vol. 15 (March, 1954), pp. 3-24.]

"Toward an Understanding of Halacha," in *Yearbook, The Central Conference of American Rabbis*, Vol. 63 (1953), pp. 386-409; and *The Jewish Frontier*, Vol. 21, No. 4 (April, 1954), pp. 22-28.

"The Spirit of Jewish Education," in *Jewish Education*, Vol. 24, No. 2 (Fall, 1953), pp. 9-20. [Hebrew transl. by "M. M.," in *Hadoar*, Vol. 36, No. 8 (De-

Bibliography

cember 23, 1955), pp. 151-153, and Vol. 36, No. 9 (December 30, 1955), pp. 166-168.]

"A Preface to the Understanding of Revelation," in *Essays Presented to Leo Baeck on the Occasion of His Eightieth Birthday*, London: East and West Library, 1954, pp. 28-35.

"Symbolism and Jewish Faith," in *Religious Symbolism* (Religion and Civilization Series), ed. by F. Ernest Johnson, New York: The Institute for Religious and Social Studies: Harper & Brothers, 1954, pp. 53-79.

"The Last Years of Maimonides," in *National Jewish Monthly*, Vol. 69, No. 10 (June, 1955), pp. 7 and 27-28. [A translation of chapter 25 of *Maimonides: Eine Biographie*.]

"The Biblical View of Reality," in *Contemporary Problems in Religion*, ed. by Harold A. Basilius, Detroit: Wayne University Press, 1956, pp. 57-76.

"Teaching Religion to American Jews," in *Adult Jewish Education* (Fall, 1956), pp. 3-6.

"A Hebrew Evaluation of Reinhold Niebuhr," in *Reinhold Niebuhr: His Religious, Social, and Political Thought*, Vol. 2 of The Library of Living Theology, ed. by Ch. W. Kegley and R. W. Bretall, New York: Macmillan Company, pp. 391-410.

"Rabbi Yitzhak of Drohobitsh" [Hebrew], in *Hadoar Jubilee Volume*, Vol. 37, No. 28 (May 31, 1957), pp. 86-94.

"The Task of the Hazzan," in *Conservative Judaism*, Vol. 12, No. 2 (Winter, 1958), pp. 1-8.

"Sacred Images of Man," in *Religious Education*, Vol. 53, No. 2 (March-April, 1958), pp. 97-102; and *The Christian Century*, December 11, 1957, pp. 1473-1475.

"The Problem of the Individual" [Hebrew], from "Proceedings of the Ideological Conference in Jerusalem" *(Sefer ha-kinnus ha-iyyuni ha-ʿolami)*, *Hazut*, Jerusalem: Ha-sifriyah ha-tziyonit, Vol. 4 (1958), pp. 312-319 and 80-84; and (abridged) *Hadoar*, Vol. 38, No. 22 (April 4, 1958), pp. 396-399.

"The Religious Message," in *Religion in America: Original Essays on Religion in a Free Society*, ed. by John Cogley, New York: Meridian Books, 1958, pp. 244-271.

"The Hebrew Prophet in relation to God and Man" [Hebrew], in *The Old Testament Conception of God, Man and the World*, ed. by Zevi Adar, Tel Aviv: Massadah Publ. Co., 1957, pp. 215-224 [Includes material from a draft version of *The Prophets*].

"The Essence of Prayer," [Hebrew] in *Ha-Tefillah*, ed. by Joseph Heinemann, Jerusalem: Amanah, 1960, pp. 3-15; and in *Essays on Judaism (Perakim ba-yahadut)*, ed. by Jakob J. Petuchowski and Ezra Spicehandler, Cincinnati: Hebrew Union College Press and Jerusalem: M. Newman, (1963), pp. 37-44.

Bibliography

[Originally written as a contribution for the *Meir Balaban Jubilee Volume,* Warsaw, 1939 which was destroyed by the Nazis before publication. It appeared in *Bitzaron,* February, 1941].

"Man as an Object of Divine Concern," in *What Is the Nature of Man?,* Philadelphia: Christian Education Press, 1959, pp. 93-105. [Originally published in *Religious Education,* Vol. 53, No. 2.]

"Yisrael: Am, Eretz, Medinah: Ideological Evaluation of Israel and the Diaspora," in *Proceedings of the Rabbinical Assembly of America,* Vol. 22 (1958), pp. 118-136.

"Prayer and Theological Discipline," in *Union Seminary Quarterly,* Vol. 14, No. 4 (May, 1959), pp. 3-8.

"Rabbi Mendel mi-Kotzk" [Hebrew], in *Hadoar,* Vol. 39, No. 28 (June 5, 1959), pp. 519-521.

["Answer to Ben Gurion" (Hebrew)], in *Hadoar,* Vol. 39, No. 38 (October 9, 1959), p. 741.

"The Moral Challenge to America," in *Proceedings of the 53rd Annual Meeting of the American Jewish Committee,* New York, 1960, pp. 62-77; also printed under the title "Who Is Man?", in *The Jewish Chronicle,* London (England), October 9, 1959, pp. 23-25. [Hebrew transl. in *Shevile ha-emunah ba-dor ha-aharon,* ed. by O. Margaliot, Tel Aviv: Mahbarot Lesifrut, 1964, pp. 11-15.]

"The Great Debate," in *The Torch* (Philadelphia), Vol. 19, No. 1 (Winter, 1960); also in *Proceedings (of) the 1959 Biennial Convention (of) the United Synagogues of America,* pp. 76-85.

"The Concept of Man in Jewish Thought," in *The Concept of Man,* ed. by S. Radhakrishnan and P. T. Raju, London: Allen and Unwin, 1960, pp. 108-157. [Spanish transl. in *El Concepto del Hombre,* Mexico-Buenos Aires: Fondo de Cultura Económica, 1964, pp. 132-195.]

"Call of the Hour" [A paper originally read at The White House Conference on Children and Youth in Washington, D.C. on March 28, 1960], in *Law and Order, The Independent Magazine for the Police Profession,* Vol. 8, No. 5 (May, 1960), pp. 14-25. [Spanish transl. in *Maj'shavot (Pensiamentos),* Buenos Aires, Vol. 3, No. 2 (July, 1964), pp. 23-32.]

"Depth Theology," in *Cross Currents,* Vol. 10, No. 4 (Fall, 1960), pp. 317-325.

"To Grow in Wisdom" [A paper delivered at The White House Conference on Aging in Washington, D.C. on January 9, 1961], published as a pamphlet, New York: Synagogue Council of America, 1961; also in pamphlet form: Salt Lake City: The Utah Religious Committee on Aging, 1963; also reprinted in *Congressional Record, Proceedings and Debates* of the 87th Congress, First Session, March 21, 1961, Appendix A 1973-1975, and again in *Congressional Record,* June 14, 1961, Appendix A 4364-4367. Extracts from this paper also in *The Beacon* (Jewish Theological Seminary of America), Vol. 4, No. 2

Bibliography

(June, 1961), pp. 5, 19-20; a version of the paper was reprinted as "The Older Person's Religious Needs," in *Geriatric Institutional Management*, ed. by Morton Leeds and Herbert Shore, New York: Putnam's, 1964, pp. 235-241.

"The Nation and the Individual," in *Conservative Judaism*, Vol. 15, No. 3 (Spring, 1961), pp. 10-26. [Contains an address given at the 1957 Jerusalem Ideological Conference in Hebrew and transl. by S. Kling and S. H. Dresner; the Hebrew text can be found in *Molad*, Vol. 15, Nos. 107-108 (July-August, 1957), pp. 237-244.]

"Ilya Schor," in *Conservative Judaism*, Vol. 16, No. 1 (Fall, 1961), pp. 20-21.

"Hillel Bavli," [Hebrew] in *Hadoar*, Vol. 42, No. 6 (December 8, 1961), p. 81.

"Hillel Bavli: *In Memoriam*" [English], in *Conservative Judaism*, Vol. 17, Nos. 1-2 (Fall-Winter, 1962-63), pp. 70-71.

"The Values of Jewish Education," in *Proceedings of the Rabbinical Assembly*, Vol. 26 (1962), pp. 83-100 ("Comments" by S. Kling and D. Lieber on pp. 101-109). A different version under the title "Idols in the Temple," in *Religious Education*, New York, March-April, 1963, pp. 127-137. [Spanish transl. by Gracie Feinstein in *Maj'shavot (Pensiamentos)*, Buenos Aires, Vol. 1, No. 4 (December, 1962), pp. 5-21.] Abridged versions of this paper have appeared in *Jewish Affairs*, Johannesburg, (South Africa), Vol. 18, No. 1 (January, 1963), pp. 4-8, and in Hebrew in *Prozdor*, Tel Aviv, Nos. 6-7 (September, 1963), pp. 41-45.

"Prophetic Inspiration," in *Judaism*, Vol. 11, No. 1 (Winter, 1962), pp. 3-13 [Contains excerpts from The Prophets, chapter 25].

"Le judaïsme concerne-t-il l'homme américain?", in *L'Arche*, Paris, Nos. 67-68 (August-September, 1962), pp. 64-67.

"The Religion of Sympathy," in *The Leo Jung Jubilee Volume*, New York, 1962, pp. 105-113 [Contains parts of The Prophets, chapter 18].

"Versuch einer Deutung," in *Begegnung mit dem Judentum: Ein Gedenkbuch*. (Stimmen der Freunde Quäker) in Deutschland, Heft 2), ed. by Margarethe Lachmund, Bad Pyrmont, 1962, pp. 11-13. [Contains the first publication of an address delivered to a group of Quakers at Frankfurt am Main in February, 1938 and secretly circulated under the Nazi régime by Rudolf Schlosser.]

"Prophétie et poésie," in *Evidences*, Paris, Vol. 15, No. 95 (January-February, 1963), pp. 45-50. [Contains French transl. of excerpts from *The Prophets*, chapter 22.]

"Two Methods in Jewish Religious Thought," [Hebrew] in *Hadoar*, Vol. 43, No. 15 (February 8, 1963), pp. 244-246, and Vol. 43, No. 16 (February 15, 1963), pp. 262-263. [Excerpts from the Introduction of *Torah min hashamayim*].

"The Religious Basis of Equality of Opportunity—The Segregation of God,"

Bibliography

in *Race: Challenge to Religion*, ed. by Mathew Ahmann, Chicago: Henry Regnery (Paperback Edition), 1963, pp. 55-71. [An abridged version of this paper originally read at the Conference on Race and Religion in Chicago can be found in *The United Synagogue Review*, Spring, 1963; a Spanish transl. in *Maj'shavot (Pensiamentos)*, Buenos Aires, Vol. 3, No. 2 (July, 1964), pp. 33-36.]

"A Jewish Response," in *The Catholic News*, New York, Vol. 78, No. 14 (April 4, 1963), p. 4 [Text of an address given on April 1, 1963 at a dinner in honor of Augustin Cardinal Bea. This ta!'., as broadcast on radio, was also printed in *The Catholic Hour* for May 26, 1963, issued by the NBC Radio Network in Washington D.C.]

[An Address on the Jews in the Soviet Union], in *The Day-Jewish Journal*, New York, September 12, 13 and October 12, 1963 [also reprinted as a broadside]. A French version appeared in *L'Arche*, Paris, Nos. 91-92 (August-September, 1964), pp. 23-29.

"Protestant Renewal: A Jewish View," in *The Christian Century*, Vol. 80, No. 49 (December 4, 1963), pp. 1501-1504.

[Address "The White Man on Trial"] in *Proceedings of the Metropolitan New York Conference on Religion and Race*, February 25, 1964, New York: New York City Youth Board, 1964, pp. 100-110.

"The Meaning of the Spirit," in *Claremont Dialogue*, Vol. 1, No. 2 (Spring, 1964), Claremont, Cal.: Claremont Community Church of Seventh-day Adventists, pp. 16-35.

"The Patient as a Person," in *Manuscripts of Addresses Presented to the American Medical Association 113th Convention, San Francisco, Calif., June 21, 1964*, Chicago: Dept. of Medicine and Religion, AMA, pp. 23-41; also in *Conservative Judaism*, Vol. 19, No. 1 (Fall, 1964), pp. 1-10; also an abridged version under the title "The Sisyphus Complex," in *Ramparts*, Menlo Park, Calif., Vol. 3, No. 2 (October, 1964), pp. 45-49.

"The Moral Dilemma of the Space Age," in *Space: Its Impact on Man and Society*, ed. by Lilian Levy, New York: Norton, 1964, pp. 176-179.

"Rabbi Nahman of Kossov, Companion of the Baal Shem" [Hebrew], in *The Harry A. Wolfson Jubilee Volume*, ed. by Saul Lieberman et al., New York: The American Academy for Jewish Research, 1965 (Hebrew Section), pp. 113-141.

Bibliography

ARTICLES AND BOOKS DEALING WITH THE WORK OF
ABRAHAM J. HESCHEL

(A selective bibliography)

Reinhold Niebuhr, "Masterly Analysis of Faith," in *New York Herald Tribune Book Review*, April 1, 1951.

Dayyan Al-Yahud, "Professor Heschel, the Creative Thinker: A Critical Study of His Works," in *The Jewish Forum*, Vol. 35, No. 8 (September, 1952), pp. 137-141; Vol. 35, No. 10 (November, 1952), pp. 189-190; Vol. 36, No. 1 (January, 1953), pp. 16-18; Vol. 36, No. 3 (March, 1953), pp. 31-38.

Edward A. Snynan, "Abraham Heschel and Prayer," in *The Bridge: A Yearbook of Judaeo-Christian Studies*, ed. by John M. Oesterreicher, Vol. I, New York: Pantheon Books, 1955, pp. 256-265.

Maurice Friedman, "The Thought of Abraham Heschel," in *Congress Weekly*, Vol. 22, No. 31 (November 14, 1955), pp. 18-20.

Joseph H. Lookstein, "The Neo-Hasidism of Abraham J. Heschel," in *Judaism*, Vol. 5, No. 3 (Summer, 1956), pp. 248-255.

Herbert W. Schneider, "On Reading Heschel's *God in Search of Man:* A Review Article," in *The Review of Religion*, Vol. 21, Nos. 1-2 (November, 1956), pp. 31-38.

Maurice Friedman, "Abraham Joshua Heschel: Toward a Philosophy of Judaism," in *Conservative Judaism*, Vol. 10, No. 2 (Winter, 1956), pp. 1-10.

Jakob J. Petuchowski, "Faith as the Leap of Action: The Theology of Abraham Joshua Heschel," in *Commentary*, Vol. 25, No. 5 (May, 1958), pp. 390-397.

E. La B. Cherbonnier, "A. J. Heschel and the Philosophy of the Bible: Mystic or Rationalist?", in *Commentary*, Vol. 27, No. 1 (January, 1959), pp. 23-29.

Ephraim Shemueli, "Be-vikuah al ha-emunah ha-yisreelit, [Hebrew] in *Perakim*, Haifa, Nissan, 1958, pp. 19-22; and Iyyar, 1958, pp. 44-50.

Fritz A. Rothschild, "God and Modern Man: The Approach of Abraham J. Heschel," in *Judaism*, Vol. 8, No. 2 (Spring, 1959), pp. 112-120 [Spanish transl. in *Davar: Revista Literaria*, Buenos Aires, No. 86, July-August-September, 1960, pp. 26-39].

Lou H. Silberman, "The Philosophy of Abraham Heschel," in Jewish Heritage, Vol. 2, No. 1 (Spring, 1959), pp. 23-26, 54.

Emil L. Fackenheim, "God in Search of Man," in *Conservative Judaism*, Vol. 15, No. 1 (Fall, 1960), pp. 50-53.

Marvin Fox, "Heschel, Intuition, and the Halakhah," in *Tradition*, Vol. 3, No. 1 (Fall, 1960), pp. 5-15.

Zalman M. Schachter, "Two Facets of Judaism," [A response to the article by M. Fox] in *Tradition*, Vol. 3, No. 2 (Spring, 1961), pp. 191-202.

271

Bibliography

Yehiel Halpern, *The Jewish Revolution: Spiritual Struggles in Modern Times* (Ha-mahapekhah ha-yehudit) [Hebrew], Vol. I, Tel Aviv: Am Oved Publishers, 1961, pp. 275-278.

Fritz A. Rothschild, article s. v. "Heschel," in *Encyclopaedia Hebraica,* [Hebrew] Vol. 15, Jerusalem, 1962.

Yaffa Leader-Levinson, "Torato shel Heschel" [Hebrew], in *Niv: The Hebrew Literary Magazine,* New York, June, 1962, pp. 12-20; November, 1962, pp. 12-15.

David S. Shapiro, "A New View on the Systems of Rabbis Akiba and Ishmael," in *Hadoar,* Vol. 53, No. 39. (September 27, 1963), pp. 769-772.

Franklin Sherman, "Abraham Joshua Heschel: Spokesman for Jewish Faith," in *Lutheran World,* Geneva, Vol. 10, No. 4 (October, 1963), pp. 400-408 [German transl by Jürgen Roloff, "A. J. H., ein Sprecher fü den jüdischen Glauben," in *Lutherische Rundschau,* Vol. 13, No. 4 (October, 1963), pp. 486-496].

David S. Shapiro, "The Prophets" [Hebrew], in *Hadoar,* Vol. 44, No. 36 (September 4, 1964), pp. 665-666.

Eliezer Berkovits, "Dr. A. J. Heschel's Theology of Pathos," in *Tradition,* Vol. 6, No. 2 (Spring-Summer, 1964), pp. 67-104.

"The Audience That Was," in *The Jewish World,* New York, Vol. 2, No. 12 (October, 1964), pp. 23-24, 68 [A journalist's report on Heschel's audience with Pope Paul VI].

NOTES

INTRODUCTION

1 *New York Herald-Tribune Book Review,* April 1, 1951.
2 *The Earth Is the Lord's,* New York: Henry Schuman, 1950, p. 56.
3 An exposition in English of Heschel's views on prophecy can be found in Harold Knight, *The Hebrew Prophetic Consciousness,* London and Redhill: Lutterworth Press, 1947.
4 II, 11.
5 I, 275.
6 II, 3.
7 *Ibid.*
8 Maurice Friedman, "Abraham Joshua Heschel: Toward a Philosophy of Judaism," *Conservative Judaism,* Vol. X, No. 2 (Winter, 1956), p. 9.
9 See H. W. Schneider, "On Reading Heschel's *God in Search of Man,*" *The Review of Religion,* Vol. XXI, Nos. 1–2 (November, 1956), p. 38.
10 II, 34.
11 II, 33 (where faith is, however, not mentioned).
12 I, 13 f.; II, 46 f.
13 II, 39.
14 II, 95.
15 I, 63.
16 II, 353.
17 See, e.g., Jakob J. Petuchowski, "Faith as the Leap of Action," *Commentary,* Vol. 25, No. 5 (May, 1958), p. 391.
18 Paul Tillich, *Systematic Theology,* Vol. I, Chicago: University of Chicago Press, 1951, p. 109.
19 II, 67.
20 II, 67 f.
21 I, 46.
22 I, 127.
23 I, 128.
24 Tillich, *op. cit.,* pp. 205–206.
25 II, 121 f.
26 I, 33 f.
27 I, 145 f.; II, 158.
28 I, 76; II, 137.
29 II, 154.
30 I, 129.
31 *Man's Quest for God: Studies in Prayer and Symbolism,* New York: Charles Scribner's Sons, 1954, p. 73. See also I, 148.
32 I, 102–104. For an analysis of how the concept of unity functions in metaphysics, science, and religion, written from a Naturalist viewpoint, see John

Notes

Herman Randall, Jr., *Nature and Historical Experience,* New York: Columbia University Press, 1958, ch. 7.
33 See, e.g., Aristotle, *Metaphysics,* Book Delta, ch. 6.
34 I, 111–123.
35 I, 122.
36 I, 109.
37 See Stephen Pepper, *World Hypotheses,* Berkeley and Los Angeles: University of California Press, 1948.
38 II, 209.
39 II, 210.
40 II, 16.
41 II, 92. Compare Schelling's "desperate question": *"Warum ist überhaupt etwas, warum ist nicht nichts?" (Sämtliche Werke,* Vol. 13, pp. 7, 163 ff., 242; also Vol. 6, p. 155; Vol. 7, p. 174.)
42 II, 16.
43 II, 97.
44 II, 211.
45 *Ibid.*
46 II, 210.
47 II, 197.
48 I, 6.
49 See Otis Lee, *Existence and Inquiry,* Chicago: The University of Chicago Press, 1949, p. 311.
50 II, 202.
51 II, 142.
52 I, 237.
53 See G. Scholem, *Major Trends in Jewish Mysticism,* rev. ed., New York: Schocken Books, 1946, pp. 260–265.
54 I, 149.
55 I, 150.
56 II, 162.
57 *Die Prophetie,* Cracow, 1936, 163 f.; II, 258.
58 Compare the use of the term *"göttliches Gewahren"* in *Prophetie,* 163 f.
59 I, 145.
60 I, 137 f.
61 I, 143.
62 I, 137.
63 I, 138.
64 *Prophetie,* 164.
65 I, 129; II, 16, 412.
66 II, 413.
67 II, 21.
68 *Prophetie,* 131. See also I, 244 f.
69 *Prophetie,* 132–138; also I, 245.
70 See E. Gilson, *God and Philosophy,* New Haven: Yale University Press, 1941, pp. 33 f.; also Joh. Hessen, *Griechische oder biblische Theologie?,* Leipzig, 1956, *passim.*
71 I, 12.
72 *Prophetie,* 164.
73 Schneider, *loc. cit.,* p. 32.
74 *Prophetie,* 176–180.
75 The root *yada'* means "to know" as well as "to have sexual intercourse" in most Semitic languages.

76 *Prophetie,* 128.
77 II, 171.
78 *Prophetie,* 165, 180.
79 II, 411.
80 I, 219.
81 I, 257.
82 II, 356.
83 II, 409.
84 II, 411.
85 II, 410.
86 I, 33.
87 II, 409.
88 I, 142; II, 410.
89 II, 411.
90 II, 211.
91 See Tillich, *Systematic Theology,* Vol. I, p. 184: "Freedom is experienced as deliberation, decision and responsibility."
92 II, 411.
93 I, 201.
94 I, 201 f.
95 I, 202.
96 I, 203.
97 I, 205.
98 *The Sabbath: Its Meaning for Modern Man,* New York: Farrar, Straus & Young, Inc., 1951, p. 97.
99 I, 206.
100 *The Sabbath,* 100.
101 *Ibid.*
102 I, 242.
103 II, 343.

PART I: WAYS TO HIS PRESENCE

Chapter 1. Three Starting Points

1 See Job 35:5; Amos 5:6, 8–9. "Meditate about the works of the Lord, for thereby you will come to know Him by whose word the world came into being." Quoted in the name of Rabbi Meir by Maimonides, *Responsa,* ed. A. Freimann, Jerusalem, 1934, 347, p. 312. See also *Wisdom of Solomon* 13:1 ff.; *Baruch,* 54:17 f. According to old legends, Abraham discovered the true faith by meditating on nature; see Louis Ginzberg, *The Legends of the Jews,* Vol. V, p. 210, n. 16. Cf. also p. 60 of this book. According to Baḥya, *The Duties of the Heart,* ed. M. Hyamson, Vol. I, p. 3, it is our duty to "meditate on the marvels as manifested in His creations, so that they may serve us as evidence of Him."

Chapter 3. Wonder

1 Charles S. Peirce, *Collected Papers,* Cambridge, Mass., 1935, Vol. V, p. 65.
2 J. Arthur Thomson, *The System of Inanimate Nature,* p. 650.
3 A. N. Whitehead, *Adventures of Ideas,* New York, 1933, p. 185.
4 *Theaetetus,* 155d.
5 *Metaphysica,* 12, 982b12.

Notes

6 See Schopenhauer, *Supplements to the World as Will and Idea* ch. xvii; Max Planck, *Scientific Autobiography*, New York, 1949, pp. 91–93.
7 Aristotle, *Metaphysica*, 847all.
8 Job 5:10–16; Isaiah 25:1–4; Psalms 107:8, 15, 21, 24, 31; Isaiah 40:26.
9 Exod. 3:20; 34:10; Joshua 3:5; Jer. 21:2; Micah 7:15; Psalms 72:18; 86:10; 98:1; 106:22; 136:4; Job 9:10.
10 Job 37:5–13.
11 *Seder Eliyahu Rabba*, ch. 2, ed. Friedmann, p. 8 (in Nahum N. Glatzer, *In Time and Eternity*, pp. 22 f.); *Pesikta Rabbati*, ch. 33, ed. Friedmann, p. 152a; *Nedarim*, 41a.
12 Kant, *Critique of Practical Reason*, trans, Abbott, London, 1889, p. 260.

Chapter 4. The Mystery

1 *Zohar*, Vol. III, p. 128a.
2 Abraham Flexner, *Universities*, New York, 1930, p. 17.
3 Gilbert N. Lewis, *The Anatomy of Science*, New Haven, 1926, p. 154.
4 According to Socrates, "God only is wise," and the man who claimed actual possession of wisdom was guilty of presumption, if not blasphemy. He called himself a lover of wisdom. *Apology*, 20 ff.
5 Oliver Goldsmith, *The Citizen of the World*, Letter 37.
6 Cf. Rashi on Psalms 9:1 and *Midrash Tehillim* (see S. Buber's remark *ad loc.*); *Bate Midrashot*, ed. Wertheimer, Jerusalem, 1950, Vol. 1, p. 251; Maimonides, *Moreh Nebukhim*, Introd.; Naḥmanides, *Commentary* on Genesis 1:1; Maimonides, *Mishneh Torah*, Yesode Hatorah, 2, 10; *Ecclesiastes Rabbah* to 12:9; *Sanhedrin* 99a and Maharsha's comment; *Berakhot* 34b and Isaiah 64:3.
7 Rabbi Isaac Meir Alter of Ger, quoted in *Sefat Emet*, Vol. III, p. 81a.
8 Cf. the rendering of the Septuagint.
9 Hegel, *The Philosophy of Religion*, vol. II, p. 122.
10 Cf. I Samuel 2:3.
11 Sophocles, *Antigone*, 951 and 133 ff.
12 Genesis 18:25.
13 Plotinus, *Enneads*, III, 8.4.
14 The Musaf liturgy for Sabbath.
15 Isaiah 63:15; see Psalms 89:50 and *Yoma* 69b.

Chapter 5. Awe and Reverence

1 *Zohar*, Vol. I, p. 11b; cf. Rabbi Mosheh Isserles' gloss on the importance of Psalms 16:8 in the opening paragraph of the *Shulḥan Arukh*.
2 *Wisdom of Solomon* 17:12.
3 See Albo, *Ikkarim*, ed. Husik, Philadelphia, 1930, Vol. III, ch. 32.
4 Deut. 10:12; see Psalms 2:11; cf. *Seder Eliyahu Rabba*, ch. 3: "I feared in my joy, I rejoiced in my fear, and my love prevailed over all."
5 See also Psalms 23:1, 4; 102:26–29; 112:7.
6 *Zohar*, Vol. I, p. 11b. See Shabbat 31b.
7 See *Wisdom* 6:10.

Chapter 6. The Glory

1 See also Exod. 16:6, 7, 10; 24:16 f.
2 See I. Abrahams, *The Glory of God*, Oxford, 1925, p. 17, in refutation of A. von Gall, *Die Herrlichkeit Gottes*.
3 See also Isaiah 59:19; 60:1–3; 66:18; Psalms 97:1, 4–6.

Notes

4 *Likkute Maharan*, I, 133.
5 See Niddah 31a.
6 Ibn Gabirol, *A Choice of Pearls*, ed. Ascher, London, 1859, p. 82.
7 Isaiah 42:20.
8 Ez. 12:1; see Jer. 5:21.
9 Ḥagigah 12b; see also R. Pinḥas Horowitz, *Hamakneh,* Preface.

Chapter 7. A Question Addressed to Us

1 *Genesis Rabbah,* ch. 39. The word *doleket* is ambiguous. It may mean *illumined, full of light,* or it may mean *in flames.* In the first sense it is understood by the "Rashi" Commentary on Genes. Rabbah, in the second by *Yede Mosheh,* R. David Luria and R. Zeëv Einhorn. For an interpretation in the second sense see ch. 33 of this book.

Chapter 9. An Ontological Presupposition

1 Cf. Philip Wheelwright, *The Burning Fountain*, Bloomington, 1954, pp. 18 f., and Abraham J. Heschel, *Man's Quest for God*, pp. 117–144.
2 George P. Adams, "The Range of Mind," in *The Nature of Mind*, Berkeley, Calif., 1936, p. 149. Cf. J. Loewenberg, "The Discernment of Mind," *ibid.,* pp. 90 f.
3 Rabbi Yehudah Loew of Prague, *Netivot Olam*, Netiv Haavodah, ch. 2.

Chapter 10. Faith

1 The liturgy of the Day of Atonement.
2 *Mekhilta,* ed. Lauterbach, II; 218 f.; Judah Halevi *Kuzari,* II:50, IV:3.
3 *Selected Poems of Jehudah Halevi,* trans. N. Salaman, Philadelphia, 1928, pp. 134–135.
4 Deuteronomy 5:19, according to the Aramaic translations of Onkelos and Pseudo-Jonathan. See also Sanhedrin 17b, Sotah 10b, and Rashi.
5 Rabbi Jacob Joseph of Ostrog, *Rav Yevi,* Ostrog, 1808, p. 43b.
6 See *Lam. Rabbah,* Proemium 25.
7 See *Masekhet Kallah,* ed. M. Higger, New York, 1936, ch. 5, p. 283.
8 Bahya, *Duties of the Heart,* Avodat Elohim, ch. 5 (II, 55).
9 Rabbi Mordecai Azulai, *Or Hachammah,* Przemysl, 1897, III, 42b.
10 Yoma 38b.

Chapter 11. Revelation

1 Cf. *Mekhilta* to Exod. 19:18; *The Mishnah of Rabbi Eliezer*, Rule 14, ed. Enelow, New York, 1933, p. 25.
2 Isaiah 40:17; see also Daniel 4:32.

Chapter 12. Response Through Deeds

1 *"Shekhinah* is the mitzvah," *Tikkune Zohar,* VI; see *Zohar,* I, 21a.
2 Shabbat 88a; *Midrash Ḥazita* 2, 10.
3 *Lev. Rabbah* 31, 4.
4 *Exod. Rabbah* 30, 9; see *Jerushalmi,* Rosh Hashanah 1, 3, 7a.

PART II: THE GOD OF THE PROPHETS

Chapter 13. The Worship of Nature

1 Sophocles, *Oedipus Tyrannus*, 1424–1429; *Electra*, 86–95.
2 *Hippolitus*, Act IV, 1116.

Notes

3 *King Lear,* Act I, Scene 2, 1–2.
4 *Cymbeline,* Act III, Scene 3, 2–7.
5 Ezek. 8:16; cf. II Kings 17:16; 21:3.
6 *The Works of Francis Thompson,* Vol. III, pp. 80–81. See Will Herberg, *Judaism and Modern Man,* New York, 1951, p. 34.
7 Diels, *Fragmente der Vorsokratiker,* Herakleitos, Fr. 30.
8 *Timaeus,* end.
9 Marcus Aurelius, *Meditations,* iv, 23.
10 Cf. Isaiah 40:26; Job 27:4–6.
11 *Adventures of Ideas,* p. 154.
12 W. Jaeger, *The Theology of the Early Greek Philosophers,* pp. 31 and 203, n. 44.

Chapter 14. How to Identify the Divine

1 Cf. C. A. Richardson, *Spiritual Realism and Recent Philosophy,* pp. 82 f.
2 Ernst Cassirer, *Substance and Function in Einstein's Theory of Relativity,* Chicago, 1923, p. 373 f.
3 Mishnah Sanhedrin 4:5.

Chapter 15. One God

1 In Hebrew the word *eḥad* means both one and unique. It is in the latter sense in which *eḥad* is to be understood in the passage of II Samuel 7:23, incorporated in the afternoon service for the Sabbath: "Thou art One and Thy name is One; and who is like Thy people Israel unique (*eḥad*) on earth." This was also the understanding of the rabbis, cf. Bekhorot 6b. The Targum renders *eḥad* with "unique" in Genesis 26:10. *Eḥad* is taken in the sense of *meyuḥad,* i.e., "unique," unlike other beings, in Megillah 28a. In rabbinic literature God is sometimes called *Yehido shel olam,* the Unique of the universe, or *Yaḥid be-olamo,* cf. Tanhuma Buber I, 49a: "because God is unique in the universe, He knows the character of every single creature and their minds!" Compare also Ḥullin 28a, 83b; Bekhorot 17a.
2 The Decalogue does not represent, as some scholars assert, a tribal henotheism in the sense that the tribe of Israel should recognize Him alone without denying the reality of the deities that other tribes continued to worship; a God, of whom no image should be made, who created "heaven and earth, the sea, and all that in them is" (Exodus 20:11), cannot admit the reality of other deities.
3 *Or Yesharim,* 87.
4 *Lev. Rabbah* 4, 8; *Deut. Rabbah,* 2, 26; cf. Berakhot 10b.
5 *Gen. Rabbah* 3, 9.

Chapter 18. The Divine Concern

1 Kant, *Kritik der Urteilskraft,* p. 121; cf. Wundt, *Einführung in die Psychologie,* pp. 31 ff.
2 Aeschylus, *Prometheus Bound,* 645 ff.

PART III: MAN AND HIS NEEDS

Chapter 23. God Is in Need of Man

1 *Sifre Deut.,* 346; cf. the interpretation of Psalms 123:1.

Chapter 25. Freedom

1 See above, ch. 17, "Process and Event."

278

Notes

PART IV: RELIGIOUS OBSERVANCE

Chapter 26. Religion and Law

1 Sanhedrin 106b.
2 I. Goldziher, *Vorlesungen über den Islam*, Heidelberg, 1910, pp. 167 ff.; D. S. Margoliouth, "The Devil's Delusion of Ibn Al-Jauzi," *Islamic Culture*, Vol. X (1936), p. 348; *Encyclopedia of Religion and Ethics*, Vol. II, pp. 842 f.
3 Romans 3:28. On the theological implications of the problem, see E. La B. Cherbonnier, *Hardness of Heart*, New York, 1955, ch. XI.
4 *Avot* 5:20.
5 *The Sabbath*, p. 15.
6 *Man's Quest for God*, ch. 4.
7 *Exod. Rabbah* 41, 6.
8 *Pesikta Rabbati*, ed. Friedmann, p. 64b; *Numbers Rabbah* 19. See A. Freimann, "Yehiel . . . on the Study of the Torah," in *Louis Ginzberg Jubilee Volume* (Hebrew), New York, 1945, p. 360.
9 *Pirke de-Rabbi Eliezer*, ch. 21.
10 R. Yom Tov Lippmann Heller, *Tosfot Yom Tov*, Preface.
11 R. Isaiah Horowitz, *Shene Luḥot Haberit*, p. 25b; see R. Mosheh Cordovero, *Pardes Rimmonim*, 23, sub "ḥumra."
12 *Genesis Rabbah* 19, 3.
13 *Jerushalmi* Sanhedrin IV, 22a. See *Pene Mosheh, ad loc.;* also *Midrash Tehillim*, ch. 12.

Chapter 27. Law and Life

1 Baḥya, *Duties of the Heart*, ed. Hyamson, I, 4.
2 Haḥayim, MS. Munich, in *Otzar Hasafrut*, Vol. III, p. 66.
3 *Sifre Deut.*, ed. Friedmann, p. 80a.
4 Baḥya, *Duties of the Heart*, I, 7.
5 Mishnah Kiddushin 4:14.
6 Berakhot 17a.
7 Cf. Sotah 22b; M. H. Luzzatto, *Mesillat Yesharim*, ed. M. M. Kaplan, p. 140.
8 *Exod. Rabbah*, 36, 3.
9 R. Mosheh Almosnino, *Tefillah Lemosheh*, p. 11a.

Chapter 28. Kavvanah

1 *Tanḥuma*, ed. Buber, *ad loc.; Jerushalmi* Shekalim I, 46b.

Chapter 29. Religious Behaviorism

1 *Tractatus Theologico-Politicus*, III, IV, XIII.
2 Kant owed his knowledge of Judaism partly to Spinoza's *Tractatus* and partly to Mendelssohn's *Jerusalem*. He maintained that Judaism is *"eigentlich gar keine Religion."* Cf. Hermann Cohen, *Jüdische Schriften*, Vol. III, pp. 290–372, and Vol. I, pp. 284 f. The same applies to Hegel; cf. his *Early Theological Writings*, Chicago, 1948, pp. 195 f.
3 *Jerusalem*, ch. 2. See Hermann Cohen, *Die Religion der Vernunft*, etc., pp. 415 ff.
4 *Ikkarim*, Part 3, ch. 25.
5 *Mevo Hatalmud*, ascribed to R. Samuel Hanagid.
6 Cf., however, M. Guttmann, *Clavis Talmudis*, I, 453.
7 Cf. *Genesis Rabbah* 85, 2.

8 *Ibid.*, 60, 8.
9 *Sifre Deut.* 49, to 11:22.
10 *Yalkut Shimoni*, Psalms, 672.
11 *Midrash Tehillim* 28, 5.
12 *Jerushalmi*, Shekalim V, beginning. Cf. *Mekhilta* to 15:26; *Exod. Rabbah* 47, 1; Ibn Zimra, *Responsa*, IV, 232; *Lev. Rabbah* 22:1; *Jerushalmi*, Megillah 4, 1.
13 *Sifre Deut.* 48; Kiddushin 30a.
14 *Midrash Mishle*, to 10:3.
15. R. Shneur of Ladi, *Shulḥan Arukh*, Talmud Torah, ch. 2, 1–2.
16 See Maimonides, *Commentary on the Mishnah*, Sanhedrin X, Introd.; Michael Sachs, *Die religiöse Poesie der Juden in Spanien*, Berlin, 1845, p. 160.
17 Elijah Morpurgo, in Asaf, *Mekorot Letoldot Haḥinnukh Beyisrael*, Vol. II, p. 231.
18 Shabbat 31a-b.
19 Mishnah Berakhot II, 2.
20 *Mekhilta*, to 20:3.
21 Yevamot 6a-b.
22 Naḥmanides on Leviticus 19:2.
23 Bava Metzia 30b.
24 See Kiddushin 32b.
25 *Midrash Tehillim* 119:13.
26 Mishnah Berakhot 9:5.
27 S. Schechter, *Studies in Judaism*, First Series, p. 151.
28 *Jerushalmi*, Peah 16a.
29 *Mekhilta*, to Exod. 14:31.
30 Mishnah Sanhedrin 10:1.
31 *Lam. Rabbah* 2, Proemium.
32 Berakhot 8a.

Chapter 30. Halakhah and Agadah

1 *Genesis Rabbah*, to 27:28.
2 *Kad Hakemaḥ*, Shavuot.
3 Baḥya, *Duties of the Heart*, IV, 91.
4 Sotah 21b.
5 Sanhedrin 98b.
6 Sukkah 28a.
7 *Commentary on Mishnah*, Berakhot 9:5.
8 *Yetzirah* vi, 6; *Ẓohar*, II, 69b.
9 *Sifre, ad loc.*

Chapter 31. The Meaning of Observance

1 *Genes. Rabbah* 44.
2 Baḥya, IV:91.
3 *Ibid.*, 91–92.
4 Yoma 39a.

Chapter 32. Mitzvah and Sin

1 *Likkute Maharan*, II, 5, 10.
2 *Genes. Rabbah* 19, 17.
3 Niddah 30b.

4 *Avot* 4:28.
5 *Selected Religious Poems,* p. 113.
6 *Avot* 2:5.
7 Berakhot 61a; see Rashi; Eruvin 18a.
8 Nazir 23a; Albo, *Ikkarim* III, ch. 28; Berakhot 17b.
9 Ḥullin 7a. (and Tosfot, *ad loc.*); Pesaḥim 118a; Nazir 23b.
10 Ḥullin 7b.
11 *Midrash Tehillim,* 118, 10. See Schechter, *Some Aspects of Rabbinic Theology,* pp. 55 f.

Chapter 33. The Problem of Evil

1 *Gen. Rabbah,* ch. 39. See above, ch. 7, n. 1.
2 Sukkah 52a; cf. Bava Metzia 32b on Isaiah 64:5.
3 Reinhold Niebuhr, *The Nature and Destiny of Man,* Vol. I, pp. 222 f.
4 *Zohar,* III, 80b.
5 *Sifre Deut.* 45; Kiddushin 30b.
6 *Lev. Rabbah* 35, 5.
7 *Mekhilta, ad loc.*
8 *Avot* 4:2.
9 *Numbers Rabbah* 15, 16.
10 *Avot* 4:17.
11 Cf. Reinhold Niebuhr, *An Interpretation of Christian Ethics,* p. 65.

Chapter 34. Prayer: An Act of Spiritual Ecstasy

1 From the daily liturgy.
2 Prayer is defined as a dialogue with God by Clement of Alexandria. See Max Pohlenz, *Die Stoa,* Göttingen, 1948, Vol. I, p. 423.
3 From the daily liturgy.

Chapter 35. Prayer: Expression and Empathy

1 Pesaḥim 117a.
2 R. Zevi Elimelekh of Dynov, *Igra Depirka,* p. 62.
3 *Tur Oraḥ Ḥayim,* ch. 61.
4 "Hear, O Israel," core of the morning and evening prayers, consisting of the following passages: Deuteronomy 6:4–9; 11:13–21; Numbers 15:37–41.
5 Cf. Sanhedrin 106b.
6 *Sefer Ḥasidim,* ed. J. Wistinetzki, Berlin, 1891, p. 6; Nahum N. Glatzer, *In Time and Eternity,* New York, 1946, pp. 88–89.
7 Ibn Gabirol, *The Choice of Pearls,* ed. Ascher, 66.
8 Ibn Ezra, *Commentary on Psalms,* 4:5.
9 Ibn Ezra, *Commentary on Proverbs,* 16:1.
10 Berakhot 33b.
11 *Siaḥ Sarfe Kodesh,* Vol. II, p. 92, para. 318.
12 The *kedushah* in the liturgy of the Sabbath morning.

Chapter 36. Prayer: Know Before Whom You Stand!

1 Berakhot 28b; *Avot de-rabbi Natan,* version B, ch. 9; Orḥot Ḥayim, 18.
2 *Jerushalmi,* Berakhot 4, 4, 8b.
3 E. S. Ames, *Religion,* p. 217.

Notes

Chapter 37. The Sabbath: Holiness in Time

1 See *Man Is Not Alone,* pp. 200 ff.
2 See Bertrand Russell, *Our Knowledge of the External World,* pp. 166 f.
3 See N. Berdyaev, *Solitude and Society,* p. 134.
4 Maimonides, *Mishneh Torah,* Teshuvah 1, 2, on the basis of Mishnah Yoma 8:8. Cf. also *Sifra,* to 23:27, and Shevuot 13a, Yoma 85b, Sanhedrin 102a, and *Tanhuma* to Gen. 49:28; Taanit 29a, Arakhin 11b. Also Pedersen, *Israel I–II,* pp. 488, 512; E. Panofsky, *Studies in Iconology,* pp. 69–93.
5 Genesis 2:3. In the Ten Commandments the term "holy" is applied to one word only, the Sabbath.
6 See *Tanhuma,* Exod. 34:1 (31); *Seder Olam Rabba* ch. 6; Rashi to Exod. 31:18. See, however, Nahmanides to Lev. 8:2.
7 Numbers 7:1.
8 *Zohar,* I, 75.
9 *Mekhilta,* to 31:13.
10 *Gen. Rabbah* 19, 3.
11 Except the prohibition of idolatry, adultery, and murder.
12 *Otzar Hageonim,* Yoma, pp. 30, 32.
13 Juvenal, *Satires,* X.80.
14 Isaiah 58:13. Cf. *Tikkune Zohar 21,* ed. Mantua, 1558, 59b.
15 *Deut. Rabbah* 3, 1; see *Midrash Tehillim,* ch. 90.
16 Quoted by Rashi on Megillah 9a; on Genesis 2:2.
17 *Genesis Rabbah* 10, 9.
18 Deut. 12:9; cf. I Kings 8:56; Ps. 95:11; Ruth 1:19.
19 Job 3:13, 17.
20 Psalms 23:1–2.
21 Shabbat 152b; see also *Kuzari* V, 10; *Yalkut Reuveni,* Amsterdam, 1700, 174a, and the prayer *"El male rahamim."*
22 Exod. 20:9; 23:12; 31:15; 34:21; Lev. 23:3; Deut. 5:13.
23 *Mekhilta de-rabbi Shimon ben Yohai,* ed. D. Hoffmann, Frankfort on the Main, 1905, p. 107.
24 *Avot* 1, 10.
25 *Avot de-rabbi Natan,* ed. Schechter, ch. 11.
26 R. Isaiah Horowitz, *Shene Luhot Haberit,* Frankfurt on the Oder, 1717, p. 131a.
27 Shabbat 12a.
28 Shabbat 119a.
29 Rabbenu Hananel, Bava Kama 32a.
30 Shabbat 119a.
31 Avot 1, 15; 3, 12.
32 *Midrash Tehillim,* ed. Buber, ch. 92, p. 403; Al Nakawa, *Menorat Hamaor,* II, 182.
33 See the special prayer for the Sabbath at the end of grace after meals.
34 R. Elijah de Vidas, *Reshit Hokhmah,* Shaar Hakedushah, ch. 2.
35 Hermann Cohen, *Jüdische Schriften,* Berlin, 1924, Vol. I, p. 325.
36 Cf. Isaiah 66:2.
37 *Tanhuma,* ed. Buber, II, 76; see Rashi to Exod. 19:1; Deut. 26:16.
38 Mishnah Pesahim 10, 5.
39 Avodah Zarah 10b, 17a, 18a.
40 *Avot* 4:22.

Notes

PART V: THE MEANING OF THIS HOUR

Chapter 39. Understanding the Bible

1 See R. Isaiah Horowitz, *Shene Luḥot Haberit*, 40a.
2 *Jerushalmi*, Makkot, II, 31d.
3 *Gen. Rabbah* 17, 5.
4 It is equated with Wisdom. See Prov. 8:22; Sirach 1:4; Wisdom of Solomon 9:9. Cf. Louis Ginzberg, *The Legends of the Jews*, Vol. V, pp. 4, 132 f.
5 Shevuot 5a.
6 R. Judah Loew of Prague, *Derekh Haḥayim*, Warsaw, 1833, p. 8d.
7 Cf. *Pesikta de-rav Kahana*, ed. Buber, 4, p. 39a, and Sanhedrin 21b.
8 Rashi on Song of Songs 1:2. See *Tanḥuma*, Balak, 14; *Numbers Rabbah* 20, 20.
9 Cordovero, *Pardes Rimmonim*, XXI, 6, Koretz, 1786, p. 165a.
10 *Shene Luḥot Haberit*, 59a.
11 R. Abraham Azulai, *Ḥesed le-avraham*, mayan 2, nahar 12.
12 See *Temunah*, Koretz, 1784, pp. 27a, 30a–31a, *et al.*
13 Sanhedrin 89a.
14 *Rav Yevi* on Psalm 18; R. Mosheh Alshekh on Levit. 9:2.
15 *Tosefta* Berakhot 3, 7.
16 *Seder Eliyahu Ẕuta*, ch. 2, ed. Friedmann, p. 172.
17 Temurah 14b.
18 *Jerushalmi*, Shabbat XVI, 1.
19 Temurah 14b; Gittin 60a.

Chapter 41. The Meaning of This Hour

1 See *Genesis Rabbah* 22, 12, ed. Theodor, pp. 219 f., and Louis Ginzberg, *The Legends of the Jews*, Vol. V, p. 141.

FREE PRESS PAPERBACKS

A Series of Paperbound Books in the Social and Natural Sciences, Philosophy, and the Humanities

These books, chosen for their intellectual importance and editorial excellence, are printed on good quality book paper, in large and readable type, and are Smyth-sewn for enduring use. Free Press Paperbacks conform in every significant way to the high editorial and production standards maintained in the higher-priced, case-bound books published by The Free Press.

**Many of these books are available in their original cloth bindings.
A complete catalogue of all Free Press titles will be sent on request**